Memory and Modernity

CRITICAL STUDIES IN
LATIN AMERICAN CULTURE

SERIES EDITORS:

James Dunkerley
Jean Franco
John King

This major series – the first of its kind to appear in English – is designed to map the field of contemporary Latin American culture, which has enjoyed increasing popularity in Britain and the United States in recent years.

Six titles will offer a critical introduction to twentieth-century developments in painting, poetry, music, fiction, cinema and 'popular culture'. Further volumes will explore more specialized areas of interest within the field.

The series aims to broaden the scope of criticism of Latin American culture, which tends still to extol the virtues of a few established 'master' works and to examine cultural production within the context of twentieth-century history. These clear, accessible studies are aimed at those who wish to know more about some of the most important and influential cultural works and movements of our time.

Other Titles in the Series

DRAWING THE LINE: ART AND CULTURAL IDENTITY IN CONTEMPORARY LATIN AMERICA by Oriana Baddeley and Valerie Fraser

PLOTTING WOMEN: GENDER AND REPRESENTATION IN MEXICO by Jean Franco

JOURNEYS THROUGH THE LABYRINTH: LATIN AMERICAN FICTION IN THE TWENTIETH CENTURY by Gerald Martin

MAGICAL REELS: A HISTORY OF CINEMA IN LATIN AMERICA by John King

Memory and Modernity

Popular Culture in Latin America

WILLIAM ROWE

AND

VIVIAN SCHELLING

VERSO

London · New York

First published by Verso, in association with the Latin America Bureau, 1991
© Verso 1991

Verso
UK: 6 Meard Street, London W1V 3HR
USA: 29 West 35th Street, New York, NY 10001-2291

Verso is the imprint of New Left Books

British Library Cataloguing in Publication Data

Rowe, William *1944*–
Memory and modernity: popular culture in Latin America. –
(Critical studies in Latin American culture).
1. South America. Central America. Popular culture
I. Title   II. Schelling, Vivian   III. Series
306.4098

ISBN 0-86091-322-8
ISBN 0-86091-541-7 pbk

US Library of Congress Cataloging-in-Publication Data

Rowe, William.
Memory and modernity: popular culture in Latin America/William
Rowe and Vivian Schelling.
p.   cm. — (Critical studies in Latin American culture)
Includes index.
ISBN 0-86091-322-8. — ISBN 0-86091-541-7 (pbk.)
1. Latin America—Popular culture.   I. Schelling, Vivian, 1952–
II. Title.   III. Series.
F1408.3.R69   1991
980—dc20

Typeset in Perpetua by GCS, Leighton Buzzard, Beds.
Printed in Great Britain by Biddles Ltd.

To Nuri and Anthony

Contents

vii

Acknowledgements

We are particularly grateful to John King and James Dunkerley for their care and generosity in responding to earlier drafts of this book. Special thanks are also due to Jean Franco for advice and suggestions. Many people have given help at different stages and we apologize to any whom we have inadvertently failed to include in the following list: John Kraniauskas, David Treece, Tony Macpharlane, Néstor García Canclini, Raquel Caravia, Emilio Yauli, the Taype brothers, Claudio Orós, Leo Casas, Rodrigo Montoya, Valdi Astvaldsson, Xaieb Alonso, Rosaleen Howard-Malverde, Octavio Ianni, José Jorge de Carvalho, Rita Segato, Luis Alberto Peluso, Jan Rocha, Padre Ticão, Renato Ortiz, Moyra Ashford, Sergio and Mundicarmo Ferreti, José Eduardo de Souza, Sebastian Balfour, Maureen Larkin, Rosy, Cristoph Hering, Polly Josefowitz-Hering, Sue Branford and Maria Alicia Ferrera. We are also indebted to the Conselho Nacional de Pesquisa, the people of Vila Aparecida and the oral poets of São Paulo, without whom some of this research would not have been possible.

Photographs are courtesy of the following: Guy Brett (Plate 9), Sue Cunningham (Plates 2 & 4), Magnum/S. Salago Jr (Plates 1 & 5), Rosaleen Howard-Malverde/Andrew Canessa (Plates 3 & 6), Julio Etchart (Plate 8), Nicaragua Solidarity Campaign (Plate 11), Rosanna Horsley.

Introduction

It is a normal condition in late-twentieth-century capitalism to be surrounded by a continuous supply of cultural goods which seem to offer an unbroken horizon. All meanings are available and transferable: from Mozart to Bolivian folk music, from *Dallas* to Brazilian *telenovelas*, from hamburgers to tacos. The tendency for products from different cultural environments to mix on a global scale is accelerating as the century draws to an end. It is a process which has both negative and positive aspects. (One of its effects is homogenization, whereby differences either between the objects themselves, or between the experiences involved in their making, or between the ways in which we receive them become eroded.) At the extreme this destructive process involves cultural death. On the other hand, the vast increase in channels of communication which flow across cultural boundaries has the effect of dismantling old forms of marginalization and domination and making new forms of democratization and cultural multiplicity imaginable.

The outcome is undecided. New forms of cultural violence and of the monopolization of power are also imaginable, and indeed have been happening for some time in Latin America. For instance, the transfer of new media and information technologies to the region is in the first place unequal: the centres of production and control are elsewhere. And in the second place, it is allowing social and political problems to be treated as merely technical ones, (as a result of which values and identities disappear as issues which can be debated.) This book is written against homogenization and its deadening effects. But at the same time it seeks to recognize the new possibilities of cultural mobility and inventiveness brought about by the proliferation of communications in the late twentieth century.

Popular culture in Latin America is easy to identify yet problematic to define. It is easily identifiable in the immediate reality of such things as *telenovelas*, salsa, carnivals, folk music, magical beliefs, and oral narratives – all conveying in some measure the idea of the popular as a distinct sphere. The problem lies in the fact that when these objects and practices are placed in their larger context, this distinctness becomes more difficult to define. Although it is a useful starting-point to define popular culture as the culture of the subaltern classes, in cases where the latter is merely a replica of ruling-class culture, the term 'popular' loses its force. To call something popular carries an implied opposition: opposed to what class or group, and opposed in what particular way? It is not enough simply to say that the dominant is what the popular is opposed to, since to do so involves making assumptions about the history of culture.

These assumptions need spelling out. They belong to three main interpretative narratives, each of which construes the history of popular culture in a different way. Perhaps the most familiar is the view, which arose with Romanticism, of an authentic rural culture under threat from industrialization and the modern culture industry – historical processes which in Latin America have tended to coincide. It is assumed that the purity of a peasant culture is degraded or forgotten under pressure from the capitalist mass media. What is lost is most often described as the experience of community. The second interpretation, a twentieth-century response to industrialization, takes the modern culture of the advanced capitalist countries as the inevitable goal towards which Latin American societies are moving. Popular culture can only take the form, according to this version, of a variety of mass culture – either a tragedy or a solution, depending on the viewpoint. The third position, whose history goes back to Marx and beyond, ascribes to popular culture an emancipatory and utopian charge, whereby the practices of oppressed classes contain within them resources for imagining an alternative future society. All three interpretations, which usually overlap and combine, have fundamental flaws. The first involves nostalgia for a static past, and a failure to acknowledge that traditional and modern worlds are no longer separate, and that many people in Latin America live in both at once. The second suffers from a lack of confidence in the inventiveness of the popular classes and in the capacity of traditional and non-Western cultures to bring about a different modernity of their own. The third has the disadvantage of tending to locate the observer in some ideal place from which everything can be judged as contributing (or not) to an emerging positive future, whereas in reality things are not so clear. It also tends to sidestep the question of how popular tactics could be formulated into a strategy for taking power, and how that power could be maintained without authoritarianism.

Although this book comes closest to the third interpretation, it nevertheless attempts to avoid a programmatic approach, seeking instead to investigate what actually occurs in the conflict of meanings and practices between social groups. We have chosen, on the descriptive level, to keep in mind those ways in which older forms of popular culture change, rather than to present them as frozen and timeless. On the interpretative level, we understand tradition as a word which should not be confined to pre-modern cultures and recognize that the modern too can become a tradition. Latin American modernity is not a replica of US or European mass culture, but has a distinctive character which varies from country to country. A major factor in its difference – probably the major factor – is the force of popular culture. It is a modernity which does not necessarily entail the elimination of pre-modern traditions and memories but has arisen through them, transforming them in the process.

We reject both Manichean and apocalyptic views of mass culture in Latin America: we do not believe either that it is destroying all that is 'pure' and 'authentic', nor that the mass media merely manipulate a passive audience. Nevertheless we believe that it is vital to be aware of the enormous amount of destruction which both preceded and accompanies current developments. The pressure to forget, the force of social amnesia, can be extremely powerful. The issue here is of both genocidal and symbolic violence; of the eradication of social groupings and of 'the gentle, hidden form which violence takes when overt violence is impossible'.[1]

In addition to the three interpretative positions we have outlined, there are two main disciplinary frameworks through which popular culture has been made into an object of knowledge and discussion: the first is associated with the idea of folklore; the second with that of mass culture. Each is associated with particular intellectual traditions and with different political commitments. Neither of the two mises-en-scène is satisfactory, in that popular culture overflows both, but they remain the principal bases for approaching the subject.

When the expressions of pre-capitalist culture are put into a kind of museum, this both makes them perceivable as cultural objects and preserves them. The word 'folklore' arose at a particular moment of European history, when the disappearance of pre-industrial cultures was accelerating. W.J. Thoms proposed the term in a letter to the British journal *The Athenaeum* in

1846. The idea was that it should replace the previous designation of 'popular antiquities'; it continued to work as preservation of the past, but with important new connotations of seriousness, since 'lore' included the meanings of teaching and scholarship and 'folk' covered both people in general and the idea of the nation. The connotation of nation connects with a German tradition, best known through the word *Volksgeist*. Associated with the philosopher Herder, and meaning the stories, songs, customs, rituals and proverbs which shaped the collective spirit of a particular 'people', the notion of *Volksgeist* arose from a Romantic response to the Enlightenment. In opposition to the analytical and generalizing categories of the scientific systems of the Enlightenment, it emphasized identity, in terms of the organic growth of national cultures as territorially specific ways of life. At the same time, it was associated with an idea of community (*Gemeinschaft*) represented by peasant life, in opposition to industrial society and the culture of the learned.

Some of this history of the idea continued in Latin America in the twentieth century, but with a number of important differences. These centre on two main issues. First, Latin American societies were more heterogeneous, in that there have been wide cultural differences within an individual country, differences sometimes so great and involving such large populations that the idea of a unitary nation is not viable. Second, in some regions (such as the Andean) the cultures referred to as folkloric have upheld their own alternative ideas of nationhood and have been capable of challenging the official state. In these circumstances, the idea of folklore breaks down, since the phenomena it refers to challenge the legitimacy of the society voicing the idea itself. Although it is difficult to generalize, it is probably valid to say that in Latin America the idea of folklore has been bound up with the idea of national identity, and has been used by the state, among other things, in order to bring about national unity. Folklore was 'discovered' in Latin America early in the twentieth century, when modernizing states were seeking ways to achieve partial integration of those rural populations which a weak capitalist economy could not fully incorporate. The term is more highly charged politically here than in Europe, both for the reasons we have given and because of the crucial fact that its referent – the cultures thought of as folkloric – can be as much part of the present as of the past. Thus the concept ranges between two extremes of usage: on the one hand, folklore is seen as a kind of bank where authenticity is safely stored; on the other, it is a way of referring to contemporary cultures which articulate alternatives to existing power structures.

4

It is probably in Brazil that the idea of folklore has most strongly represented a critical alternative to capitalist mass culture. The Brazilian anthropologist José Jorge de Carvalho has argued that folklore is where collective memory is conserved – as opposed to its being destroyed by the mass media, which tend to produce passivity in their audience.[2] However, this utopian view of folklore entails a number of problems. The way in which cultural actions come to be called folklore needs to be understood as a historical process, involving changes in the practice both of its producers and of those who seek to interpret and control it. The action of the state and of anthropologists and other intellectuals, as exemplified in Mexico in the 1930s and later, involved the promotion of peasant handicrafts as symbolic of the nation; this became a stable arrangement which brought economic benefits to the producers. In Peru, state promotion came somewhat later (in the 1940s and '50s) and centred on music.[3] The important difference, however, was that attempts to control the performance of Andean music – in particular to preserve the authenticity of costume in the face of the hybridizing force of the modern urban environment – had to be abandoned: the explosion of rural migration, the proliferation of performance of Andean music, and the migratory drift of styles made such control impossible. For the performers of music and dance, the classification 'folkloric' meant an offer of recognition within the national arena, making it possible for them to give new signification to their products or performances. The Peruvian example of the war-dances from Toqroyoq, which we describe in Chapter 2, shows how a performance from a relatively isolated highland village can become charged with meanings which resonate on a national scale, but can also exceed the frame implied by folklore and challenge the state itself.

Thus the term folklore emerges as part of a wider set of historical circumstances. It needs stressing that whatever implications of uniformity it may have in a European context, its meanings in Latin America differ between countries. In Argentina it has tended to take on a reactionary charge, as part of a paradigm of national culture that stresses the mystical qualities of the land and attempts to ignore the social divisions produced by capitalism; early urbanization, large-scale immigration from Europe and the defeat of recalcitrant rural groups contributed to this process. In Mexico, after the Revolution, it was a key part of an official state policy of integrating rural populations. In Brazil, it has been adopted by intellectuals as a utopian alternative to corrupting aspects of the modernization imposed by authoritarian regimes in recent decades. In Peru, Bolivia, Guatemala and Paraguay, the strength of native and *mestizo* cultures makes the term folklore and the approach associated with it (the preservation of rural performances and artefacts by members of the other, modern culture) incapable of containing the phenomena they are supposed to frame.

A critical approach to the notion of folklore would need to include the following points. The term has a built-in backdating tendency, implying a museum made by others in a territory which is not that of the producers. For example, there is a permanent exhibition of Latin American folklore in the Monumento a America Latina, a huge cultural centre in São Paulo which was opened in 1989. Although it is probably the best such exhibition in the world, in terms of the quality of the objects displayed, it does very little to indicate the contexts of their production and use. The result is that differences of use and meaning become lost: the aesthetic aspect is highlighted to the detriment of the practical and the symbolic, giving a superficial impression of similarity between products of different regions. When difference disappears in this way, the popular is made to appear as a single thing rather than a multiplicity. This notion that there is one popular culture is a mark of populism: the long-lasting appeal of folklore in Mexico, Argentina and Brazil needs to be understood, therefore, in connection with the persistence of populism as a force.

The academic study of folklore focuses on local communities and ethnic groups in a manner that isolates them from the broader structural constraints of a society which, with the expansion of capitalism and the culture industry, has altered the characteristics and function of practices traditionally carried out by and for the peasantry. Moreover, the implicit assumption in many such studies that what is being recorded are disappearing customs, prevents one from recognizing that the process of modernization in Latin America does not always, as we shall see, entail the elimination of modes of production, such as the making of handicrafts, which are not part of capitalism but very often retains them in a state of partial integration.[4] Finally, the utopian connotations of 'community' with which folklore has tended to be loaded have encouraged the idea that music and the visual arts are usually collectively created. That this is far from always being the case is demonstrated by a study of panpipe styles in the Peruvian altiplano, where it emerges that a particular well-known style supposed to belong to a whole community was in fact the invention of an individual.[5] The fact that musical pieces and objects of visual art are anonymous does not mean that they were created collectively in the strict sense of the term. The desire that they should be, and the making of collective creation into a positive value, reflect the urge to set up an opposition between the collective as authentic and the individual as alienating.

(Mass culture is a term associated with the expansion of cinema, radio, comics, *fotonovelas* and, above all, television.)It has been taken by some to spell the end of any genuinely popular culture and by others to be the only form that popular culture can take in the late twentieth century. The first view can be traced back to Adorno and Horkheimer's influential theory of the culture industry, which argued that the subordination of culture to the capitalist market turns cultural forms into standardized products which reduce the consumer's capacity to think critically or to acquire experiences which transcend the status quo. Elaborated during the authors' exile from Nazi Germany, this is a powerful indictment of the totalitarian potential of the electronic media. However, a problem with this theory is the way it uses the notion of the genuine work of art as a yardstick against which to measure the degeneracy of the mass media: 'genuine art', in this argument, tends to mean European high culture. Also, no allowance is made for the variety of ways the media are actually received, and the fact that they can be vehicles for popular traditions and for resistance to social control by authoritarian capitalism.

The negative view of mass culture and the notion that popular culture by definition means opposition to the mass media is present in many analyses of the mass media in Latin America in the 1970s.[6] The passivity of the public is seen as axiomatic; in addition, popular culture is taken to be that which does not penetrate and is not penetrated by mass culture. It is fairly clear that such purity does not exist. Obviously we are not suggesting that popular culture and mass culture are one and the same, and we would resist the notion that mass culture can be defined as popular because of the sense of sheer scale of its circulation and ratings. Popular culture means something else, but before entering into definitions, certain other issues should be set out.

If the idea of folklore gives popular culture an ontological solidity, that of mass culture appears to empty it of any content.(With folk or pre-capitalist cultures the popular can be pointed to as a set of lived practices which include rituals, handicrafts, narratives, music, dance and iconography)This makes it possible to think of popular culture as a whole way of life.)With the mass media, however, these specifics no longer hold. Where can the popular be located, as a practice, if one is talking about television? This problem contributes to the tendency to be pessimistic about the effects of the mass media. Whether defined by the technology employed or by their presumed ideological effect, the mass media can appear to involve a one-way process whose manner of reception is predetermined by the built-in 'message'. Such an approach dehistoricizes the media, removing them from the different

7

historical conjunctures in which they are used. Too often, the particular ways in which the modern nation was consolidated by mass society in the USA are taken as a model for understanding the mass media, as though their relationship with a particular society were inherent in the media themselves. On the contrary, the different historical moments at which the culture industry becomes established give rise to crucial differences. Whereas in Europe the culture industry mainly arose after the consolidation of nation-states, and could thus appear as a threat to high culture, in Brazil, for example, the culture industry created in the 1960s became a means for unifying the nation. It thus took on some of the aura of high culture. Modernity arrived with television rather than with the Enlightenment, and television supplied the cultural capital of the middle classes.

The most important contribution in recent years to rethinking the role of the media in Latin America has been that of Jesús Martín-Barbero, who has laid the groundwork for an understanding of media as 'mediations'. In place of the one-sided view which assumes the manner of reception to be moulded entirely by the medium in question, Martín-Barbero demonstrates the need to pay attention to the cultural characteristics of the receiving public and to see the mass media as vehicles or mediations of particular moments of the 'massification' of society, and not its source: 'the historical constitution of the mass [*lo masivo*], rather than being a degradation of culture by the media, is actually tied in both with the long slow process of development of the national market, state and culture, and with the patterns [*dispositivos*] within which this process caused popular memory to enter into complicity with the mass imaginary.'[7] The mass media in Latin America enter societies in which the secularization of popular memory is only partial; societies shaped by the mixing, or *mestizaje*, of modern Western and traditional native and African groups whose magical beliefs and practices continue to be part of everyday life. The majority of television viewers in Latin America at the beginning of the 1990s, although they are exposed to the mass imaginary of television, nevertheless continue to participate in symbolic systems which combine pre-capitalist and capitalist worlds. Magic may not figure in television pro-grammes, but it does in the site at which they are received. If 'mass culture is not something completely external, is not something which comes to invade the popular from outside but is actually a development of certain potentialities already within the popular itself',[8] what we are dealing with is an intermingling of popular traditions and a mass imaginary (as is shown in the second part of Chapter 2). This does not mean that they are identical. What need investigating are the particular codes of perception and recognition which specific popular memories bring to the reception of the media, and the particular items of popular traditions which are included – though transformed – as genre, style or theme in the media. Thus the *telenovela* (to take an example), while offering to the majority of viewers the glamour of higher social status, can also be studied in terms of how it includes features of popular memory and how its reception is multivalent; for instance its intense emotionality does not exclude irreverence, parody and the grotesque. The research on these acts of negotiation still has to be done; Chapter 2 offers an outline of entrances to the problem.

The emergence of mass forms of society as a historical process began in Latin America around 1880, and had two main effects: it offered an entry to the advantages of urban life, and access to cultural improvement. It was thus both a mode of enforced integration of the peasantry and urban poor into 'society' and a way of asserting their rights to share goods and services which the privileged minority had previously monopolized.[9] This key ambivalence of the media becomes lost to view if they are assumed simply to be instruments for imposing the ideological messages of ruling groups. It is therefore crucial to keep in sight the fact that media are not mere conveyors of messages but meeting-points of often contradictory ways of remembering and interpreting. To approach the media in this way requires attention to the cultural contexts of their reception, the variety of ways in which they are received and used.

At this point, another approach to the problem of locating the popular in relation to mass culture should be mentioned. This is the use of the notion of a market for symbolic goods, as a means of defining what happens to cultural products in a consumer society. The popular then becomes defined by the unequal access of the subaltern classes to this market. This way of defining the popular, as developed by Néstor García Canclini,[10] combines Pierre Bourdieu's approach with that of Gramsci, and is useful in that its vocabulary permits both the investigation of culture as power and an analysis of the impact of the capitalist market.[11] Any study of popular culture must be indebted to Gramsci's crucial concept of hegemony. It breaks with the crude application of Marx's thesis that the ruling ideas in any period are those of the ruling class, and emphasizes instead the ways in which particular social groups become hegemonic through obtaining consent within the cultural arena to the general direction which they impose on society as a whole. The term hegemony is therefore essential for the study of popular culture in that it highlights the negotiations which take place on a cultural level between dominant and subaltern groups. This means that culture is not simply derived from class, as if it were a crude form of ideology, but on the contrary plays a primary role in challenging or maintaining given social relationships. The major limitation to the concept of hegemony, with its basis in consent obtained by non-violent means, is its lack of or at least diminished relevance to situations of violence, which have prevailed in a number of Latin American countries.[12]

(Gramsci's great contribution to the study of culture is the understanding that culture is inseparable from relationships of power.) One way of developing his insights is to take popular culture not as a given view of the world but as a space or series of spaces where popular subjects, as distinct from members of ruling groups, are formed. The stress in this case would be democratic rather than utopian, in the sense of recognizing actual differences between the subjectivity of different classes, rather than creating ideal models which assume that there is – or should be – a single popular identity. On the other hand, it seems likely for the time being that in Latin America popular culture will continue to have utopian connotations. When the variety of popular cultures is unified by using the term in the singular, this expresses in some degree a utopian political programme; if we have in this book used it in the singular as well as the plural, this is in recognition of the transitional state of current thinking.[13] Actually existing popular cultures have an inter-penetrative relationship with mass culture. Historically, the unification of the cultural market, which was vital for the establishment of a national culture industry (Mexico and Brazil are prime examples) has only been achieved by incorporating forms of popular memory already in process of massification, as happened with the Mexican film industry.)

When the popular is defined not as an object, a meaning or a social group, but as a site – or, more accurately, a series of dispersed sites – then it generates a principle of opposition to the idea, imposed by authoritarian liberalism or by populism, of the nation as a single body. As the Mexican Ezequiel Chávez put it in 1901, the Mexican people had not yet been 'ground by the mortar of centuries so as to form a single body with a certain homogeneity'.[14] The drive for homogeneity throughout Latin America in the twentieth century meant either the suppression of popular culture or its appropriation by the authoritarian state. The notion of dispersed sites is not the same as pluralism. Pluralism belongs to the liberal theory which allows that society consists in a plurality of interests, but gives to the state the role of mediating them. The study of popular culture is incompatible with ascribing to the state a fictitiously neutral function, since what states have actually done is to seek to homogenize culture in order to consolidate the power of ruling groups.

At the same time, the assumption that the culture of subaltern groups is necessarily the expression of resistance to state authority creates problems of its own. To place the relationships between dominant power and the popular inside a vocabulary of conformity versus resistance entails simplification and distortion of the issues. To say that something is resistant is often part of a political agenda, usually unspoken: certain cultural forms are taken to represent popular resistance without clarifying what in real terms is being resisted or what alternative notions of sociality the resistance implies. Also dubious is the dualistic thinking which conformity/resistance can generate: each side of the opposition becomes unified, as though a monolithic dominant structure were faced with an equally coherent popular resistance. The problem can be seen clearly if one looks at the processes by which cultural formations arise, rather than abstracting them as finished products. (Both resistance and conformity can occur simultaneously, as for instance in popular religiosity, where fatalism combines with the desire for change.[15]) Thus, to shift terms but continue the same debate, dominant and subaltern are not already constituted collective subjects, or intrinsic properties, but modes of conflict which link discourses and practices.[16]

However, the problems of vocabulary cannot be resolved by multiplying terms. On the contrary, one must be alert to the different theorizations and constructions of the field which particular terms entail. For example, a slippage tends to occur from subaltern to resistant to emancipatory, whereas the usefulness of the term subaltern is its emphasis upon the straightforward fact of subordination without connotations of an alternative political project. The problems begin with the mythical or ideological assumption built into such words used simultaneously as descriptive and programmatic. 'Counter-hegemonic' is in this sense a more useful term, since it places emphasis clearly and openly on the idea of an alternative power structure. On the other hand, there is no set of 'correct' terms which will solve all the problems. When the field to be described and analysed has shifting boundaries, as popular culture does, then some mobility of terms and concepts is appropriate. One of the priorities is neither to dissolve nor to rigidify the ambiguities of the shifting cultural map. The concepts of reconversion, resignification and resemanticization are particularly appropriate to popular culture as ways of handling the constant refashioning of cultural signs which keeps alive the sites of the popular and prevents them being wholly absorbed into the dominant power structures. The types of temporal, spatial and symbolic shifts we refer to can be exemplified by the linking of pre-Spanish Indian war-dances with a modern political project in Peru, or parading the community-based radio station in a Brazilian shanty town as though it were a saint in a religious procession, or using the iconography of Superman to articulate the demands for adequate housing from the Mexican state by inhabitants of shanty towns.

The investigation of popular culture poses the rethinking of the whole cultural field, from the practices of everyday life to artistic production. Its proper documentation shakes up influential paradigms of cultural history (both folklore and media studies, for example), challenges discourses of identity (populist ones, for example), and undermines literary and art-historical theories (magical-realist ones, for example). Inevitably a multi-disciplinary action, it requires taking the cultural sphere as neither merely derivative from the socio-economic, as a merely ideological phenomenon, nor as in some metaphysical sense preceding it. Rather, it is the decisive area where social conflicts are experienced and evaluated.

Popular culture in Latin America has tended to be ignored by the paternalistic Enlightenment rationalism of the Left but not by the culture industry. In recent years the traditional political parties, relying on pre-modern forms of social communication and social relationships, have lost ground to the mass media. The kinds of issue which seem likely to become particularly important in the 1990s centre on globalization of the media on the one hand, and the defence of cultural multiplicity on the other. The first needs to be confronted without apocalyptic pessimism and the second defended without attempts to preserve 'purity'. Both are traversed by movements for democratization throughout the geographical region. Popular culture is vital in this respect as the recognition of collective experiences which are not acknowledged by the established political culture. In the past decade, a new tradition of Latin American cultural criticism has been emerging; important new theoretical and empirical work has been produced, in which the experience of massive social destruction under the dictatorships of the 1970s and '80s and the study of popular culture have been the key impetus. The redistribution of cultural power and access and the revaluation of popular culture by the Sandinista government in Nicaragua, which drew in turn on the experiences of Cuba and of various radical traditions in Latin America, stands as a major achievement. The New Right rejects cultural nationalism and, in the face of the labour movement's and the traditional ruling groups' loss of prestige, reduces culture pragmatically to the prestige necessary for a given social group to retain power. The cognitive and creative dimensions of culture are abandoned: the only questions are technical ones. Nevertheless, the diagnosis that previous bases of political power are no longer viable seems correct. The discourse of the New Right, now becoming dominant in Latin America, can only be countered by a careful rethinking of the whole cultural field and its history.

The selection and distribution of material in this book has initially been shaped by the division between folk or rural culture and mass, urban culture. However, in the study of particular examples, we have sought to problematize critically such divisions, especially where cultural forms move across geographical and social boundaries. The ideal goal of a study of popular culture in Latin America would be to create the 'nocturnal map' of which Martín-Barbero speaks: 'We need to have at our disposal something like a "nocturnal map" which will allow us . . . to establish articulations between the *operations* – of withdrawal, rejection, assimilation, refunctionalization, redesign – the *matrices* – of class, territory, ethnicity, religion, sex, age – the *spaces* – habitat, factory, neighbourhood, prison – and the *media* – micro like cassette recordings and photography, meso like the record or the book, macro like the press, radio or television.'[17] The map is nocturnal because the terrain has still to be made visible. The present study seeks to establish and explore this new terrain by drawing on history, ethnography, sociology, literary criticism and communications theory. A synthesis on this scale has not been attempted before, and we hope that the gaps we leave will be instigations for future work.

In the present book, descriptive material is concentrated in the second chapter, where a series of examples of different popular cultures is offered. These show something of the exuberant variety of cultures in Latin America, and of the changes they have been passing through in the twentieth century. It has been impossible to embrace all countries and geographic areas. We have not considered the highly significant phenomenon of border culture, where migrants to the USA elaborate inventive responses to their experience, to be within our purview.[18] However, those areas included have been selected because they are paradigmatic in particular ways. The three other chapters take the form of essays which explore the broad issues arising in the study of popular culture in Latin America: its history, the ways it has been appropriated politically, and its relations with high culture. Chapter 1 gives a historical view of the continuities and discontinuities which have marked popular cultures from the time of the Spanish and Portuguese Conquest until the earlier twentieth century. Chronologically, Chapter 3 begins approximately where Chapter 1 left off, and seeks to trace the main uses made of popular culture by populist political movements in the twentieth century. The final chapter tests the validity of differentiations between popular culture and high culture and looks at the part played by popular culture in the work of some major twentieth-century writers.

Notes

1. Pierre Bourdieu, *Outline of a Theory of Practice*, Cambridge 1977, p. 196.

2. José Jorge de Carvalho, 'Notas para una revisión conceptual de los estudios de la cultura poplar tradicional', Ponencia para le Segunda Reunión Interamericana sobre la Cultura Popular y Tradicional, Caracas 1987, p. 6.

3. See Eve Marie Fell, 'Du folklore rural au folklore commercial: une expérience dirigiste au Pérou', *Caravelle*, No. 48, pp. 59–68.

✗ 4. See Néstor García Canclini, *Las culturas populares en el capitalismo*, Mexico 1982, and Rodrigo Montoya, *Producción parcelaria y universo ideológico*, Lima 1979.

5. Tomas Turino, paper given at the Institute of Latin American Studies, London, 16 March 1990. The individual in this case was a schoolteacher, indicating the influence of modernization and folklorization. The music, nevertheless, was presented to the outside world as collectively created, in line with the ideology of folklore.

6. For example, in Armand Mattelart and S. Siegelaub, eds., *Communication and Class Struggle*, New York 1979.

↗ 7. Jesús Martín-Barbero, *De los medios a las mediaciones*, Barcelona 1987, p. 95. Cf. Jesús Martín-Barbero's statement at the Symposium on Media in Latin America held by the Centre for Latin American Cultural Studies, London, 25 May 1990: 'mass is a category created by the European Right in the nineteenth century which the Left never revised. And the criticism of communication media in Latin America was anchored in a vision of mass media as a product rather than as part of the massification of the whole social structure: that is, of the emergence and visibility of the masses on the national scene.'

8. See Martín-Barbero, *Procesos de comunicación y matrices de cultura*, Mexico n.d., p. 96. For further discussion of the non-passivity of consumers of mass media, see Michel de Certeau, *The Practices of Everyday Life*, London 1988, pp. xii, xv, 18.

9. Martín-Barbero, *De los medios*, pp. 172–3.

↘ 10. Néstor García Canclini, '¿Reconstruir lo popular?', ponencia presentada al seminario 'Cultura popular: un balance interdisciplinario', organizado por el Instituto Nacional de Antropología, Buenos Aires, September 1988.

11. Some caution is needed in using Gramsci's thought, as José Joaquín Brunner's objections to García Canclini's approach help to make clear: if one respects Gramsci's definition of culture as a 'conception of the world', which implies that it must be 'organized' and coherent in its own terms, then popular culture is not something that actually exists in Gramsci's sense of a culture, but is only a project for the future. (See Brunner, *Un espejo trizado*, Santiago 1988, pp. 159–61.) One of the many issues arising here is the possibility that Gramsci's formulations, which belong to a different historical moment, are not necessarily appropriate in an age of simulations and hybridization: perhaps the notion of popular culture as a world view, given the degree of totalization that term implies, is no longer possible or useful at the end of the century.

12. The separation of hegemony from violence is not simple, as is shown by Gramsci's own mixing of a vocabulary of consent with one of warfare.

✗ 13. For a critical review of current thinking, see Jean Franco, 'What's in a Name? Popular Culture Theories and their Limitations', *Studies in Latin American Popular Culture*, Vol. I, pp. 5–14.

14. Roger Bartra, *La jaula de la melancolía*, Mexico 1987, p. 132.

15. Marilena Chaui, *Conformismo e resistencía*, São Paulo 1986, pp. 9–47, 84. Also useful is Michel Foucault's notion of the polyvalence of discourse (in *The Archaeology of Knowledge*, London 1974) whereby no discourse is purely dominant or oppositional but is always in some degree both. See Alan Sheridan, *Michel Foucault: The Will to Truth*, London 1980, p. 186.

16. 'Gramsci con Bourdieu', unpublished paper.

17. Martín-Barbero, *Procesos*, p. 135.

✗ 18. See Néstor García Canclini, 'Escenas sin territorio: Estética de las migraciones e identidades en transición', *Revista de Critica Cultural*, Vol. I, No. 1, pp. 9–14, and *Tijuana: la casa de toda la gente*, Mexico 1989. See also Harry Polkinhorn, 'Chain Link: Towards a Theory of Border Writing', *La Linea: Ensayos sobre literatura fronteriza México-Nortamericana*, Calexico n.d., Vol. 1, pp. 37–43.

ONE

Breaks and Continuities

The history of popular cultures in Latin America is a subject of vast scope. A full-length overview has not, to our knowledge, been attempted. This chapter offers a chronological view of key processes and moments which may serve as guides to how a more complete map might be drawn. This approach, as opposed to an overall survey, has been chosen in order to draw attention to all the variety of possible perspectives. Another factor is the paucity of research in this field. Excellent new work has been appearing in recent years, but a great deal of basic investigation remains to be done. The account which follows aims to trace some of the historical continuities in the cultural life of the popular classes, from the time of European Conquest to around 1940.

Certain conditions, such as the mixing of European and native American elements, have continued through the whole period; some features, such as magical rather than rationalist ways of thinking and seeing, have remained fairly constant over the long term. Particular forms, such as the Andean dance and song known as the *huayno*, have a continuous presence from pre-Conquest times to the twentieth century, while others, such as the Argentinian and Uruguayan tango, span the past hundred years. These greater or lesser continuities are cut across by discontinuities which break or transform them: the idea that there has been a smooth accumulation of popular traditions is not viable. The discontinuities include changes in communication media (newspapers, radio), social revolutions, industrialization and population migrations; the main break, which includes all of these, has been the effect of modernization. The tango, for instance, coincides with

17

the period of modernization, and in the process changes from a rural to an urban form. The *huayno*, under the impact both of immigration to the cities and of the recording industry, has metamorphosed into the hybrid musical form of *chicha*. *Chicha* can be heard in New York, an example of the increasing international migration of styles. In Peru, alongside such hybrid forms, the traditional *huayno* still continues. Old, new and hybrid forms coexist, thus invalidating those approaches which assume that there has been an evolution in which the old is superseded by the new. Latin America is characterized by the coexistence of different histories: this chapter offers an introduction to some of the complexities involved.

Among the key concepts for drawing a historical map of Latin American culture are acculturation, *mestizaje* and transculturation. Acculturation refers to a one-way process of conversion and substitution of native cultures by European ones. *Mestizaje*, a word denoting racial mixture, assumes a synthesis of cultures, where none is eradicated. The difficulty with the idea of *mestizaje* is that, without an analysis of power structures, it becomes an ideology of racial harmony which obscures the actual holding of power by a particular group. Furthermore, debates about cultural *mestizaje* can founder through failure to distinguish between different modes and levels of cross-cultural influence.[1] Transculturation, a term arising out of anthropology, is used to counter critically the assumption that acculturation is the only long-term possibility for Latin America: it is concerned with the mutual transformation of cultures, in particular of the European by the native. Although none of these concepts is adequate to the complexity of the real historical process, they are useful for indicating some of the main ways of seeing it.

While acculturation and transculturation belong to twentieth-century debates, the term *mestizo* dates from the early colonial period. (The *mestizos*, born of Spanish fathers and Indian mothers, were held in very low esteem.) Their reputed ungovernability and instability mirrors the projected anxiety of the colonial ruling elite at the fact of inter-cultural mixing.[2] Racial purity was an essential symbol for the dominant, an inheritance which continues to affect present-day Latin American societies. However, from the time of emancipation from Spain and Portugal in the nineteenth century there begins a positive re-evaluation of *mestizaje*, and of 'our America' as vitally distinct both from its European colonial metropolises and its increasingly powerful northern 'neighbour'.

Colonization, Magic and the Limits of Obedience

The definition of the Spanish colonial action as Conquest, with its assumption of the rights of 'just war' and its echo of the reconquest of Spain from the Arabs, was rejected by Bartolomé de Las Casas, the Spanish Dominican friar. For Las Casas, the great defender of the Indians in the sixteenth century, the only appropriate word was invasion.[3] Reversing the terms of the justificatory epic of conquest, he called the Spaniards 'wolves' and the Indians 'lambs', and considered the Spanish actions to be destructive of any basis of law or rationality. For this reason, his account of the atrocities perpetrated by the Conquistadors in *Breve relación de la destrucción de las Indias* (*Brief Account of the Destruction of the Indies* 1552) constantly moves towards the edge of the unthinkable and unspeakable which threatens like a black hole to destroy all meaning.[4]

However, it is to the native and *mestizo* accounts of the invasion that we need to go in order to reconstruct the native experience. These native versions of the Conquest have been given increasing prominence in recent years, for instance by Miguel León Portilla.[5] The first attempt properly to document this other side of history is Nathan Wachtel's *The Vision of the Vanquished*, which makes pioneering use of the continuing historical memory of peasants in Middle America and Peru, particularly in the form of popular plays representing the Conquest, still performed to the present day.[6] Wachtel, however, overemphasizes the 'destructuring' of native cultures. It is true that one can now recognize the decimation of native populations by war, forced labour and disease as perhaps the worst genocidal action of history. And certainly the idea of an 'encounter' between two worlds, now being orchestrated – not without some remnants of imperialist arrogance – by the current Spanish government in preparation for the five-hundredth anniversary of 1492, is a cynical use of the modern fashion for cultural plurality in order to obscure the tremendous destructiveness of the actual events. Nevertheless, mutual transformations of both the European and the native cultures did occur, in different degrees and different directions. In spite of Las Casas's conclusion that the only constant factor was a law of increasing destructiveness, forms of Spanish and Portuguese civilization were established throughout the Indies, as the territories were called, and these were modified to different extents by the surviving native cultures – although in some cases nothing of the latter remained, as in Hispaniola, where within thirty years of the first arrival of the Spanish, the total native population had disappeared.

The main thrust was towards the colonization of native consciousness and this met with varying degrees of success. Colonial Mexico exemplifies very effectively the processes of acculturation, native resistance and *mestizaje*, given the extent to which the native population, except in Yucatán to the South, was successfully acculturated over the three centuries of colonial rule. Up to around the middle of the sixteenth century, the modes of expression of the two cultures combined in a multiplicity of ways, opening up the possibility of a mixed or *mestizo* culture. By the late sixteenth century, the elimination of the native nobility, experts in native script and painting – the most powerful vehicles for native knowledge – and the decimation by disease of the vast majority of the non-Spanish population had aborted the possibility of a free interaction of cultures. Before that, there had begun to flourish a multiplicity of simultaneous practices and expressions, including glyphs; pictographic and alphabetic script; painted images and engraving; pre-Hispanic and Christianized oral transmission; native languages, with Nahuatl as lingua franca, as well as Latin and Spanish; and juxtapositions of native and Christian calendrical and mathematical notation.[7] By 1541, twenty years after the Conquest, some Spaniards were nervous about the number and excellence of native scribes, who were now able to assemble a complete knowledge of the country – an alarming possibility given the assumption that this was an accomplishment 'which previously was impossible for them'.[8] However, the question of how far two entirely different traditions might combine was pre-empted by Spanish campaigns for the extirpation of idolatry, and the weakening of native populations by disease. By the end of the sixteenth century the material basis of native memory had suffered drastically: informants who had memorized 'the words of the ancients' had died; techniques for recording and reading pictographic information had been lost; documents had disappeared, confiscated by the Spanish religious orders, destroyed by the Indians or simply neglected insofar as they had become indecipherable.[9] In fact by this time the speed of acculturation had greatly accelerated due to the effacement of native concepts, of the material supports of information (native screen-folds, 'idols', and so on), and of the human beings themselves. As happened during this same period in Peru, a wave of suicides and infanticides occurred in response to the destruction of the native universe.

Nevertheless, after this first destruction, a number of sites of resistance evaded suppression. Despite attempted effacements by Western mapping, the landscape retained its traditional cosmological meanings, in the form both of place-names which the Spanish could not replace and of the remembered magical significance of land features. At the same time, Christian ideas were used as disguises for the preservation of native thinking. For example, the doctrine of the resurrection of the dead was reused by natives to express their traditional belief in the continued existence of ancestors as guardians of village tradition.[10] One of the places where an alternative memory of this kind was preserved were the *títulos primordiales*, false land-titles which served as counter-documents to those of the colonial administration. These date from the second half of the seventeenth century and continue even up to the end of the nineteenth century.

The aspects of life most intensely and persistently captured by the Church did not necessarily correspond with the intensities of native life. One of the sites which tended to escape the extirpation of idolatry, the term used to refer to native religion, was the house, the hub of everyday life. Here peasants gathered together bundles of diverse objects, which might include statuettes, bracelets and hallucinogenic mushrooms; although not to be touched, these nevertheless offered a continuity with ancestors, 'a sort of symbolic and material capital'.[11] In a broader sense, idolatry involved a way of thinking which clashed with a Western rationality based on Aristotle's philosophy. The native world was characterized by a non-Aristotelian fluidity of time and space, a permeability of things and beings, a multidimensionality, which undermined the stable categories of Western thinking, upheld by the Church against Satan, who was held responsible for such destabilizations of natural order.[12]

The Jesuits were probably the most determined and inventive of the religious orders in their efforts to emplace a Christian subjectivity which would reduce the multiplicity of the native cosmos to a duality of good and evil. It was Jesuit policy to use native traditions of song, dance and theatre to make acculturation as penetrative as possible; for instance they wrote Catholic hymns in native languages and set them to native music. In the northeast of Brazil they established a tradition of religious plays, which interpreted history as a struggle between God and the Devil, and these became a key feature of *sertão* culture, as in Glauber Rocha's extraordinary film, *Deus e o diabo na terra do sol* (*Black God White Devil* 1963).[13] The film shows how Jesuit ideology has been transformed into popular Manicheism, with its belief in the possible reversal of the social order.

Two issues begin to emerge. First, there is the question of how far the Christian intellectual grid distorted native thought. A central point in this sense was idolatry, the belief that the sacred is present in objects. By defining native culture as idolatrous, the Spanish were reconstructing native thought in

21

terms of its magical-religious aspects and intensifying these as markers of evil and of difference. Second, there are the ways in which Christian concepts are changed and in greater or lesser degree reappropriated into native or non-orthodox codes. The distinction is necessarily crude at this stage, and will be refined shortly. The gaps which Christianity could not reach had to do particularly with the individual and domestic spheres, whereas the public domain was more permeable to Christianization. Gruzinski speaks of the 'silences of the Church on illness and birth, on the rapport with nature and the elements, but equally on the domestic group'.[14] Native practices tended to continue especially in relation to misfortune, illness and death. And in this matter of counter-acculturation, women rather than men often played the major role. In divination, for example, the experts tended to be women: 'It is most often women who locate objects and animals which have become lost, find lost companions and re-establish the domestic equilibrium when it has been disturbed.'[15]

Over time, the native practices dubbed as idolatry broke increasingly adrift from the comprehensive context of meanings they originally reproduced. Idolatry remained a repertory of actions, conducts and ruses capable of giving coherence to the emotional states of the person but at the same time running the risk of no longer being a way of interpreting the cosmos and 'an organized semantic memory' but becoming instead isolated and esoteric formulae. This decontextualization, however, was one of the conditions for the success of practitioners such as *curanderos* (curers, sometimes translated as witch-doctors) among other social groups, including Spaniards. The more they were able to answer the needs of other classes, the more their rituals and symbols became disconnected from pre-Hispanic native knowledge. At the same time, native iconography and religious terminology were becoming detached from their traditional contexts as a result of Western modes of reading. It is perhaps useful to introduce here the distinction made by Soviet semiotics of culture: if a measure of the strength and viability of a culture is its capacity both to store information and to process new information, then what we have described constitutes a reduction of this capacity on the part of native cultures, though by no means their disappearance.[16]

One of the phenomena that occurred as a result of the redistribution of cultural practices was a convergence, which can be termed 'colonial magic'.[17] Arising from a variety of origins – popular European, African, as well as native American – it broke the Church's monopoly of the supernatural and served as a way of getting round the inequalities of colonial hierarchy. 'This cascade of gestures, substances, formulae, these discrete connections . . . just as much as corruption, give colonial society its dynamism and plasticity.'[18] This was particularly true of erotic magic, which could be used to overcome the numerous barriers of caste in order to gain the sexual attentions of someone who was socially forbidden. Such minor everyday practices occurred within the interstices of the rigid hierarchies of colonial society, and over time formed a key stratum of popular culture.[19] In this sense, the marvellous, on which twentieth-century magical realism is based, has its origins in the colonial period, and was transmitted above all by women. The transmission occurred in the gap between tactical obedience and pragmatic evasion: 'obedezco pero no cumplo' ('I obey but I do not accept'), in the Spanish phrase. Women adapted black and indigenous religion to practical uses and invented new ritual practices. Magic responded to a lack of mechanisms for mediating relationships in colonial society: Spanish women for instance were supplied with herbs by blacks, and with drugs by Indians. Magical practices did not cohere into a body of belief nor fuse into a movement of resistance; nevertheless they were used where there were no social mechanisms for resolving conflict and they fed into a substratum of popular culture which changed little until the onset of modernization. Such historical continuities of popular culture should not simply be assumed to recur automatically, as if they were archetypes. There is always the question of how something was actually transmitted, by whom and in what circumstances. In what we have described above, this body of popular attitudes was transmitted by women, in those spheres of life which most eluded the controls of the colonial institutions.

Native visions of the Christian supernatural, which above all took the form of appearances of the Virgin Mary, began to occur in Mexico very soon after the Conquest. Cultural incompatibilities become diminished in dreams and visions, where elements from different sources can combine more freely than where verbal representations are involved. Visions, a major conduit for the acculturation of natives by missionaries, can also facilitate an opposite native use of Christian iconography within native structures of belief. Doubts about the direction of the process – colonial penetration or native appropriation – form a major part of the early history of the Virgin of Guadalupe, whose shrine was to become the most important of all Christian holy places in the New World and whose image became the most significant icon of emergent Mexican nationalism. 'The Virgin was the standard of the Indians and *mestizos* who fought in 1810 against the Spaniards, and a century later she became the banner of the peasant armies of Zapata.... The feast day of Guadalupe, December 12, is still the feast day par excellence, the central date in the emotional calendar of the Mexican people.'[20] The image, now housed in a church specially built for it, is fronted by a moving floorway, to keep the endless crowd of pilgrims flowing before it.

The eventual power of the symbol resided in its capacity over time to represent a convergence of Indian and creole consciousness. When an image of the Virgin first appeared to an Indian in 1531, the Catholic Church was suspicious. The appearance occurred just north of Mexico City, at Tepeyac, the place of an Indian shrine to Tonantzin, a major Aztec divinity whose name means 'our mother'. For Sahagún, a Franciscan friar committed to the extirpation of native religion, this syncretism of native and Christian belief was very dangerous, 'a satanic invention to palliate idolatry'.[21] However, by the late sixteenth century, the Church had had to bow before the shrine's miraculous powers. In the seventeenth century, the Virgin of Guadalupe became a key icon for growing creole nationalism. As a social group, creoles were people of Spanish descent who had been born in the New World. This increasingly large group was excluded from high public office and their growing frustration made them the source of incipient Mexican nationalism. Metropolitan Spain's view was that New Spain, as Mexico was then called, owed its origin to the Spanish evangelical mission, entrusted by the Pope as God's representative, in converting Indians from paganism to the true faith. For the creoles, it was necessary to counter the claims of Spanish historiography by asserting the originality of Mexico as a country existing in its own right. The Virgin of Guadalupe supplied a basis for arguing both that the Indians were not idolatrous and that God had bestowed great spiritual favours upon Mexico, without the mediation of Spain.[22] Guadalupe could be considered as important as the great Spanish Virgen de los Remedios, invoked by the Conquistador Hernán Cortés.

Independence: Official Versions and Popular Versions

Guadalupe became an ideal symbol of nationalism because she could serve as an emblem of common identity between creoles and the lower social orders. In this context, Benedict Anderson's insistence upon literacy as the basis for nationalism, not only in Europe but in Latin America, is somewhat misleading.[23] He argues that a national society cannot be fashioned out of traditional local relationships but needs to give its members a new, broader sense of belonging. This, he claims, is supplied above all by the novel, a form which generates a shared space-time whose inhabitants need not know each other directly provided they share the sense of 'meanwhile', of other similar lives occurring simultaneously. The weaknesses of Anderson's scheme lie precisely in its omission of the role of popular culture. It cannot account for the extent of popular participation in the independence movements; the fact that this participation depended not on literacy but on oral transmission and iconography; and the fact that popular identity did not and does not necessarily correspond with the nation and its boundaries as state but may involve other allegiances of a regional, ethnic or class nature. In some areas of Latin America, these are unfinished struggles, even in the late twentieth century.

Anderson's omissions are highlighted by Yolanda Salas's study of the metamorphoses of Simón Bolívar in popular consciousness. Of all the figures involved in the political emancipation of Latin America, Bolívar is the best known. He was born of creole parents and inherited a sizeable landed estate. His own vivid and succinct characterization of the situation of creoles was that they were neither 'Indians nor Europeans, but rather a species in between the legitimate owners of the country and the Spanish usurpers'.[24] There are a variety of popular traditions in Venezuela which reveal the distance between creole concerns and popular ones. The latter reinterpret the figure of Bolívar and have him born in a black region, and of a slave mother. As Salas points out in her account of these popular interpretations, 'the notion of the hero and saviour originating within the oppressed group elevates the status of that group both socially and ethnically'.[25] These versions rely entirely upon oral transmission, which raises particular issues of continuity and authenticity, dramatized in the words of an informant recorded in the mid 1980s: 'It is still said, there are people who give it voice [that Bolívar was born there], but it is not given any hearing. It is not given any belief, because a person living today cannot say I saw him or not. But everyone living now has had parents, and one's own parents have had grandparents, and those are people who come dragging that secret along with them.'[26] The actual process of passing remembered information from one person to another over time and thus building a history is conveyed in the vivid physicality of the words: *vocifera* (shout or give voice), *escucha* (hearing), *arrastrando* (dragging). The other main way in which the figure became known at popular levels was through the iconography of coins and matchboxes.

Salas also found that in present-day Venezuela, Bolívar is both a shaman with healing powers and a spirit who, when invoked in the correct way, will come down and intervene in the present. A striking feature of the popular versions is how symbols elaborated elsewhere (by the Spanish or creoles) are resemanticized into counter-symbols. This happens with Bolívar's white horse. In the Spanish historical imagination, the white horse belongs to Santiago (St James), patron saint of the Conquistadors. In the popular Venezuelan historical imagination the white horse of Bolívar had magical powers: it could fly, pass through mountains, or disappear behind white smoke. This was why Bolívar was never touched by a bullet: the horse protected him, making him invisible behind the smoke, or carrying him from one place to another with extraordinary speed.[27] To think in this way is to disperse the sacred, so that it takes the form of magic or 'superstition', as it was called by the Enlightenment – an attitude which clashes with the Church's centralization and monopolization of the sacred. The very disorder which Bolívar sought so persistently to eradicate during his life, with constitutions which enshrined higher moral and civic virtues, here seems to have taken revenge upon him. Programmes to educate the lower social groups about liberal institutions and republican virtues have made little headway among Salas's informants, whose polymorphic interpretations of history are attempts to establish their own power both as actors in history and as recorders of it. Similar phenomena occur throughout much of Latin America.

The first Bolivian constitution was written by Bolívar himself, whose name had of course been chosen for the new republic which was founded in 1825. His proposals included the institution of censors, who would be the guardians of the secular religion of the state: 'the censors exercise a moral and political authority which has some resemblance with that of the Areopagus in Athens or the Censors in Rome. They will be the guardians against the Government to ensure that the Constitution . . . is observed with religion.'[28] Although this measure was not eventually included in the constitution, it exemplifies the discrepancy between institutions and reality which characterizes the majority of post-Independence Latin American states. Bolivia, at the time of Independence, had a majority Indian population. In spite of this, as far as liberal-creole historiography is concerned, Indians have been silent in the republican history of Bolivia.

Indian and creole interpretations of the symbols of the Republic competed with each other. For the creoles, the 'liberation of the Indian is taken as the central ideological justification of the Wars of Independence from Spain'. One of the forms the justification took was a hammered gold sheet, commissioned for display in the new parliament, depicting 'a beautiful Indian girl, symbolizing America, seated upon the remnants of a lion and beneath a canopy, formed by the flags of the continents' countries'. In addition, Bolívar and Sucre (another Independence hero) are 'seen in the act of decorating her with the cap of liberty'.[29] However, against the creole iconography, in which the virgin to-be-liberated was quickly convertible into virgin (land) to be possessed, there existed an Indian counter-iconography, concentrated around the key image of the Virgin as *pachamama* (literally earth-mother), symbol of reproductive increase. This symbol was deployed by Indians to legitimate their claims to the land, as against such creole representations as for example a medal showing the Liberator (Bolívar) 'at the top of a ladder formed by guns, swords, cannons and flags ... placing on the Mountain [of Potosí] the cap of liberty'.[30] The designs of liberty upon the Potosí mountain, the richest silver mine of the Americas, reveal their agenda of economic appropriation. The village square is another place of interpretative convergence and collision, where the tree in front of the church can stand variously for the republican tree of liberty or the Indian sacred tree. 'A "sacred tree" growing in front of the church in the central square is today a common feature of many old Indian towns ... in Potosí. It is rooted in a square which is thought of as an expression of the Virgin (*wirjin*), or *pachamama*, thus symbolizing the lands of the local ethnic group. In this way the parish tree becomes a symbol of local regenerative increase.'[31]

Law, Order and the State

Independence from Spain was secured throughout most of the subcontinent by the 1820s, though Cuba remained a Spanish colony until 1898. The popular classes did not necessarily support the creoles against Spain; they often took the opposite side.

Popular culture, in the post-Independence period, cannot be separated from the process of state-formation. The construction of nation-states, which was the goal of the creole elites, was impeded by the inheritance of colonial forms of society. Among the latter were *caciquismo*, the institution whereby members of native ruling groups had been allowed to retain local power in exchange for loyalty to the colonial regime, a power which tended to keep rural populations in the semi-feudal position of retainees; *latifundismo*, the organization of land into very large estates; and clientelist politics, which were an obstacle to the achievement of national as opposed to local loyalties. Political liberation – from Spain – was not the same as social emancipation, as the great nineteenth-century thinker Andrés Bello pointed out. Republicanism did not necessarily free peasants from feudal landholding institutions; in many cases it reinforced the power of landlords, as with the sugar *usinas* in Brazil or the *haciendas* (large estates) in the Spanish-speaking countries. The popular classes, whose formation was linked with colonial institutions, or who recognized that the new liberal institutions offered them little benefit, were for the creoles the recalcitrant element which had to be brought into line.

Argentina offers a particularly useful example of these issues. The clash of different social formations is revealed most sharply in the cities, especially in Buenos Aires. 'In matters of form', as one historian puts it, 'this is a modern and near-perfect European metropolis; in matters related to quotidian social and political behaviours, however, the record of Europeanization is checkered.'[32] Buenos Aires continued to be 'a terminus of rural and pastoral behaviours, while becoming the hub of South Atlantic trade with Europe'. This highly contradictory situation made it a testing ground for the ideology of progress.[33]

The Wars of Independence brought a breakdown of authority. Subsequently, the control of the masses (the *gente de pueblo*) became a persistent and elusive concern of the creole elites (the *gente decente*). The principal goal of the latter was 'the institutionalization of stable systems of community, mechanisms by which links could be established that would be capable of binding a public that shared a common space and heritage'.[34] However, for the *gente de pueblo*, the bonds of community were not felt towards the city or the nation, but towards the *barrio* (neighbourhood) and the *casa* (house). Moreover, the popular classes consumed little in the way of European goods. 'Women seldom owned more than a couple of shawls and blouses, perhaps as many as three skirts, and one pair of shoes or sandals. Undergarments were similarly few, and most men's clothing was comparably limited.'[35] The further one moved away from the Plaza de Mayo, the administrative centre of Buenos Aires, the greater the percentage of people wearing ponchos, *chiripás* and other rural clothing.

Consolidation of the power of the state required the legal and bureaucratic regulation of the population. Mobility of population was severely restricted and those authorities who failed to carry out regulations were threatened with condemnation as enemies of the fatherland. The use of criminalization as social control is revealed in the fact that, after robbery, the most common crime was insult and insubordination, in other words offending social superiors.[36] Lower-class vagrancy was a repeated worry voiced in the newspaper editorials read by the *gente decente*. 'The streets swarm with vagrants and the billiard halls are crowded with boys'; 'boys . . . roam through the streets, engaging in indecent games and annoying passers-by'.[37] In the provincial cities, the *gente decente* and the lower classes tended to share the same pastimes: 'walks in the plaza, patriotic and Church holidays (especially the pre-Lenten festivities of *Carnaval*), the theatre and special visiting attractions, horse races and equestrian competitions, cockfighting, public dances, billiards and cards, and bathing in the river'.[38] Nevertheless, as the cities grew larger, the separation of activities along class lines increased. The *gente decente* began to build their own race tracks and cockpits at the edge of town, and to establish clubs for their own use, leaving heavy drinking as an exclusively lower-class pastime.

Laws against vagrancy and the systematic marking of class distinction were among the preconditions of the formation of the modern Argentinian nation-state. Another essential step was the elimination of the Indians, not just from the lands to the south of Buenos Aires, but from the national conscious-ness – or perhaps it would be more accurate to speak of the consolidation of a national consciousness through a process of exclusion. The Indians of Argentina, proportionately a much smaller part of the population than in Bolivia, are also absent from official history. But their absence takes on an entirely different kind of importance. In a nation where ruling groups have repeatedly made use of popular voices in order to build a national identity, they are a reminder of what the official use of the popular excludes, in fact violently eradicates. In this sense, David Viñas's powerful book, *Indios, ejército y frontera* (*Indians, Army and Frontier* 1982), is written against the grain of liberal history. Viñas documents how the formation of the modern Argentinian state was completed with the military campaign of General Roca in 1879, which drove the Indians south of the Río Negro and opened up the pampas for capitalist exploitation. Within thirty-five years the pampas region was 'markedly more advanced than the rest of the country. It was covered by a dense network of railways. Its landed estates were clearly demarcated by barbed wire, its landscape dotted with small towns.'[39] It was also the source of over half the subcontinent's foreign trade. Roca's campaign brought about a new rigidity of geographical and cultural frontiers. The old frontier, based on a series of small forts, had permitted a multiplicity of identities, an interchange between Indians and non-Indians without imposed assimilation: 'these forts, rather than opposing the Indians, served as authentic market fairs where feathers, blankets, ponchos and skins were exchanged for herbs and sugar'.[40] The new frontier was based on genocide. The new mobility of the army, purchased by the 'Holy Trinity' of telegraph, Remington rifle and railways, immobilized cultural flows and meant that movements of population would in future be those of immigration to the capital.

Viñas's study highlights a characteristic of the ruling classes of most of Latin

America to this day: their continuing use of conquest ideology, of a vocabulary reaching all the way back to Columbus, which justifies the elimination of those elements believed to be a danger to the body politic. The Indians are the unassimilable-to-be-eliminated, they are the disappeared, as opposed to the gaucho who is always there as official voice of the popular. The gaucho would be remembered, the Indians forgotten. Viñas points to the ways in which the military government of 1976–85, responsible for the disappearance of some 30,000 people, saw itself as fulfilling the same providential history.[41] Having become in the nineteenth century the core institution of the state, its 'hidden god',[42] the army in its most recent period of rule was able to place its policy of mass extermination inside a language which enshrined the need to purify the body of the nation of 'subversive' elements, giving the nation the aura of the mystical body of Christ.[43]

By the 1880s, the speed of technological modernization was increasing. This period also serves as an approximate marker for major changes in popular cultures in most of Latin America, as a result of urbanization and massification. The lives and attitudes of the popular classes show considerable continuity from the seventeenth century, once the colonial regime was consolidated, until the late nineteenth century, which brought changes greater than those occurring with Independence early in the same century. At the level of habits and mentalities, the 1880s mark a major division; to give the same meaning to Independence is to accord 'explanatory power to the constitutionality of the political state', a flawed position given that the state represented a small proportion of the population.[44]

The term 'modernization' has implications wider than technological change. One of the difficulties involved in its use has to do with the frequent assumption that the updating of certain sectors of the economy will, by some trickle-down effect, improve the situation of the whole population. On the contrary, the effect is often to reinforce the partial marginalization and super-exploitation of pre-capitalist sectors of the economy, especially those involving the peasantry. Moreover, modernization of the economic infra-structure does not necessarily bring social modernization with it, but often proceeds alongside feudal and paternalistic features. Overall, modernization in Latin America was uneven (affecting mainly the coastal regions), partial (benefitting the landed elites and their successors rather than the majority) and distorted (with inadequate infrastructure and the continuation of monocultural production). It was under these conditions that the phenomenon of authoritarian liberalism, the combination of economic liberalism with social authoritarianism, came into being in nineteenth-century Latin America, especially in Argentina.

We therefore use the term modernization to refer to technological and economic changes without the assumption that these necessarily lead to modernity, itself a much-debated idea.[45] The most useful deployment of the term modernity is Beatriz Sarlo's notion of 'peripheral modernity', where 'peripheral' is used ironically, to expose the paternalistic assumption that Latin American countries are incapable of a proper modernity – like that of the 'advanced' countries – and to assert that Buenos Aires did achieve its own modernity in the early twentieth century. This lends support to the notion of a distinct Latin American modernity, with a specific character of its own, the nature of which will emerge in later chapters of this book.

Argentinian history is characterized by the state's employment of a 'popular' voice, purportedly that of 'the people'. The major manifestation of this phenomenon is Peronism, to be discussed in Chapter 3. For the present let us consider briefly what in some ways was its prelude: the use of the gaucho as a vehicle for the construction of a national consciousness. The gauchos were a nomadic group of *mestizos* who lived off the herds of wild cattle on the immense grassy plains of the pampas. Their lifestyle collided absolutely with any notion of capital accumulation. When hungry they would kill an animal, cut out the best part, the tongue, roast it on the spot and move on, leaving the carcass to the vultures. During the Independence struggles, the gauchos were recruited into the patriotic armies. But from the point of view of the landowning elite who were attempting to fashion a modern nation and for whom the pampas were the basis for the expansion of capital, which required land enclosure, the gaucho was an anomalous social element who had to be disciplined by the law. Those who failed to acquire employment as peons (labourers on the landed estates) – that is, to become sedentary – were condemned as *vagos* or *delincuentes* (vagrants or delinquents).

In an important recent book, Josefina Ludmer investigates the ways in which the gaucho was used in gauchesque literature, a genre which made use in written texts of the oral forms of gaucho song. The most famous books in this tradition are José Hernández's *Martín Fierro* (Part I 1872, Part 2, 1879) and Ricardo Güiraldes's *Don Segundo Sombra* (1926). The genre is built within the semantic opposition between the gaucho as 'vagrant' and the gaucho as 'patriot', terms which dramatize the process of nation formation.[46] While the gaucho's body is used by the army, his voice is deployed by the gauchesque writers, a voice within which 'imported' words such as liberty and *patria* – the universals of the European Enlightenment – can be enunciated and generalized as a genuinely 'popular' national consciousness. At the same time an exclusion is operated, against the 'bad' gaucho, for example in the figure of the deserter from the patriotic armies.

The gauchesque is one strand in the making of a popular urban culture. While Part I of *Martín Fierro* was phenomenally successful, it was mainly sold in the countryside, and read aloud in the *pulpería* (a cross between a bar and a general store), as earlier gauchesque poetry was read, to groups of peasants. Part II, however, was a success in Buenos Aires. This change corresponds to two main factors. In Part I (1872) the hero, conscripted to fight the Indians, deserts, becomes an outcast and goes to live with the Indians. Part II (1879), however, has Fierro return to civilization and express a programme of social reconciliation. The second factor has to do with major technological and social changes in the pampas, which brought about the disappearance of the gaucho as a distinct cultural entity and his integration into national society.

The speed of change in the pampas was considerable: from 1860 British capital began to build an industrial infrastructure, particularly in the form of railways; by the 1870s over a thousand miles of track had been laid. Beef was at the core of these developments: salt beef had been the first industrial product of the region; made from the meat of free-roaming native herds, it was not acceptable in Europe, even to the proletariat, and so the market, limited to the crews of sailing ships and Brazilian slaves, could not be expanded. From the 1880s, a series of major changes occurred: from stringy native breeds to imported shorthorn stock, from free-roaming herds to enclosed land with wire fencing, from pampas grass to cultivated alfalfa, and from the salt-meat plant to refrigerated exports. At the same time, a massive flow of immigration was taking place, from Europe to Argentina, and from the countryside to Buenos Aires. Argentina's population figures are as follows: 1869, 1,800,000: 1895, 4,000,000: 1914, 8,000,000. By the last of these dates, the population of Buenos Aires had risen to one and a half million.

The rapid expansion of Buenos Aires, making it the first modern city in Spanish America, coincided with the eclipse of the gauchesque genre. With the linguistic unification of the nation-state, the non-standard language of the gaucho could no longer function as the voice of the *patria*. And the materials of nineteenth-century rural life passed into new forms, which included the tango. Although histories of literature emphasize *Don Segundo Sombra*, far more widely read at the time were the popular novels produced by writers such as Eduardo Gutiérrez for what was becoming a mass urban public.

Between 1880 and 1910, a massive literacy programme reduced illiteracy to some 4 per cent, although the number without an effective capacity to read was clearly higher.[47] A measure of the scale of rural immigration to the capital is given in the fact that, in 1892, one fifth of the population had recently arrived from the provinces. These lived in some 2,192 *conventillos*, tenement buildings with one room per family. At the same time, over a third of the population of Argentina were foreign immigrants, the greater part from Italy. Nevertheless, it was the voices and images of rural culture which offered a model of communality, not only for the internal immigrants but also for the foreign ones.

> The plasma which seemed destined to unite the various fragments of the racial and cultural mosaic was constituted from a particular image of the peasant and his language; the projective screen upon which the various components sought to symbolize their insertion into the society was intensely coloured by all the signs and paraphernalia of the creole lifestyle, even though at that time this style was losing its specific supports: the gaucho, more or less free roaming herds...[48]

The period spanned by this literature is approximately 1880 to 1910. By the 1920s, with the loss of links with the old style of peasant life and the increasing social weight of the working class, it was definitely in decline. Its role, therefore, had been a transitional one, offering an imaginary continuity.

If one broadens one's gaze to other forms and to other Latin American countries, the transition towards modernity passed principally through the following: newspapers, the *folletín*, the circus, popular theatre, and photography. One of its best exemplifications of this transition is the work of the Mexican engraver José Guadalupe Posada (1852–1913), whose prints were published in newspapers and as broadsheets. They combine a traditional iconographic style with modern printmaking technology; the appearance of pre-industrial woodcut technique is deliberately created without actually being used: Posada in fact used more modern, industrial procedures. The prints are accompanied by texts in ballad form, a form which had not changed since the colonial period. The traditional is thus resignified inside the modern – or, equally, the modern is arrived at through tradition. At the same time, Posada was engaged in the construction of the popular as a social space which was not rural, or proletarian or middle-class. This is shown particularly well in a print entitled 'Project for a monument to the people', which reuses the classical motif of the figure of Laocöon. There are three figures in it: on the left, an Indian representing 'the indigenous race', on the right a man wearing a cap, representing 'the proletariat', and in the centre 'the people', a man who looks like a peasant but is wearing black trousers rather than the white trousers worn by peasants in Mexico.[49]

The new urban popular culture differed both from rural traditions and from high culture. It was assumed by the educated elite to be degraded. For instance the literary establishment was intensely scathing about the novels of Gutiérrez and others: 'this is the most pernicious and unhealthy literature ever produced in this country'.[50] The objection was not just to vulgarity, to a vocabulary drawn 'from *conventillos* and prisons', but to the fact that all the protagonists were 'drunks, criminals and killers' – that is, they represented the *gaucho malo*, the bad, anti-social gaucho, not the good gaucho, the patriot. There was also a vast gap between the very small print-runs of 'serious' literature, a thousand copies being not unusual, and the tens of thousands of copies sold of popular *criollista* (creolist) literature. The new readership had been shaped by the rise of mass circulation newspapers. In 1882, for a population of some three million, the total number of copies produced per day seems to have been over 300,000.[51] Gutiérrez's most successful novels, the best known of which was *Juan Moreira*, were all published in *folletín* (serial) form by the newspaper *La Patria Argentina* and immediately thereafter as books under the imprint of the same newspaper. At the same time, the *gaucho malo* entered into other circuits: *Juan Moreira* was presented as a pantomime in Buenos Aires in 1884, and the eponymous hero became a key figure in the creole circus – where it was not uncommon for spectators to jump into the ring in order to defend him from the police. Moreira also figured in the Carnival, the main popular celebration in the streets of Buenos Aires at the turn of the century. The most fashionable disguises were gaucho ones, and the favourite seems to have been Moreira. The wearers of the disguises were *compadritos*, the term for peasants newly arrived in the city. These were men with a reputation for macho courage and violence, living at the edges, both cultural and geographical, of the city. But by the early years of the twentieth century the Moreiras in the Carnival processions had become permissive masks for office employees, whose lives took place in the city centre and were disciplined by work hours, leaving no place for knife-fighting, the traditional expression of the *gaucho malo*.

The *compadrito* figure, transitional between the rural and the urban, the traditional and the modern, has his equivalents in other Latin American countries. In Mexico, there was the *pelado*, 'a type of urban peasant . . . who has lost the rural Eden but has not found the promised land'.[52] At the same time, in early-twentieth-century Buenos Aires a different cultural stratum was being formed, without reference to gaucho or *compadrito* traditions. Explored by Roberto Arlt (1900–1942) in his urban novels, its repertory included science (aviation, guns, the chemistry of explosives) and urban crime, as well as spiritism, classical mythology, European history and the

Bible.[53] One of Arlt's central concerns is 'the unequal distribution of culture' and his response is to display a 'modernization from below', an alternative to the imposition of modernization from above.[54] There are similarities here with anarchist ideas of education, anarchism having exerted a major influence upon working-class organizations. But there is also something less programmed: the formation of a new cultural archive, of the working class and those parts of the petty bourgeoisie living at its fringes. The *criollista* repertory to some extent overlapped with it; for instance, socialist and anarchist publications used creolist symbols.[55] However, by the 1920s *criollismo* was losing its power as a bridge between rural and urban experience. The *centros criollos* (creole centres) set up from the 1890s by rural immigrants as meeting places where traditional rural music was performed, were in decline. There had been at least 268 of them, named after the regions their members had originated from, or inspired by Gutiérrez's characters (for example, 'The Desert Bandits' ['Los matreros del desierto']), or – and these were the majority – invoking their legitimacy in the language of nationalism, with titles such as 'The Patriotic Gauchos' ('Los gauchos patriotas') or 'Glory, fatherland and tradition' ('Gloria, patria y tradición').[56] From the 1920s the *centros criollos* were also places where the tango was played, an indication of the rise of a more restrictedly urban popular culture.[57]

Up to around 1917 the tango had been predominantly a dance performed in the suburbs (*orillas*), where the rural presence was strongest. During this *orillero* stage it retained a connection with the rural musical and song forms of the *payada* and the *milonga*. Where emphasis was given to the song element, this included the denunciation of conditions in the overcrowded *conventillos* and expressed the hostility of the *orillero* to the *cajetilla* (the city dandy or dude associated with the centre of town) or to the industrialization and proletarianization of the city:

> Where is my barrio, my cradle of rogues?
> Where is the nest, the refuge of yesterday?
> Asphalt has erased with one stroke of the hand
> The old neighbourhood where I was born....[58]

A variety of elements converged in the tango. Musically it was a combination of the Argentinian *milonga*, the Spanish-Cuban *habanera*, the Spanish *contradanza* and the black African music played by ex-slaves in Buenos Aires.[59] It was danced by couples, closely embraced, and replaced the older more polite dances, which were performed in groups. It permitted a display of male sexual domination, both contained and provocative, associated with the machista code of the *compadrito* and with an ambience of prostitution and knife-fighting. Thus 'to accept the tango was a form of rebellion against civic virtue and morality'.[60] However, once the tango migrated from the suburbs to the city proper, it left behind the *compadrito*, the prostitute and the knife, and the social themes were replaced with a new repertory based in individualized emotion. Through radio and sound-films it became part of mass culture, and through figures like Carlos Gardel, who took the tango to Paris and New York, it entered the middle-class cultural repertoire. From around 1920 to the 1940s, the tango became popular in the three main senses of the word: quantitatively, it reached a mass audience through the mediation of the culture industry; qualitatively, it still retained some remnants of the popular as oppositional, a claim made by Humberto Solanas's films, *Tangos: el exilio de Gardel* (*Tangos, The Exile of Gardel* 1985), and *Sur* (*South* 1988); it had also, however, become a populist form, as in Fernán Silva Valdés's nostalgic composition, 'El tango':

> Tango of *milongas*,
> tango of *compadritos*
> which you dance with intensity
> but as if without intensity,
> as if on slow rails:
> you are a state of mind of the masses.[61]

Popular Culture and the State

In Brazil the struggle over the course of modernization was intimately connected with the ruling elites' attempt to control and define the role of the subaltern groups in this process. Despite a series of republican conspiracies, Independence reflected primarily a power conflict between creole and Portuguese elites which was resolved through the establishment of a constitutional monarchy in 1822. During this period a number of European ideologies were adopted and articulated in order to reconcile the contradiction between the liberal aspirations of the modernizing elites and the anachronistic nature of a slave-owning monarchy.

Social Darwinism, which had emerged in Europe and interpreted European predominance as an example of the superiority of the white race, was used in Brazil as an explanatory framework to account for Brazil's backwardness in terms of its black and Amerindian racial inheritance.[62] The transposition of European evolutionary thinking to the Brazilian context gave rise to a peculiar ideology of whitening, according to which the pattern of racial miscegenation was gradually producing a whiter population, genetically better endowed with the capacity for the building of civilization. The possibility that the tendency to generate mulatto offspring reflected sexual exploitation by white upper-class males or the attempt by free blacks to achieve social mobility by marrying a person with lighter skin was conveniently ignored by evolutionary determinist theories.[63]

The ambiguities and ironies of a society simultaneously slavist and liberal are brought out by the great Brazilian novelist, Machado de Assis. In a key essay for Latin American cultural history, 'As idéias fora do lugar' ('Ideas Out of Place'), the Brazilian critic Roberto Schwarz explores the dislocations between liberal ideology and a slave-owning monarchy: 'although it was the fundamental relationship of production, slavery was not the effective nexus of ideological life'.[64] The latter took place within the relationship between the free population and the large slave- and landowners, a relationship dependent on *favor*, the paternalistic favours granted by the powerful through which access to social status and material benefits was gained. Although a product of the colonial period, the system of *favor* has in Schwarz's view continued to permeate Brazilian society to the extent that it 'is our virtually universal mediation'. *Favor* creates dependence within all the social strata and is a flaw in the whole modernizing project. It contradicts the central ideas of liberalism – individual autonomy, equality before the law, the authority of reason – and evaluates persons on the basis of particular characteristics and personal relations rather than impersonal standards of achievement and efficiency. In this context, liberal ideas have not been lived as expressions of the Adam Smith model of a free market society but ornamentally, as a decorative screen behind which relationships of patronage have continued.

This juxtaposition of a modernizing ideology and a 'backward' milieu has had important consequences for the analysis of culture, relevant not only to Brazil but also to other Latin American countries. The discrepancy between representation and reality generated in Schwarz's terms an 'improper discourse', a form of thinking which is dislocated. However, far from being a merely negative fact this discrepancy allows for critical distance from forms of thought claiming dubious universality, appearing as 'one dress among others, very much up to date but unnecessarily tight'.[65] As will become clear in the following chapters this incongruity finds expression in popular culture in the form of a keen sense of the absurd and satirical irreverence towards the pretensions of the ruling group, while also potentially creating a basis from which to elaborate alternative representations of reality and models of society.

In 1888 slavery was abolished, followed a year later by the declaration of the Republic. However, as in the case of Brazil's Independence, the republican regime was established from above with a coup d'état, favouring primarily the new coffee-planter class of the South at the expense both of the sugar-owning landowners in the North and of the emergent urban middle classes who wanted to create an industrial base and a larger internal market. This entailed in effect abandoning the path of independent economic development and accepting neo-colonialism, whereby Brazil embraced economic liberalism by exchanging primary products for imported European manufacturers. Nevertheless, although the patrimonial social relations inherited from the colony and empire prevailed, Brazilian elites became receptive to European cosmopolitanism and the current belief in progress and enterprise. This new attitude is clearly revealed in the transformation of the capital, Rio de Janeiro. The old colonial houses, narrow streets and alleyways were demolished and replaced with sumptuous avenues, statues and even nightingales imported from Europe. As Nicolau Sevcenko points out, this metamorphosis was based on four principles: 'the condemnation of the habits and customs connected to the memory of traditional society; the negation of any element of popular culture which disturbed the civilized image of the dominant society; a strict policy of expulsion of the popular classes from the centre of the city, available now for the exclusive use of the bourgeois strata; and an aggressive cosmopolitanism, profoundly identified with the Parisian lifestyle.'[66] With the new emphasis on time as money, the alleged laziness of the rural population, popular religiosity and popular festivities came under attack from the state. This is the historical moment in which the binary opposition of tradition versus modernity becomes a cornerstone of intellectual debate reinforcing the earlier proposition propounded in Argentina by Sarmiento in *The Life of Juan Facundo Quiroga: Civilisation and Barbarism,* that Latin America must overcome its 'barbaric' past and become civilized through adopting European models.

The attempt to extirpate the unsightly 'barbarian' elements – forms of social life and culture connected to blacks, mulattoes, Indians, peasants, illiterates – from the fabric of Brazilian society is manifested in a set of ideas, policies and state actions. Immigration policy between 1890 and 1920 aimed at recruiting Europeans, in particular North Europeans, to work as agricultural labour. This policy was based on the belief that immigrants of European stock were abler than the descendants of former slaves and that this would contribute to the gradual whitening of the population.[67] At the level of ideas, positivism with its emphasis on science and authoritarian social engineering provided a rationale for economic development without popular participation or change in the land tenure system. The positivist motto of 'order and progress' emblazoned on the Brazilian flag encapsulates the view among governing elites that modernization from above would establish Brazil as a civilized nation.

While the expansion of commercial agriculture and the process of urbanization in the South may have justified the belief that modernization was indeed advancing, social life in the backlands exposed the gap between the 'classical' model of European development and the 'barbarian' reality of Brazil all the more glaringly. This discrepancy was painfully laid bare in 1896 when a key conflict arose; it was caused by the totally unexpected resistance on the part of the rural backlands, where concepts of the political were still religious, to the intrusion of the modern secular state, and revealed clearly the manner in which the 'popular' and 'the people' as an element to be civilized were being constructed. However, in order to grasp fully the significance of this conflict, it is necessary to look briefly at some of the essential features of the social structure of the Northeast.

During the period of colony and empire, and to a large extent even today, the system of land tenure in the Northeast was characterized by large estates, or *latifundios*, producing primary products for export abroad. These were located in large part in the coastal regions and a vast territory of land stretching into the hinterland – the *sertão* – sparsely populated by groups of semi-nomadic peasants living within a subsistence economy. The social relations which emerged in this context centred around the large and self-sufficient *engenho* or *fazenda*, the sugar-mill or cattle-rearing estate. These belonged to a few powerful families, organized around a patriarchal figure who ruled over his domains and dependants in the manner of a feudal lord. Given the export-oriented nature of agriculture, large tracts of land remained uncultivated when demand on the world market fell. The concentration of property made technological innovation in order to increase productivity unnecessary, while also preventing the growth of subsistence crops and medium-sized landholdings. Together these factors created profound social inequalities: power and wealth in the hands of a few landholding families and a mass of peasants and landless labourers living in extreme poverty and servile subordination to the landowner. With no secure claim to the land, and threatened with hunger and destitution during recurrent periods of drought, the rural poor formed semi-nomadic groups of migrants wandering through the vast expanse of the Northeast in search of shelter and food.

In 1896 during a particularly severe drought, Antonio Conselheiro, religious and political leader of the rural poor in the backlands of the state of Bahia, brought together a number of peasant communities who were resisting the measures introduced by the republican regime, among them the collection of taxes and the imposition of the metric system of measurement. In Canudos, the site of an abandoned cattle ranch, Conselheiro and his followers founded a city of roughly 25,000 inhabitants based on a form of primitive communism, with its own administrators, warriors, doctors, internal commerce, fields of subsistence crops and pastures for cattle.[68]

Between January and October 1897 over 5,000 men were dispatched to impose the authority of the Republic. Field Marshall Floriano Peixoto, dictator from 1891 to 1894, declared, 'as a liberal, which I am, I cannot want for my country the government of the sword; but, and there is no one who does not know this, because the examples are there for everyone to see . . . this is the government which knows how to purify the blood of the social body, which, like our own, is corrupted.'[69] As in Argentina with General Roca, the military granted itself the sacred role of fulfilling a sacrificial mythology. The expeditionary force sent to put down the Canudos rebellion was an expression of this programme. Euclides da Cunha, sent to report on the campaign, wrote in one of his first articles, 'We shall soon be standing on the earth where the Republic will surely give the final shock to those which perturb it', interpreting the conflict in terms of a paradigm derived from the French Revolution, whereby the new Republic was facing a final monarchist revival, as in the French Vendée.[70] What followed changed his life, and provided the material for one of the greatest texts of Latin American culture, *Os sertões* (*Rebellion in the Backlands* 1902).

Military engineering became the leading edge of enforced modernization from above, its ability to establish rectilinearity in the desert, as da Cunha puts it,[71] making it the protagonist of rationality against chaos. The adversary, who practised communal ownership of the land, was 'an unconscious brute mass, which, without organs and without specialized functions, continued to grow rather than evolve, through the mere mechanical juxtaposition of successive layers, in the manner of a human polyp'.[72] As well as recognizing the destabilizing threat of the body without organs,[73] da Cunha's writing also reveals how the state projectively constructed this popular force as its own adversary. Spontaneous, purposeless growth, without evolution, is the nightmare of the positivist; for the state, it must be expunged from the national territory.

However, witnessing the conflict changed da Cunha and diminished his faith in positivism. The army degenerated: 'The last remnants of a meaningless formality were now abandoned: deliberations on the part of the commanding officers, troop manoeuvres, distribution of forces, even bugle calls; and, finally, the hierarchy of rank itself was practically extinguished in an army without uniforms which no longer knew any distinctions'.[74] At the end, as the last defenders fall into the ditch they had dug to die in, the soldiers' gaze is paralysed as they stare at their own destructiveness. This genocidal campaign, which da Cunha sees as an act of madness on the part of the government – or the nation – can be understood in part in terms of a necessity to destroy the uncontrollable. In some of da Cunha's descriptions of the settlement, 'a Babylon of huts', the adobe walls which could so easily be penetrated take on a malign elasticity: 'Canudos ... possessed the lack of consistency and the treacherous flexibility of a huge net. It was easy to attack it, overcome it, conquer it, knock it down, send it hurtling – the difficult thing was to leave it.'[75]

For a consciousness shaped by reasons of state, the people of Canudos could only be understood as fuelled by mysticism or fanaticism. In this sense, Vargas Llosa's novel, *La guerra del fin del mundo* (*The War of the End of the World* 1981) merely prolongs da Cunha's account. The defence of land rights, and of a particular way of life, disappear as motivations. And the Brazilian army, for its part, immediately overcame its moment of paralysis, without acknowledgement or memory. The memory of Canudos, now submerged by an irrigation scheme, is available to us mainly thanks to da Cunha's book. What is preserved is invaluable evidence of what modern states have destroyed, and therefore of those necessities of capitalist state formation with which popular culture has come into collision or found accommodation. Da Cunha discovered that paradigms of universal history could not simply be applied to interpret local history. The fissures in the European model of explanation, those things which it could not account for, created a problematic sense of identity: 'there occurs, in the consciousness of the ex-colonized person, a simultaneous *identification* and *rejection* of the identity both of the former colonizer and of the original native, revealing the tension between the project of integration into civilization and the differential construction of the idea of nation'.[76] This space between European models and local contexts would over time be opened up by anthropology and by the modernist movement in the 1920s and 1930s. With the First World War Brazil's export economy was disrupted and capital investment was directed towards the creation of an industrial base. The preconditions for the growth of an independent national identity had emerged. This sense was articulated above all by the modernist movement which called upon the intelligentsia to 'discover Brazilian reality', to recuperate those elements categorized by official culture as barbaric: Brazil's black and Amerindian cultures, the syntax of spoken Portuguese, the social conditions of the rural hinterland, the tropical landscape.

One solution to this problem of identity was put forward by Gilberto Freyre in *Casa Grande e Senzala* (*The Masters and the Slaves* 1933). In Freyre's account, the free sexual relationships between white masters and black slaves brought about a new *mestizo* race which transcended the old racial divisions and made possible the cultural integration of the nation. Shifting the debate from positivist racialism, which had stressed the inferiority of the blacks, Freyre introduced an anthropological orientation, which emphasized culture not race as the marker of distinction. He thus has a major responsibility for the myth of Brazil as a 'melting-pot of races',[77] which in the Getulio Vargas's regime (1930–45) became a key feature of a populist programme of national integration.

Freyre transformed the *mestizo*, previously seen as tainted by black blood, into a positive member of the nation. 'The ideology of *mestizaje*, which had been imprisoned in the ambiguities of racial theories, could now be propagated socially and become common sense, ritually celebrated in everyday relationships, or in the great public events such as carnival or football. The *mestizo* becomes national.'[78] This version of cultural syncretism was ideological. It offered a picture of Brazilian society which transcended class boundaries just at the moment when a large industrial workforce was being created. Freyre himself recognized, not long before his death in 1987, the incompatibility of his vision with the working-class movement: 'what wrecked everything was the factory'.[79] Thus although Freyre's anthropological approach and his positive evaluation of Brazil's ethnically mixed civilization superseded the racialist determinism of the nineteenth century, his view that Brazil was characterized by 'racial democracy' reinforced the ideal of whitening because it led to the widespread notion that Brazil's racial problems were being resolved through ethnic integration, whose goal remained white civilization. The black playwright Abdias do Nascimento points to a crucial consequence of the persistence of this ideal, namely the absence of a significant black consciousness movement: 'the underlying objective of this ideology has been to deny blacks the possibility of self-definition by depriving them of the means of racial identification'.[80] In his view concepts such as miscegenation, acculturation and assimilation are in fact euphemisms for the sexual exploitation of African women and the gradual annihilation of African culture. Taking Nascimento's critique into consideration, it is therefore necessary in analysing forms of black popular culture in Brazil and indeed in

Latin America as a whole, to avoid a culturalist approach which regards these forms merely as a continuation of African culture. Such an approach overlooks the profound alterations they suffered as they became part of a society founded on slave labour as a result of which they were transformed – to use Bastide's definition – into a class subculture.

The slave trade destroyed clans, villages and lineages; it brought together groups from diverse civilizations settled along the western half of Africa. In the boats in which they were transported and in the markets in which they were sold, forest peoples mingled with farmers, matrilinear with patrilinear civilizations, members of kingdoms with members of tribes and totemic clans, all reduced to a single common denominator by slavery. With all the original forms of ethnic solidarity destroyed, it was not possible to reproduce the African cultures in their new social habitat. Instead, residual and new configurations developed in the few interstices in the new social system through which black cultures were able to manifest themselves, becoming in the process a class subculture. African culture thus 'ceased to be a communitarian culture encompassing society as a whole, in order to become exclusively the culture of a social class, of a single group in Brazilian society, of an economically exploited and socially subordinate group'.[81]

In Chapter 3 we will focus in greater detail on the main devices through which black culture was articulated with Brazilian society. For the present discussion of continuities and discontinuities in the formation of popular culture it is important to note that although the abolition of slavery and the declaration of the First Republic changed the formal status of blacks, the continuing prevalence of the past economic structure meant that 'slavery's terms permeated, and corroded, all social relations, and extended to free persons'.[82] This explains partly why despite the emergence of an urban trade union movement and political parties demanding greater participation in the formation of the new society, the subaltern groups – *mestizos*, Indians, blacks, peasants, workers, domestic servants – did not acquire the status of citizens. The phrase 'the social question is a question for the police' was frequently used to describe the attitude of the state to the popular classes and their culture.

As indicated earlier, significant social changes took place in the 1920s, the most important being the development of industry and the emergence of new social classes – in particular an urban middle class – who would eventually break the great landowners' monopoly of power and witness the emergence of a state favourable to their interests. In 1930, following an uprising against the republican regime, the populist leader Getúlio Vargas became president and began a programme of state-led industrialization.

The year 1930 is regarded by historians and sociologists as a watershed in Brazilian history, marking the emergence of an urban-industrial civilization often referred to as Brazil's 'bourgeois revolution'. It is important to note, however, that these developments differed quite considerably from their European counterpart in a way which would have significant repercussions for the formation of popular culture. Given that industrialization was in part achieved with capital no longer used to grow coffee, due to the fall in demand during the First World War and subsequently during the Depression, the new class of industrialists belonged in part to the landowning strata. Moreover, since the foreign currency needed to support industrialization was obtained through selling primary products abroad as before, the colonial *latifundio* system prevailed as did the extreme poverty of the rural population who tried to ameliorate their situation by migrating to the city. While the acquisition of urban worker status was considered a form of social mobility, its effect in fact was to attenuate the growth of class consciousness. Thus in contrast to Europe, in Brazil the development of a modern capitalist society was not accompanied by the formulation of a distinct urban-industrial ideology or a radical programme of social transformation. In a manner which has come to be seen as characteristically Brazilian, social change was achieved less through a radical break with the past than through a conciliatory accommodation of divergent interests and moderate social reforms introduced by the state. Capitalist development and modernization in Brazil went hand in hand with the creation of a heterogeneous mass society, an urban population with fluid class, regional and ethnic identifications whose participation became essential for the legitimacy of the state but which was nevertheless carefully controlled from above.

In this period 'the people' became a major political, literary and ideological category. Popular cultural forms became important sites where, on the one hand, traditional, ethnic and local identities were articulated by the state within the project of national integration and development, and, on the other, they became a means through which the subaltern groups struggled to participate in the formation of the new urban social order, using popular cultural forms to represent their new identity, to make their presence as citizens felt. This two-way process will be explored in greater detail in Chapter 3. At this stage it is important to keep this constellation of forces in mind because it enables one to make sense of the fact that modernity in Brazil – and to some extent in other Latin American countries where parallel processes have occurred – contains, as Octavio Ianni points out, 'a multiplicity of concepts, themes and national realities which are both new and old and in which the different cycles and periods in Brazilian history intermingle as in a unique kaleidoscope of realities and imitations'.[83] Popular culture, it is suggested, is a privileged vehicle through which this kaleidoscope of multiple intermingled realities, rural and urban, pre-modern and modern, local and non-local can be fruitfully studied.

Notes

1. In this connection, Serge Gruzinski's study of Mexico between the sixteenth and eighteenth centuries, *La colonisation de l'imaginaire* (Paris 1988), is extremely valuable for the comprehensiveness with which it distinguishes between different levels and modes of interaction without reducing them to the binary of dominant versus subordinated.

2. Roger Bartra, *La jaula de la melancolía*, Mexico 1987, p. 131.

3. 'What they [the Conquistadors] call conquests, being violent invasions on the part of cruel tyrants, condemned not only by the law of God, but by all human laws.' Bartolomé de Las Casas, *Brevísima relación de la destrucción de las Indias*, Madrid 1987, p. 105.

4. See Bartolomé de Las Casas, *The Devastation of the Indies*, New York 1974, with Introduction by Hans Magnus Enzensberger.

5. Miguel León Portilla, *Visión de los vencidos*, Madrid 1985. See also Gordon Brotherston, *Image of the New World*, London 1979.

6. Nathan Wachtel, *The Vision of the Vanquished*, Hassocks 1977.

7. Gruzinski, p. 90.

8. Ibid., pp. 80–81.

9. p. 108.

10. Ibid., pp. 144–5.

11. Ibid., p. 199.

12. Ibid., p. 214.

13. Cf. Virgílio Noya Pinto, *Comunicacão e cultura brasileira*, São Paulo, Editora Atica, 1986.

14. Gruzinski, p. 197.

15. Ibid., p. 203.

16. Jurij M. Lotman and Boris A. Uspenskij, 'Sobre el mecanismo semiótico de la cultura', in Lotman, *Semiótica de la cultura,* Madrid 1979, pp. 67–92.

17. Gruzinski, pp. 257–9.

18. Ibid., p. 259.

19. This point was made by Jean Franco in 'Women and the Vernacular', paper presented to the 1989 Congress of the Latin American Studies Association, Miami. In what follows, we are indebted to this paper.

20. Octavio Paz, Introduction to Jacques Lafaye, *Quetzalcoatl and Guadalupe*, Chicago 1976, p. xix.

21. Lafaye, pp. 211–16.

22. Ibid., pp. 62–3.

23. Benedict Anderson, *Imagined Communities*, London 1983.

24. Simón Bolívar, *Escritos políticos*, Madrid 1969, p. 69.

25. Yolanda Salas de Lecuna, *Bolívar y la historia en la conciencia popular*, Caracas 1987, p. 46.

26. Ibid., p. 42.

27. Ibid., pp. 59–61.

28. Simón Bolívar, p. 130.

29. Tristan Platt, 'Simón Bolívar, the Sun of Justice and the Amerindian Virgin', unpublished paper, p. 8. To be published in Marcusz S. Ziolkowski, ed., *Regional Cults in the Andes*.

30. Ibid., p. 10.

31. Ibid., pp. 11–12.

32. Mark Szuchman, *Order, Family and Community in Buenos Aires 1810–1860*, Stanford 1988, p. 2.

33. Ibid., pp. 1–2.

34. Ibid., p. 3.

35. Ibid., pp. 7–8.

36. Ibid., p. 23.

37. James Scobie, *Secondary Cities of Argentina: The Social History of Corrientes, Salta, and Mendoza, 1850–1910*. Stanford 1988, p. 212. The quotations are from Corrientes newspapers but the attitudes are similar to those of the ruling groups of Buenos Aires.

38. Ibid., p. 213.

39. David Rock, 'Argentina in 1914: The Pampas, the Interior, Buenos Aires', *Cambridge History of Latin America*, V (1986) p. 397.

40. David Viñas, *Indios, ejército y frontera*, Mexico 1984, p. 90.

41. See *Nunca más (Never Again)*, London 1986.

42. Viñas, *Indios*, p. 13.

43. On the authoritarian concept of culture in Argentina, see Andrés Avellaneda, *Censura, autoritarismo y cultura: Argentina 1960–1983*, Buenos Aires 1986, pp. 19, 22.

44. Mark Szuchman, ed., *The Middle Period in Latin America: Values and Attitudes in 17th–19th Centuries*, Boulder 1989, p. 11.

45. See Marshall Berman, *All That is Solid Melts Into Air*, London 1983; Perry Anderson, 'Modernity and Revolution', *New Left Review*, No. 144, March–April 1984, pp. 96–113; and Berman's reply to Anderson, in *New Left Review*, No. 144, pp. 114–23. For the debate about modernity and postmodernity in Latin America, see Fernando Calderón, ed., *Imágenes desconocidas: La modernidad en la encrucijada postmoderna*, Buenos Aires 1988.

46. Josefina Ludmer, *El género gaucheso: un tratado sobre la patria*, Buenos Aires 1988, pp. 27–31.

47. Adolfo Prieto, *El discurso criollista en la formación de la Argentina moderna*, Buenos Aires, 1988, p. 13.

48. Ibid., p. 18. For a denser discussion of the use of rural voices and imagery, see Beatriz Sarlo, *Una modernidad periférica: Buenos Aires 1920 y 1930*, Buenos Aires 1988, Chapter 2.

49. See *J.G. Posada: Messenger of Mortality*, London 1989, p. 111. We are grateful to Tom Gretton for these points.

50. Prieto, p. 56.

51. Ibid., p. 35.

52. Bartra, p. 52.

53. For example in *El juguete rabioso*, 1926.

54. See Sarlo, p. 51, and Berman, pp. 219, 224, 231–2.

55. For example, *El cancionero revolucionario ilustrado* (1905), Prieto, p. 165.

56. Prieto, p. 130.

57. Ibid., p. 146.

58. 'Puente Alsina', quoted in Julio Mafud, *Sociología del tango*, Buenos Aires 1966, p. 31:

> Dónde está mi barrio, mi cuna maleva;
> Dónde la guarida, refugio de ayer;
> Borró el asfalto de una manotada
> La vieja barriada que me vio nacer . . ..

59. Simon Collier, *The Life, Music and Times of Carlos Gardel,* Pittsburgh 1986, p. 55.

60. Mafud, p. 50.

61.   Tango milongón,
       tango compadrón
       que a pesar de bailarse con todas las ganas
       se baila como sin ganas,
       como en carriles de lentitud:
       eres un estado de alma de la multitud.
El tango (antología), Buenos Aires 1969.

62. T. Skidmore, *Black into White,* New York 1974.

63. Ibid.

64. R. Schwarz, *As ideias fora do lugar,* in *Ao vencedor as batatas,* São Paulo 1977, pp. 15–16.

65. Ibid., p. 23.

66. Nicolau Sevcenko, *Literatura como missão,* São Paulo 1985, p. 30.

67. Skidmore.

68. Rui Faco, *Cangaceiros e fanaticos,* Rio de Janeiro 1978.

69. Quoted in Roberto Ventura, 'A nossa Vendéia: Canudos, O mito da revolucão francesa e a constitução de identida de nacional-cultural no Brasil (1897–1902)' *Revista de Crítica Literária Latinoamericana,* Vol XI, No. 24.

70. Ventura, p. 1.

71. Euclides da Cunha, *Rebellion in the Backlands,* Chicago 1975, p. 396 (Translation modified).

72. Ibid., p. 149.

73. Deleuze and Guattari, *A Thousand Plateaus,* London 1988.

74. E. da Cunha, *Rebellion in the Backlands,* p. 474.

75. Ibid., pp. 424, 260.

76. Ventura, p. 20.

77. David Treece, obituary for Freyre in *Independent,* 27 July 1987.

78. Renato Ortiz, *Cultura brasileira e identidade nacional,* Saõ Paulo 1986, p. 41.

79. Quoted in Carlos Guillermo Mota, *A ideologia da Cultura Brasileira* [1933–1970], São Paulo 1977, p. 60.

80. Abdias do Nascimento, *O genocidio do negro brasileiro,* São Paulo 1978, p. 79.

81. Roger Bastide, *As religiões africanas no Brasil,* São Paulo 1985, p. 98.

82. Sandra Graham, *House and Street: The Domestic World of Servants and Masters in Nineteenth-Century Rio de Janeiro,* Cambridge 1988, p. 110.

83. Octavio Ianni, 'A ideia do Brasil moderno', unpublished paper, p. 33.

TWO

The Faces of Popular Culture

I RURAL CONTEXTS

The development of rural and urban life in Latin America and thus their respective popular cultures was crucially conditioned by its position on the periphery of the world capitalist system. One of the most important consequences of this predicament was the creation of great disparities between different regions and between the so-called traditional and modern sectors of society, where, as Marxist theorists have pointed out, (the traditional frequently is dependent on and finances the development of the modern.)

The Conquest had catastrophic consequences for the Andean and Mesoamerican civilizations. Their existence as states with political, economic and religious organization was destroyed by the conqueror's superior military power, by disease and the disarticulation of their cosmogonies by the Christian Church. Despite this, (neither the colonial nor the republican regime has been able to expunge the memory of an Andean, Aztec and Mayan civilization; at a more local level, pre-Hispanic types of organization have endured along with various forms of ritual and symbolism.) These have not, however, remained unaltered by the incorporation of Latin America in the world capitalist system, initially as a provider of silver and gold and subsequently as an outlet for European goods and a source of cheap labour. This led to the emergence of complex mixed forms of social life, characterized by the articulation of pre-capitalist and capitalist elements.

Thus for example, in the Southern Andean highlands, the Indian *ayllu*, an extended web of kinship ties descended from mythical ancestors and based on a collective relationship to the land and reciprocal exchange of labour, continues to exist as also does the *iglesia andina* (Andean Church), a semi-clandestine pagan priesthood. Nevertheless, the introduction of commodity circulation and commercial principles by the conquering powers had disintegrative effects on the Indian communities. Commodity circulation undermined exchange based on reciprocity; *ayllu* members migrated to the mines and cities. After Independence, liberal economic policies attempted to transform Indian communal lands into private property; these lands, due to the growing demand for cash crops, were expropriated by the expanding estates or *haciendas*. Indians became an impoverished subsistence peasantry drawn to a lesser or greater extent into a money economy while a modernized sector, related to exports and foreign investment, emerged mostly in the coastal areas. (Thus while the Indian cultures of Latin America are attached to traditional pre-capitalist forms of social life, their characteristics are as much an expression of a tradition which goes back to the pre-Columbian period as a product of the way in which regional disparities and inequalities have developed.)

In the Brazilian Northeast, where the Indian influence has been less marked than in the Andean and Mesoamerican areas, popular cultural traditions have essentially arisen in the context of the interaction between the large estate or *fazenda*, producing primary products for export, and a parallel peasant subsistence economy. The marked presence in this area of an oral culture, of religious beliefs and practices going back to sixteenth-century Portugal, thus also needs to be related to the unequal development of different regions.

Of course these social processes have affected the formation of not only rural but also urban areas. Due to existing inequalities between the city and the country, rural–urban migration becomes a common response to the disparities. In contrast to Europe, urbanization in Latin America was connected first to the colonial enterprise and subsequently to the primary product exporting company. Urbanization was not initially the result of industrialization but rather the expression of the expansion of commerce, finance and the liberal professions. When subsequently industrialization arrived, it was insufficient to absorb the mass of poor peasants and rural labourers, leading to the growth of 'exploding' cities and the coexistence of a wealthy minority, frequently working in the modern foreign sector, and a large mass of under- and unemployed 'traditional' migrants, living in the shanty towns on the peripheries of the city.

The first part of this chapter will be concerned with the Andean region, Mexico and Brazil, regions in which, as we shall see, pre-capitalist and capitalist forms of life have been articulated in different combinations, giving rise to specific forms of popular culture. In the second part, we will concentrate on urban popular culture. The socio-economic context briefly presented above is intended not as an all-explanatory framework of the forms of rural and urban popular culture, but as a provisional map for locating the materials we present.

Rebellion in the Andes

Andean culture embraces a very large geographical area, stretching from northern Chile to southern Colombia and centred on the highlands of Peru and Bolivia at altitudes of 7,000 to 15,000 feet. This area approximates to the limits of the Inca empire in the early sixteenth century. To refer to Andean culture as a unified concept is perhaps to risk too great an abstraction in the face of local differences; nevertheless it is possible to identify certain common features. Of all the regional cultures of Latin America, it is the one which can most strongly lay claim to being an alternative civilization, a possibility which has been implicit in a number of social conflicts and which came closest to realization in the Great Rebellion of 1780, led by Tupac Amaru II.[1] His claim of direct descendency from the Inca ruling group was a major component of his assertion of legitimacy, in opposition to Spanish rule, the re-establishment of a neo-Inca state in one form or another being a primary component of Andean politics.[2] The transformation of the Inca past into a utopian image of the future began in the sixteenth century, not long after the Conquest, and utopianism has been one of the main strands of historical coherence in the Andes, as Alberto Flores Galindo has shown in his excellent book, *Buscando un Inca* (*The Search of an Inca*, 1986).[3] An early example is the writing of the Inca Garcilaso (1539–1616), a first-generation *mestizo* chronicler, son of an Inca princess and a Spanish soldier. His depiction of Inca rule claims that it fulfils precisely those ideas of good government which renaissance kings and princes sought to embody, and his implicit message is that the Europeans destroyed the very thing they were looking for. Although his view of the past was undoubtedly idealized (it inspired the twentieth-century work *The Socialist Empire of the Incas*),[4] it powerfully delegitimated the Spanish colonial regime. It is therefore no surprise that his *Comentarios reales* (*Royal Commentaries* 1609) was much read by Tupac Amaru

II.[5] In the present-day context, ethnohistory and politics intersect, in the sense that new discoveries about Inca social and political structures offer new support for an alternative Andean politics.[6] Thus the Indian Politics movement which we discuss in Chapter 3 has made use of the recently proposed idea that Inca rulers were elected. In 1989 the movement held in the Sacred Valley of the Incas a meeting of Indians claiming descendency from the Inca ruling group; this assembly was part of their campaign for an Indian response to 1992, emphasizing that 1492 was not a 'meeting of two worlds', the phrase which the official commissions for the celebration are using, but an invasion.

If utopianism offers a large-scale historical goal, it is important, when considering the ways in which the past is used as a resource for imagining an alternative future, to bear in mind that the peasant population of the Andes, who reproduce and modify the traditions we are referring to, do not hold standard Western notions of time and history. Their ideas are embedded in everyday life, and it is on this level that we need to look if we are to appreciate how Andean conceptions of the world are experienced and passed on. Let us consider the dawn rituals practised by the Laymi, an Aymara-speaking group from the northern Potosí region of highland Bolivia. In the diffuse light of first dawn, before the first sunrays cross the horizon, sacrifices and offerings are made to the divinities of the lower world, *manqhapacha*. Subsequently, 'when the sun rises, people move away from the places of the offerings and salute and congratulate each other saying *suma wina ura* ("the moment is good"). Then, as they abandon the divinities of below, they make libations to our father the sun.'[7] The lower world in Andean space-time is the pre-civilized age, when crops grew and clothing wove itself spontaneously, without human intervention. This hidden world of half-light is simultaneously the region of the dead, ambivalent, monstrous and chaotic, but also fertile.[8] The emerging of the sun is not only an opportunity to celebrate the continuing alternation of worlds in the day–night cycle, it is also made to signify the coming of a new age in the series of historical ages: the one inaugurated by the Incas, which brought about civilization, and which continues through the four hundred and fifty years of colonial and republican neo-colonial rule.

Having mentioned ritual as a formalization of everyday life through which cosmology and history are reasserted, it is important to recall that for an oral culture, like the Andean, meanings are registered and transmitted without writing. This does not mean, as some books on orality suggest, that sound becomes the privileged vehicle for information, but rather that encoding is dispersed over a variety of actions and locations, which include ritual, theatre, music, pilgrimages, artefacts, narratives and all the ways in which the earth itself is perceived as patterned with lines and significant points.[9] These patternings add up to a multitude of 'graphies', of 'writings' available to be 'read', and in which the native cultural 'archive' is stored. Hence the contemporary belief among the Laymi that people knew how to write long before the Conquest but that the Spaniards disqualified this Indian writing; or the view held in Huánuco, Peru, that with the coming of the Christian catechism, both human beings and the land became 'dumb'.[10] Nevertheless, native knowledge has been preserved, often in disguised or semi-clandestine ways, and Andean culture remains one of the most crucial challenges to the notion that modernization, United States style, is the destiny of Latin America.

There has been a struggle for cultural control, which has reached a relative equilibrium over long periods. Our approach will be to separate out a few significant moments and practices which will show that in important senses it is 'their' culture which is processing 'ours', rather than vice versa. How can that be, it may be asked, if an oral culture has to compete with one where writing enshrines order, intelligibility and the storage of information? It will help to take the most extreme example first: that is, where native culture confronts the other upon its chosen ground of written texts, using the technology of writing to preserve and transmit a cultural archive which had previously been predominantly non-written.[11] Two authors above all have attempted this: Felipe Guamán Poma de Ayala, in the late sixteenth century, and José María Arguedas, in the mid twentieth century. Quechua – with Aymara, the main Andean language – is the mother tongue of both, but they use Spanish in order to strengthen the native tradition and extend its scope. Where they succeed, it is as a result of a very complex process of reinterpreting and redeploying European paradigms in the light of Andean ones.[12] No full historical description or theoretical understanding of such a cross-cultural process exists. The transformations involved can in a sense be thought of as translations, provided we keep in mind both the etymology of the word (= moving something from one location, in this case culture, to another) and the fact that a good translation will alter the receiving language/culture. The same process is involved in the examples we give below, except that the linguistic issue, of bringing the effects of the very different grammar and semantics of Quechua into Spanish, gives way to the vaster one of how the meanings which make up a whole cultural field are constituted.

In Tristan Platt's example of how the Christian festival of Corpus Christi is surrounded by native ritual and reinterpreted by it, a whole Andean cosmology is shown to be mobilized in order to control the Christian meanings. As Platt puts it, there is a Christian text, the liturgical rite of the mass, which is punctuated and surrounded by native ritual actions, the Andean 'marginalia', which make the Christian text comprehensible to the Indians.[13] Platt takes a particular example of Corpus Christi celebrations in the Macha region of Bolivia as a test case for the degree to which Andean culture has historically become Christianized. Juxtaposed with the Christian elements of this two-and-a-half-week festival, occurring at summer solstice, are the actions which form a native 'exegesis', drawing on the tradition of Andean solar theology, in which the sun is the central deity of the upper world. The result is the assimilation of the Christian God to the sun and of the Devil to the realm of the deities of the earth or lower world [Plate 3]. Nor does the Andeanization stop here, since in accord with the Andean notion of evil as a relative concept, the Indian exegesis brings the upper and lower deities into fruitful relation with each other, refusing the Manichean propensities of Christian thought. The process can therefore be seen as one where the text is subverted and appropriated by the marginalia, which themselves mesh with the mapping of time and space through the ritual elaboration of the annual cycle of seasons, work and desire.[14]

Each ethnic locality produces its own particular calendar. In the Andean region as a whole, it is possible to conceive of the constitution of an inter-ethnic space through the way in which these 'interlocking calendars fan outwards, weaving ever wider areas and an increasing number of ethnic groups into a single social and religious design, whose outlines, in the present state of our knowledge, can only dimly be perceived.'[15] The beauty of this conception, however, needs some qualification. The idea of a single design is, on an empirical level, unlikely. Intellectually, it bears the marks of a search – or desire – for coherence, but such coherence belongs to a scriptural rather than an oral imagination.

Limitations of space do not allow us to describe the huge variety of Andean oral narratives: once again a single example will give some idea of the whole field. We use the term narrative rather than myth in order to avoid the polarization of ideas into either myth or history, since most Andean narratives are neither purely one nor the other. Thus in the Inkarrí cycle, reference is made to a series of historical ages, but this does not constitute a fully historical view of the world. The numerous and varied versions, all of them collected in the past four decades, centre on the civilizing figure of Inkarrí, who is destroyed by the Spaniards and whose return will bring a new historical age. In one of the versions the cultural battle is described as follows:

Our Father the Sun [father of Inkarrí] had another son called Españarrí.

'Why is my brother so powerful, why can he do everything?', Españarrí asked himself. 'I ought to be respected, because I'm very brave, because I'm very strong and I've an enormous penis, not my brother with his bloody feet.' This is what Españarrí, son of the Sun, said. He spoke with much hatred, and even the mountains trembled; and then, looking for his brother, he left some writing. When the writing struck Inkarrí in the eyes, he shouted furiously: 'What animals, what birds have dirtied this white leaf with their feet?' This he said.

. . . they say that Inka left a knot of strings [a *quipu*] for him, this knot is made out of threads.

'What filthy person do these shreds of clothing belong to, these old clothes?', was what Españarri said.[16]

In several of the versions writing is crucial to the initial defeat of Inkarrí, but this one stands out for the way in which it advances the claim that *quipus*, the system of knotted strings used by the Incas, were a form of writing denigrated and disqualified by the Spanish.

History is referred to in the Inkarrí cycle through the idea of a temporal series of three ages: of God the Father, of the Son and of the Holy Spirit. The idea derives from the millenarian teaching of Joaquin de Fiori (1142–1202), whose belief system was the most powerful in European history until the rise of Marxism, and was brought to the Andes by Franciscan missionaries. He was condemned as a heretic for preaching that the future age of the Holy Spirit would bring salvation on the earth, and at a particular time. The Joaquinite third age becomes in the Andes a utopian future, in which existing power structures established by Spanish colonialism will be reversed. Here the Christian idea of the Last Judgement is reinterpreted in the light of the Andean concept of *pacha kuti*, the turning upside down and inside out of time and space.[17] In all of the versions, Inkarrí's dismembered body (whose severed head has been taken, variously, to Cusco, Lima or Spain) is coming together again, underground. Thus the notion of historical change is also articulated with the idea that the lower or inside world (*manqhapacha* in Aymara, *ukhupacha* in Quechua) will exchange places with our present world. The lower world, region of chaos and fertility, becomes the source of the future, an extension of the belief that the dead return to present time and space during the growth season (November–March), engendering the growth of crops – in some areas, for instance, they are believed to push up the potato plants through the earth.[18] It would be wrong, therefore, to assume, as Henrique Urbano appears to, that Andean culture needed Western utopianism in order to construct an idea of futurity.[19] Repetitions of the annual cycle or calendar are not, moreover, thought of as occupying exactly the same space-time, but as forming a spiral. A factor of linearity or seriality, predicated on the succession of human generations, is included and is figured for instance in a yellow spiral seed whose Quechua name, *kuti waynitu*, means 'the child which doubles back on itself'.[20]

Ideas of history are also expressed in various forms of theatrical performance, deriving both from Inca theatrical traditions and the latent theatricality of rituals and festivals. The Spanish Conquest, their predominant theme, is represented as an epochal event whose meanings are still being lived in the present. As Nathan Wachtel has shown, these Conquest plays, found also in Guatemala and Mexico, elaborate a native interpretation which resists the European version, something we have already pointed to in the Inkarrí cycle. The central figure of the plays, which go back to the sixteenth century, is Atahuallpa, the Inca ruler murdered by the Spanish in Cajamarca. In the play performed each year in Oruro, Bolivia, 'the actors are divided into two groups, Indians and Spaniards, twenty yards apart. The *ñustas*, Indian princesses who form the chorus, wear white embroidered dresses and gold paper coronets. To add to their dignity they put on sunglasses . . . .'[21] Modern signs of social status and role are combined with ancient referents, so that this is not evasive costume drama but a yearly renegotiation of the historical basis of modern society. The main events of the plot are the death of the Inca at the hands of Pizarro and the appearance of the Spanish king, at the end, to punish Pizarro for killing a legitimate monarch. The final imaginary episode is not simply wish-fulfilment; it expresses a native juridical strategy which is also used by Guamán Poma. At the climax of the action, when Atahuallpa is taking leave of his people, his son 'wishes to die with him but his father makes him promise to retreat to Vilcabamba with his faithful subjects and refuse the Spanish yoke; one day their descendants . . . will drive out the bearded enemy'.[22] Vilcabamba was the site of final resistance of the Inca regime; the last Inca leader, Tupac Amaru I, was beheaded in Cusco in 1572.[23] The play also makes reference to the role of language and writing in the process of domination: whenever Pizarro speaks, he simply moves his lips, nothing is heard until Felipillo, the Indian interpreter, speaks. In one scene a letter is delivered to the Inca by the Spanish: it is represented by a leaf of maize, and produces bewilderment and incomprehension in the Indians.

There are many places where Conquest plays are performed, and as yet there is no full record of them. The details of the dramatic action depend on the social characteristics of each place, specifically on the relative predominance of Indians or *mestizos*. Flores describes a performance in Chiquián

(Ancash, Peru) where the *mestizo* majority assert their control over local culture and their historical vision: not only is there no redress against the Spanish victory, but the festival ends with a bullfight, 'a way of affirming that in Peru the fundamental culture is Spanish'. The *mestizos* of Chiquián 'do not imagine a Peru without Spaniards'.[24]

Andean song, dance and music also move between the poles of Indian and *mestizo* expression, depending on localities and occasions of performance. There is no clear and simple division, just as the search for purely Indian expression is romantic and anti-historical, and actually leaves the Indians deprived not only of those dimensions of their culture which the Conquest destroyed but also of the European materials and technologies which they appropriated for their own use. In the case of Indian music, for example, all stringed instruments are 'imported', but this does not mean they have not become native instruments. A major difference on the Indian side of the divide is that compositions are not considered to be the work of individual authors, but the product of collective creation. Each year, the peasant *ayllus* or *comunidades* (traditional ethnic units, granted legal status by the Spanish) mark the vital moments of the annual cycle with songs and dancing. In some cases these are repeated from one year to another, and in others new compositions have to be generated each year. Consideration of a particular example will enable us to chart some of the basic characteristics of Andean song.

In the small town of Toqroyoq, in southern Cusco, members of the local *comunidades* have produced performances which combine song, music, dance and theatre. What is unusual about these is that their referent is the recent history of the locality, and not the Christian liturgical calendar, or the native agricultural cycle, or the Conquest, although all of these are implicated, less directly, by the performance. The historical material has been researched both in archives and in local oral memory, by the leader of one of the *comunidades*, illustrating the desire and capacity of Andean groups to investigate and express their own history. The events concerned are the peasant rebellion of 1921 in Toqroyoq, led by Domingo Warka Cruz. This was one of a widespread series of peasant uprisings in Peru in the 1920s, which marked the crisis of the traditional hegemony of large landowners and the upsurge of *indigenismo*, a politico-cultural movement which took Indian culture as a model for reform or revolution. The performances are designed to take place in the town square of Toqroyoq, on 29 June each year, which has been renamed the Day of Domingo Warka. The immediate politics of this action includes a demand that the official name of the town be changed, something the state-appointed authorities resist. Larger historical dimensions are also involved: in the first 'Scene of Domingo Warka', composed for the 1983 performance, the landowners drag Warka out of town on their horses and behead him. As Flores points out, popular memory has here fused together details of the quartering of Tupac Amaru II in 1781 and the beheading of Tupac Amaru I in 1572.[25] In this connection it should be mentioned that one of the tenets of the 1920s movement was the establishment of an Andean state.

The songs transform the various layers of the past into an incitement of future action. The first Scene ends with:

> Domingo Warka
> was a man like a devil (*repeat*)
> loving his people
> he found death
> loving his people
> he gave up his life
>
> Wouldn't I
> do the same . . .?

The second Scene, performed in 1984, describes Warka's capture by the local landowners, and ends with words which recall those of Atahuallpa in the Conquest play mentioned above:

> Domingo Warka
> always said (*repeat*)
> those who come after
> rise up and rebel (*repeat*).[26]

A written account of the performances cannot reproduce the immediate impact of the music and dance: the reader must imagine the emotional power of the whole occasion, of which this description can only give an impression. The action takes place in the town square of Toqroyoq, and involves thirty-two dancers and a horse. The dance style is that of a pre-hispanic war-dance, another layer in the extraordinary density of dimensions, aesthetic, ritual, political and historical which give an epic quality to this mobilization of Andean traditions. The fact that the 'Scenes' have been presented at a number of other folklore festivals, as well as in Toqroyoq itself, opens up the question of how to place them historically as communicative actions. The folklorization of peasant culture involves some degree of spacio-temporal removal from its original place of production and reception [Plate 6]. Folklore festivals began to occur in Peru in the third and fourth decades of this century: for instance, the Inca solsticial feast of Inti Raymi was first recreated in Machu Pichu in the 1940s, and later moved to Sacsahuaman in Cusco. This disconnection from the annual ritual calendar involves gain as well as loss since the new spaces of representation (provincial and departmental capitals and sometimes the national capital) can challenge the national political order and its versions of national identity.

The disconnection is only relative with the Toqroyoq performances, which inventively combine old and new forms. Other types of Andean song have become entirely separated from ritual cycles. At one extreme there is the music known as *chicha* which combines an Andean melodic style with tropical rhythm and electric guitar as lead instrument. The lyrics refer not to collective experience but to individual lives in a context of urban dispersal where the traditional Andean universe has become fragmented. In terms of record sales, it is the most popular of all music in Peru and has a predominantly urban audience. *Chicha* developed out of the *wayno* or *wayñu*, an originally pre-Columbian musical form, and it is difficult to decide whether it represents an Andeanization of international styles or an internationalization of the Andean; whether it is an impoverished dilution of the elements it mixes or on the contrary an exciting crossing of frontiers and a matrix for new musical departures.[27]

A classification proposed by José María Arguedas can be used to produce a tentative historical map of the various stages of Andean poetry – the term is justified in that, excepting the recent appearance of individual authors, Andean poetry consists in anonymous and/or collective compositions in the form of songs. During the colonial period and until the twentieth century, Arguedas suggests, 'cosmic solitude' has been the characteristic attitude of Quechua poetry: it is a response to the partial destruction of the Andean universe by Spanish·colonialism.[28] The traditional cosmos is still available through all those ways in which earth, sky and underworld continue to be a repository of a native symbolic order, in spite of Spanish impositions. The effect of solitude in this context is isolation (from the *comunidad* or from a lover) within nature, not separation from nature. What begins to occur in Quechua poetry in the 1940s, coinciding with the increased penetration of the highlands by roads and other forces of modernization and the onset of mass immigration to the cities, is the expression of a purely individual solitude, where the connective bonds of language, culture and kinship give way to diversification, dispersal and fragmentation. The impact of these changes is seen not only in the content of the songs, but also in their form: the semiotic

59

regime of dense interconnection between human beings and the land, flora and fauna – called 'the logic of the concrete' by Lévi-Strauss in the sense that physical and semantic properties coincide – gives way to an individualization of feeling and a discontinuity between the person and the environment.[29] The first lines of a popular *wayno* illustrate the transition:

> Vicuña from the toughest steppe grass
> Why is it you that's crying?
> Are you me to cry like this?[30]

The initial invocation of the vicuña is in the 'cosmic solitude' mode, where the animal and the human stand in mutual equivalence. The next two lines, however, explicitly reject those semantics, and introduce us to the regime of individual solitude.

José María Arguedas was one of a small but increasing number of poets writing directly in Quechua. As this work is clearly 'indigenous' rather than 'indigenist', we will discuss it here rather than in the later chapter on popular culture and high culture, where Arguedas's novels will be referred to. A crucial characteristic of his poetry is its refusal both of the immobility of cosmic solitude and of the dispersal effect of individual solitude. Instead, it mobilizes the Andean cosmos as an autonomous and alternative cultural universe, whose exemplary creativity can direct the transformative power of twentieth-century technology towards the making of a new civilization, a task in which the various national governments of the nineteenth and twentieth centuries have spectacularly failed.

Arguedas's most powerful poem is probably the 'Hymn to Our Creator and Father Tupac Amaru', which weaves together into a dense epic the mythical meanings of the following: *Amaru* as serpent associated with the generative powers of the underworld; the historical struggle of Tupac Amaru II for an Andean state; the twentieth-century invasion by the Indians of the coastal cities of Peru, centres of Western culture; and imagery of social revolution. In another poem, 'Ode to the Jet', traditional Andean dieties and space-time concepts are not abandoned but transformed in a new epoch where human creativity replaces all creator gods and controls technology: 'God the Father, God the Son, God the Holy Spirit, Mountain Gods, God Inkarrí: my chest burns. You are me, I am you, in the unending power of this Jet; Great Jet of the World Above'.[31] Just as Tupac Amaru has translocated the gods of the world below into revolutionary historical action, the jet has replaced the gods of the world above, giving a new content to the traditional Andean idea of the age of the Holy Spirit, in which, according to the Laymi, 'everyone will have wings . . . there will be no more aeroplanes'.[32] No one has developed further than Arguedas the possibilities of Quechua poetry, in particular its capacity for innovation without abandonment of tradition. A prime claim of his writing is that Andean civilization can do the same.

Andean music displays a combination of traditional and innovatory features. The enormous range of music in the Andes is not reflected in the versions available in European metropolises. For instance, the ancient *wankas* or *harauis* sung on important ritual occasions by women who hold hands or skirts over their mouths and strive to achieve the very highest pitch possible, bear little relation to Western tonality. Wind instruments, such as the *quena* or Andean flute, and the *zampoña* or panpipes, usually played on their own or with drum accompaniment, are associated with native rather than *mestizo* styles of music. Stringed instruments, however, all of which arrived through European influence, are more used by *mestizos*. There are, as might be imagined, plenty of exceptions, such as Indian use of the bugle or the *charango* (a small, guitar-shaped instrument, sometimes built with an armadillo shell). The wealth of incorporations and metamorphoses of non-Andean elements includes the scissor-dancers of Ayacucho and Huancavelica (Peru) which draw on mediaeval Spanish motifs, or the widespread use of saxophones in the Mantaro valley (Peru) introduced through the experience of conscripts in military bands.

The past twenty years, with the mobility and transferability brought about by recording and new communications, have produced an increase in folklorization, standardization in conformity with Western tonality, and internationalization (for example, 'El cóndor pasa' recorded by Simon and Garfunkel). Nevertheless, in the southern highlands of Peru and throughout the altiplano region of Bolivia, music remains embedded in the annual cycle of the seasons and its ritual and symbolic corollaries: themes and instruments are closely tied to particular moments of the year and in this sense are not transferable. Wind instruments are associated with the rainy season, the lower world and the dead, while stringed instruments belong to the dry season. The meanings of the division extend into water versus wind: water is linked with the disembodied energy associated with death, a form of energy homologous with the collective work on the land which dominates the wet season, while wind characterizes the dry season and corresponds with the more individualized process of private appropriation.[33] The above are only a few of the multiple connections between music and everyday life. Music is used to mark particular qualities of time, in ways which still have to be

61

researched. It is also taken to be an extension of particular cosmic forces, as in the yearly offering of music instruments beside a stream or waterfall, so that the water can give new tunes.[34] These are places of particular danger, since the *sirenas* who preside over them can make a person mad. *Sirena* means siren and, as so often with Andean beliefs, the use of an 'acceptable' European term (usually Christian) has served strategically to protect native practices from persecution.

From the other side, the attempted superimposition of Christian concepts upon native ones by religious orders in the sixteenth century was, like the building of churches on native sacred sites, intended to facilitate Christianization. As test cases of the extent of this Christianization one can take the great Andean festivals and pilgrimages. These are the prime social and political events on a regional and inter-regional scale, and contrast with the far lesser importance of yearly national Independence celebrations. There has been considerable discussion as to how far the carnivalesque mocking of Spanish colonial power in festivals like the famous Virgen del Carmen in Paucartambo, Peru, constitutes an effective political resistance or whether the representation of temporary reversals of power structures has a merely compensatory effect.

The question is a complex one and a satisfactory answer would need to consider two sets of problems. The first concerns Andean concepts of history. If it is correct, as Olivia Harris has maintained, that the succession of past ages returns each year in the cyclical ritual of the seasons, and if that cyclical movement becomes a spiral movement projecting into the future, then the alternations or the overturning and restoration of power structures are not necessarily indicative of a static and unchanging outlook.[35] The second problematic area concerns the mutual relationships of the two cultures, Andean and non-Andean. Let us consider some of the ways in which festivals and pilgrimages can provide a context for discussion, before moving finally to the issue of class consciousness and ethnic consciousness.

The convergence of Andean and Christian cultural traditions must be understood as in one sense arising from the 'will to understand the European invasion and its consequences'. At the same time, however, it is important to remember that convergences do not necessarily entail the existence of a single meaning: the signs will be '*read* differently according to the cultural universe of the perceiver'.[36] With this point in mind, the famous devil figures of the Oruro festival in Bolivia can be taken as a convergence whose interpretation (either native underworld figures connected with mining or Christian representations of evil) will vary according to the position of the observer.

There is also the vital factor of competition for control over 'symbolic capital', that is, to possess and manipulate the signs of cultural legitimacy. This is particularly marked in the largest of all Andean pilgrimages, C'ollor Riti, in southern Cusco, which is notably multi-ethnic in its representations (including both jungle tribes and highland groups) and widely differentiated in the range of participants (urban and rural, *mestizo* and Indian). There is also increasing competition between the Church and traditional Indian authorities for control over the central liturgical actions and the disciplining of participants.

One of the many interesting features of C'ollor Riti is the money games, where offerings are made of toy banknotes or of capital in the form of miniature lorries, the purpose being to promote increase in value. The convergence here is between agricultural rituals for the growth of crops, and the capitalist notion of value and growth. Is this an instance of an Andean capacity to 'respond creatively', in Platt's phrase, to modern Western concepts? The vocabulary one uses will of course crucially affect the way one handles the phenomena. Let us widen the field of discussion here to include the impact of modernization on the Andes.

Recent research on Bolivian miners has given the lie to the Weberian assumption that ethnic consciousness is 'being swept away by the expansion of the market'.[37] Platt asks whether the process of identification between the miners and the *tío* (an underground devil figure to whom llamas are sacrificed for protection) is one of shamanic possession or a demonstration of class solidarity, and suggests that the Oruro dances could be interpreted either way; there is a 'transformational continuity' between the collective representations of peasants and of proletarianized miners.[38] Michael Taussig's view, that the devil represents a peasant rejection of capitalist production, especially its effect of commodity fetishism, would seem to be misleading in the Andean case on more than one count. In the first place, the devil for Andean peasants is a composite and not solely evil figure, not reducible to the Christian idea of evil. In a wider sense, capitalist production is assimilated, for interpretative purposes, to those concepts of energy and power surrounding agricultural production. As a result, the Andean attitude to commodity fetishism is to reinterpret it as a form of sacrifice which is not an act of 'resistance' but a recognition and exposure of capitalist 'magic', in other words, of the irrationality of capitalism in its sacrifice of human beings to production for profit.[39] Work – particularly mining because it represents a violation of the mountain spirits – needs to be surrounded by ritual actions in order to control the productive process through its sacrificial dimensions. In this sense Andean ritual converges with class consciousness, another way of taking control.

In the light of all the above, we need to find ways of analysing how cross-cultural processes in Latin America involve occasions of simultaneous but different meanings. This would allow, for instance, that the placing of Christian shrines at ancient sacred sites was 'not so much a "super-imposition", however much the evangelizers wanted it to be, as a cohabitation of duplicated religious forms, which erases neither the one nor the other'.[40] This capacity to handle inventively simultaneous heterogeneous sets of signs is possibly something that people were used to doing in a pre-Spanish multi-ethnic Andean state. Certainly, it is the homogenizing dynamic of modern culture which makes it hard to understand the duplication or duplicity, depending on where one places oneself in interpreting the strategies of colonized people.

Journey to the Museum

If we move geographically to Mexico, the issues connected with cultural plurality also shift. A change in the uses of the word 'folklore' serves as an initial probe into the differences. Because since the 1920s the Mexican state has used peasant cultural traditions as marks of national identity, the word folklore is charged with positive connotations of national unity, giving a positive valuation to the decontextualization it implies. This sense of folklore as national heritage is now the predominant one in most Latin American countries. At the same time, in Mexico the process of acculturation has been more complete, in terms both of the much sparser survival of native languages and of the inclusion of native religious beliefs and practices within Catholic symbolism and iconography. Historically, religion has always been the site of the main thrust of acculturation, a point which will be developed shortly. First, we will consider the production and consumption of peasant artefacts as a way of tracing some of the key features of encounters between modern urban and traditional rural cultures in Mexico. Our frame of reference deliberately excludes southern Mexico and Guatemala, areas of the strongest presence of native culture, and focuses instead on places where cultural boundaries are more fluid. In this way it will be possible to test how far received distinctions between pre-capitalist and capitalist culture still hold.

The best study of handicrafts and their various contexts of production and consumption in Mexico is Néstor García Canclini's *Las culturas populares en el capitalismo* (Popular Cultures under Capitalism 1982),[41] and what follows is a presentation of his main arguments. In the current context, the urban and tourist consumption of these artefacts causes them to be increasingly decontextualized and resignified on their journey to the museum and the boutique. In broad terms, their uses on the land, in the household and in rituals are replaced by exclusively aesthetic appreciation, a process which in turn affects their form and the materials from which they are made. Extreme cases are the trivializing miniaturizations of 'airport art' or where *artesanos* become artists and enter an entirely different circuit of production and consumption.

Historically, the journey to the museum received its first main impulse when, on the centenary of Independence (1921), President Obregón inaugurated an exhibition of handicrafts, which in those days were called 'popular art' or 'typical industries'.[42] In 1938, the Regional Museum of Popular Arts and Industries was opened in Pátzcuaro, where two years later the first Indigenist Congress approved a resolution calling for the 'protection of popular indigenous arts by national organizations'. Official organizations multiplied over the years, culminating in the 1970s with the establishment of FONART (National Foundation for the Promotion of Handicrafts), which runs shops, organizes exports and international exhibitions, and has been in the forefront of the internationalization of Latin American folklore. The promotion of handicraft production benefits both peasants and the state: the former are enabled to 'feed and keep united their family in the village they always felt part of', and, for the state, 'handicrafts are an economic and ideological resource for limiting peasant immigration, the constant invasion of the cities by a labour force which industry cannot absorb and which aggravates already serious deficiencies in housing, health and education'.[43]

It is important to remember that over the past twenty-five to thirty years the majority of the population of Latin America has become urban – for instance, some 70 per cent in Brazil – and that while the rural population has moved massively to the cities there has been a reverse flow of urban influences into the countryside, most significantly the spread of the labour movement in earlier decades and the penetration of the mass media more recently. So it would be misleading to conceive of urban and rural cultures in a pure state, just as it would be to attribute greater significance, as do many anthropologists, to those groups who have less contact with cities or who are less bicultural.[44] As García Canclini points out, tradition and modernity become articulated through mutually dependent needs: peasants consume industrial products, and there is a demand for *artesanías* in the cities. The peasant household combines industrial products such as clothing, butane gas stoves and aluminium cooking pots with hand-produced local objects, such as pottery and small amounts of woven cloth. The latter offer a way of holding on to a local collective memory, which mass-produced objects could not convey. This situation is not 'transitional' between ideal stereotypes of the urban and the rural, but a stable cultural pattern throughout most of rural Latin America. However, this does not necessarily mean that the peasant household combines 'the best of both worlds', since the penetration of consumer goods into rural areas frequently generates a crisis. New needs for industrialized goods are created, forcing the peasant household to rationalize production and work harder and longer hours, thus making it difficult for the peasant family to continue participating in traditional magico-religious practices. Nevertheless, with regard to the future of handicrafts, this should clearly depend on the decision of the producers themselves as to how far traditional forms, techniques and materials should be preserved or varied, since it is their own livelihood which is at stake.

The *artesanos* of Ocumicho, Michoacán, began in the late 1960s to produce ceramics depicting devil figures [Cover illustration]. The devils 'tend to be associated with elements of the modern world which are non-existent in the village: police, motorbikes, airplanes. The largest ceramic I saw in Ocumicho, sixty centimetres long, is a bus with happy devils leaning out of the windows and on the front the words: "Ocumicho-Mexico-Laredo", the latter two being cities where migrants go to look for work'.[45] García Canclini suggests that the devils provide a way of controlling the destructive effects of modernization, by placing it within a traditional repertory of symbols. When he asked an *artesano* why in one of his pieces various devils were pushing and crowding to see themselves in a mirror, the reply was 'The mirror is appearance. You look at yourself and you're there. You take away the mirror and you're not there any more.'[46] This prompts the further suggestion that the devils before the mirror are a way of negotiating the uncertainty of social identity introduced when modernization removes the stability of fixed communities. This would relate to a process described by the Mexican poet Octavio Paz in *El laberinto de la soledad* (*The Labyrinth of Solitude* 1950) whereby marginalized Mexican immigrants in the USA have at their disposal nothing except a series of masks from which to construct an identity. Paz takes this Mexican experience of a lack of essential identity to be emblematic of that of all human beings. His argument omits the key effect of transition from a rural peasant culture and adopts instead a style of decontextualized universality, common until recently among Mexican intellectuals.

The broader context of these changes is a transition from religious meanings to a secular and aesthetic attitude on the part of producers and consumers. A similar change occurred in European art, with the transition from mediaeval to renaissance works. José María Arguedas, in an essay on Joaquín López Antay, the great *escúltor* (sculptor – the local word for this type of *artesano*) from Ayacucho, Peru, notes the effect of changes of clientele upon his work.[47] López Antay was a maker of *retablos*, a type of portable altar consisting of a wooden frame with doors which open to reveal two scenes with plaster figures. Traditionally, the upper scene shows animals with their patron saints, and the lower has a more secular character, depicting local ceremonial occasions such as the branding of animals. The treatment of the animals, which include non-domestic species, introduces a native animist or magical dimension. His traditional clientele had been landowners needing the *retablos* for ceremonial use. But when he came to the notice of *indigenista* painters, collectors of popular art from Lima and tourists, they began to demand different themes from him, and he began to present in his *retablos* a variety of local scenes, no longer limiting himself to the traditional one, and eventually also replacing the religious upper storey with the depiction of secular customs. Arguedas celebrates López Antay's capacity for inventive adaptation without abandoning the richness of the tradition or, to adopt a modern terminology, his artistic autonomy. Just as the work shifts, from the ritual or ceremonial sphere to the artistic, so does the terminology appropriate to it. López Antay was given the Peruvian National Prize for Art in 1975. In the 1980s, *retablos* from the Ayacucho region began to depict scenes relating to the guerrilla war between Sendero Luminoso and the army.

Mirko Lauer traces the confluences which make possible the *retablo* as object: the Catholic portable altar was originally a military necessity, permitting an intersection between on the one hand Indian animism or 'idolatry' where the object itself is an 'effective presence' and on the other the symbolic representations of orthodox Catholicism. As a result of its mobility, the *retablo* approximates perhaps more than any other object of *artesanía* to the framed canvas, 'abstract and universal representation of space'.[48] Neverthe- less, the framed canvas does not have to be the destiny of *artesanías*, nor is becoming an artist in the Western sense the only option open to the producer: art in Peru is still an 'expression limited to the aspirations of the bourgeoisie of the capital city'.[49] The complex interactions and subversions between handicrafts and art resemble those between oral narratives and the book, a main theme of Chapter 4 below.

Some final observations about terminology and translation can now be made. The problem of appropriate terms arises from the fact that 'popular art' (*arte popular*) and 'folk art' (*artes folklóricas*) presume an integration of different worlds which may be wishful thinking. *Artesanía*, in Spanish, has no such pretension, and is now the preferred term. There is no satisfactory English translation, however, given that the term 'handicrafts' conveys little sense of collective production or local symbolism. Sometimes a circumlocution such as 'three-dimensional portable objects', though awkward, can be useful for describing aesthetic creations which do not fit the categories of Western art.[50]

Popular Catholicism

Distinctions between native and Hispanic, and pre-capitalist and capitalist formations should not be taken to coincide. (Popular Catholicism in rural Latin America tends to be a combination of native pre-Columbian elements, Spanish popular Catholicism of the sixteenth century and the teachings of the official Church.) The relative equilibrium between Spanish and native elements reached in the colonial period has often continued to reproduce itself with relative stability until the past thirty years, during which the isolation of rural communities has decreased drastically. Let us consider briefly the historical context before tracing the characteristics of popular religion and then exploring what it reveals about the transitions and exchanges between pre-capitalist and capitalist formations. We will be concentrating first on Mexico.

The vocabulary to describe the non-Christian other has been through significant historical changes. (In the colonial period idolatry was the word used for paganism, the eradication of which was the chief legitimation of the Conquest.) The Spanish concept of idolatry refers to the effective presence of the sacred in objects, typical in the Spanish view of native Indian religions but unacceptable to official orthodox Catholicism. However, this concept of the condensation of the divine into particular and unique objects belonged to an intellectual grid which did not necessarily fit native religions, whose notions of the sacred tended to be more fluid and dispersed. Thus idols were often the product of Spanish imagination or of native keenness to fulfil Spanish expectations.[51] The problem of how religion is defined arises here. The Spanish brought with them an interpretative grid of gods, temples and sacrifices which failed to grasp that the feast (*fiesta*) was the main basis of native religion. The opposite of idolatry was not a successfully imposed orthodox Catholicism, but a de facto syncretism mixing native practices and beliefs with the Catholic liturgy and iconography. A particular factor which made this possible was the fact that the Conquistadors brought with them the popular Catholicism of sixteenth-century Spain, which could easily accommodate the notion of effective presence.

The most famous of all examples of the continuation of native religion inside Catholic iconography is the Mexican Virgin of Guadalupe, which, as was seen in Chapter 1, combines the Catholic Marian cult with that of Tonantzin, the Aztec mother goddess. The incomplete suppression of native religions became a particular concern of the Church in the seventeenth century, when 'extirpators of idolatry' were appointed to interrogate native populations: idolaters were now seen not so much as pagans in the simple sense but as perverse and intelligent people, able hypocritically to mix two religions. The accounts of idolatry are invaluable sources for reconstructing the history of native religions. After idolatry, the next key word is superstition, a post-Enlightenment and therefore post-Independence word, which stresses less the non-Christian character of beliefs than their supposed irrationality. It is a word used by the European-oriented elite to separate themselves from popular culture. (Superstition in fact includes much of popular Catholicism.) In the twentieth century, the combined interventions of anthropology, surrealism and literature brought about a revaluation of superstition as magic, particularly in the idea of 'magical realism', which receives further discussion below.

Indian recalcitrance towards Catholicism emerges in the following sixteenth-century report on Indian attitudes in the Viceroyalty of Peru: 'They express doubt and difficulty about certain aspects of the faith: principally the mystery of the Holy Trinity, the unity of God, the passion and death of Jesus Christ, the virginity of Our Lady, the Holy Communion, universal Resurrection.'[52] The author, Diego de Torres, does not go on to say what was left: not much, presumably, apart from the saints. The broad differences between popular and 'cultivated' Catholicism in the twentieth century are the following: popular Catholicism tends to lack a conception of salvation, and its idea of sin is at variance with orthodox theology; the sacraments receive little emphasis, and the priest is viewed principally as a functionary of the Church, not as a mediator with God, a role which is fulfilled by the cult of the saints who are often seen as being 'effectively present' in the images and sculptures which represent them; domestic liturgies are given more importance than the formal rites of the Church.[53] Insight into how the saints became vehicles for native meanings is afforded by the fact that the early Spanish evangelizers in Mexico translated 'saint' into the *Nahuatl* word '*ixitla*', which in fact indicates effective presence and immanence rather than representation.

Present-day religious values in the Mexican countryside are concerned not with any idea of supernatural or invisible transcendence but with immanence and everyday life. Nor are inner spiritual values such as moral 'perfection' or the peace of the soul important; what matters is the everyday livelihood of self and family for whose benefit the assistance of the saints is sought.[54] In this context it is worth adding that the idea of the *fiesta* as a transcendental interruption of everyday time does not correspond with local conceptions, in which the occasion is a way of affirming what a hostile nature or an unjust society deny.[55] Another influential distortion of popular experience in obedience to dominant ideas of national identity is Carlos Fuentes's notion of the Aztec past as having gone 'underground', into some mythical latency. If the pre-Columbian past is present in Mexico, this is because it remains embedded, in perfectly evident ways for those who wish to look, in the lives of Mexicans. Otherwise, we are dealing with the dubious construction of a Mexican unconscious, much as Jung constructed a European unconscious, conveniently available as symbolic capital but fenced off from the practical lives of Mexicans, especially those in rural areas.[56] Both Paz and Fuentes made extensive use of Séjourné's work on Aztec religion, which transcendentalizes and Christianizes.[57]

As Giménez points out, 'Official religion . . . confronts popular religion with a power of symbolic aggression, a cosmopolitan prestige and a pretension to universality which place localism . . . and the cultural codes particular to peasant civilization in grave danger.'[58] Conserving local senses of the sacred is therefore a crucial way of preserving autonomy and identity. A typical expression of local religiosity is the pilgrimage, which involves almost the whole local population in 'a vast operation of cooperation and solidarity'. Giménez's example is the yearly pilgrimage to the sanctuary of Chalma, to the southeast of Mexico City. Chalma is the site of a pre-Hispanic shrine, an 'idol'. One of the official histories reveals the symbolic violence involved in the establishment of the Christian shrine: 'the detestable idol suffered total ruin and defeat, thrown humiliatingly to the ground and reduced to tiny fragments in front of the sacred image'.[59] Nevertheless, not only present reality but also historical identity are synthesized in the figure of the patron saint, which by embodying and protecting the whole community plays a role similar to the tutelary deity of the *calpulli*, the pre-Columbian tribal group, which under Spanish rule became redefined as the *barrio*.

Syncretism does not indicate weak adherence to Catholicism: 'the greatest dedication to the saints and other Catholic customs occurs in traditional communities, those that most preserve pre-Hispanic religious beliefs and practices'.[60] In contrast to the Andean region, where native religious practices exist alongside Catholic ones, what has happened in central Mexico is that where elements of the pre-Hispanic would have persisted they 'are embedded in, and subordinated to, Catholic beliefs and symbols'. An interesting feature of the historical process of acculturation is the selective alliance with indigenous gods, 'the identification of the supernatural patrons of the indigenous elite with the forces of evil, and the supernatural advocates of commoners with Adamic and holy figures in the Christian pantheon'. In the past three decades the Church, seeking to promote modernized Catholicism, has once again entered into the attack against popular religion. One example is the 'Pan-American Mass' with mariachi bands and South American folk music, put together by a Mexican bishop and designed to be a tourist attraction. A more powerful force for change is the fact that the cost of costumes and sponsorship increasingly goes beyond the means of peasant households; expenditure on the *fiestas* prevents capital accumulation for improving the land.[61]

Popular beliefs – superstition or magic, depending on your position – have shown remarkable persistence throughout Latin America. At the risk of folklorizing them, by removing them from the historical and social contexts outlined above, we give here a brief sample, drawing on those mentioned by J. Ingham and adding others. The condition of *susto* is considered dangerous because it causes the soul (or one of them) to leave the body; there is perhaps an equivalence with depression or anxiety in Western medicine. When the soul leaves the body, for this or other reasons, a variety of ritual cures are resorted to, such as invoking the names of saints in Nahuatl while stroking the patient with corn kernels. Death beliefs, which involve complex ideas about the soul or souls, or where pre-Columbian and/or European popular Catholic notions have persisted most strongly. The best known example is the common practice of giving food to the dead on All Saints Day. Various rituals, together with herbs, are used by wives to control husbands and prevent them from running off with other women: in Mexico, *toloache*, in Peru, *chamico*. Rituals are also practised for controlling the weather: in Mexico, the key officiators are *graniceros*, people who have been struck by lightning. Other areas of popular belief are concerned with *los aires* or *mal de viento, mal de ojo*, and *daño*, all of which have to do with notions of evil influence and methods for its removal.

Such lists are potentially misleading, because they remove the differences not only between diverse types of thinking but also between very different historical situations and therefore between very different meanings. There are

71

no permanent meanings to be drawn on, as some folklorists would want, but different histories which intersect, with varying stabilities and instabilities. Let us consider the case of José Gregorio Hernández, a Venezuelan popular saint. Hernández was a medical doctor who practised in a rural area. 'Soon after his death [in 1919], rumours began to spread regarding favours that had been obtained through his intercession, and stories began to circulate concerning the miraculous cures effected at the graveside.'[62] He is currently the object of massive devotion and is being considered by the Vatican for canonization. However, his popular sanctification began during a period when Venezuela was changing from a coffee economy to a petroleum one and as a consequence the isolation of the rural masses was coming to an end. The Hernández cult includes elements from both tradition and modernity, and reveals the negotiation of transition by the popular imagination. For instance, he only cures natural diseases, not supernatural ones, but as a ritual intervention. His image embodies his qualities, but also has 'contagious powers', or 'effective presence'. By synthesizing these elements, it 'served to dispel some of the structural dissonance that is a frequent accompaniment to social change'.[63] The painting 'Declaration of Love to Venezuela' by the Colombian J.C. Uribe makes use of the Hernández image inside a series of ironical dissonances. The shape of the Sacred Heart, central symbol for the Catholic basis of official national identity, is made by a mass of cheap coloured lithographs, which 'form the shape not only of a heart, but also of lips'.[64] The heart is enclosed in some forty-two images of Hernández (wearing suit, tie and hat), also mass-produced. (In this ironical space come together the sixteenth and the twentieth centuries, the sacred and the profane, anonymous popular imagery and signed pop art, the shrine and the museum, miraculous images and mass-produced ones.)

Encounters between pre-capitalist cultures and modernity have engendered a very important debate about acculturation and cultural resistance. Michael Taussig's *The Devil and Commodity Fetishism in Latin America* has been a major contribution to that debate. He argues that capitalism also has its 'magic', such as the attack and invasion of human beings by the parasitic forces of commodities and money. Therefore we should think of pre-capitalist fetishism as a resistance to capitalist fetishism; thus devil beliefs should be interpreted not just as a negotiation of modernity but also a criticism of it. In 1914, the Cauca valley in central Colombia was opened up to the world market by a railway line across the Andes to the Pacific. The current situation of the peasantry in that area is one of semi-proletarianization: they own small plots of land, but these are insufficient for all the needs of subsistence. In this sense they stand 'between two epochs and two worlds, proletarian and peasant'.[65] At this liminal moment, the 'preexisting cosmogony of the workers becomes a critical front of resistance, or mediation, or both'. The devil-contract occurs when 'male sugar-plantation workers . . . make secret contracts with the devil in order to increase productivity, and hence their wages'.[66] The contract, however, entails that the proceeds cannot be invested in improving the land, but must be consumed immediately, and the contract leads to premature death. Taussig finds here an image of the barrenness and destructiveness of capitalist growth, based on exchange value, in contradistinction to a system of reciprocity and self-renewal based on use value.

The issues are fundamental to how one defines and interprets popular cultures. One of the problems that arises with Taussig's approach is that resistance must include the reproduction of its own conditions of survival. In this connection, he isolates symbolic actions inside a predicted resistance of pre-capitalist culture to capitalism, a resistance which does not necessarily occur, at least at that level of generality. What he does not analyse with appropriate depth is all the ways in which, both at the economic and the cultural level, different modes of production coexist and interconnect. Exchange value is presented solely as a negative force; there is no acknowledgement that its freeing of social relations from inherited fixities and territorializations is a potentially positive aspect which, for example, makes possible the migration of human beings, artefacts and symbols. Perhaps, rather than being opposed, the two fetishisms mirror each other, a possibility suggested by the role of Andean demon beliefs referred to above. If this is the case, then finding in pre-capitalist cultures a source of resistance to capitalism is less viable. Nevertheless, Taussig's conclusion makes a valid challenge: 'A community can in many ways be affected and controlled by the wider capitalist world, but this in itself does not necessarily make such a community a replica of the larger society and the global economy'.[67] Lauer, similarly, insists that different outcomes to the encounter between Andean tradition and capitalist modernity in Peru are possible: not only does the former have its unique cultural forms, but the latter is 'radically different from the different local and regional patterns of capitalism' in the advanced countries.[68] It is also important to bear in mind García Canclini's caveat: 'Although capitalist development tends to absorb and standardize the forms of material and cultural production which preceded it, the subordination of traditional communities cannot be total given the inability of industrial capitalism itself to give work, culture, and medical attention to all, and given the resistance of the ethnic groups who defend their identity.'[69]

In the following sections we turn to rural popular theatre and oral poetry in the northeast of Brazil, in order to elucidate further the relationship between a given form and peasant culture and the way in which the pressures of modernization affect the form.

The Dancing Ox: Peasant Life and Popular Theatre

As we saw in Chapter 1, the nature of the process of colonization in Brazil created the basis of traditional rural society, giving rise to forms of popular culture which, despite the rapid expansion of an urban culture industry, continue to exist, particularly in the north and northeast of Brazil.

Social life centred around large clan-like groups or *parentelas* based on complex networks of kinship and bonds of gratitude between various generations of landowning families, their dependants and workers. These relationships based on reciprocity diminished social distance between the dominant landowning strata and their subordinates, mitigating social conflicts which might arise as a result of the unequal distribution of land. Conflict arose more frequently between families, due to disputes over land, cattle or an attack on family honour. To pre-empt such conflict, it was the custom to travel from one *fazenda* to another, to arrange marriages and to form alliances with other families. Courage and fearlessness constituted the means through which individuals acquired prestige and social status.

Given these conditions, the only alternative for those who preferred to remain independent was to survive on the margins of the colonial agricultural enterprises through the development of a particular kind of subsistence economy on the areas unoccupied by the *latifundio*. This involved relinquishing more advanced methods of tilling the soil and adopting indigenous traditions of extensive agriculture. When the land was exhausted, new areas were opened up while the nourishment obtained was complemented by hunting, gathering and animal husbandry. The abundance of land, and the fear of being expelled from it by the expansion of the *latifundios*, discouraged the use of more advanced agricultural techniques. Moreover, due to the absence of markets, little or no money was needed, while the distance which separated this itinerant population from urban centres contributed to the emergence of a form of social life closed in on itself and immune to social change. By the end of the colonial period, an area extending from the South to the hinterland of the Northeast, Maranhão and Amazonia had been populated by small groups of peasants – respectively called *caipiras*, *sertanejos* and *caboclos* – living in precarious improvised adobe huts which could easily be left and rebuilt elsewhere when the soil had become poor.[70]

Despite the industrialization and modernization of Brazil which began in the 1920s, this rural social structure, consisting of large estates and a stratum of peasants living at subsistence level, remained largely unchanged until well into the mid twentieth century. (An exception was the South, where European immigration, the use of more advanced agricultural techniques and the existence of smaller landholdings introduced significant changes.) Although subsequently, due to the massive influx of rural migrants to the city and the rationalization of agriculture, this traditional rural society became less significant, the social relations it generated and the cultural forms in which they were embedded need to be considered in order to understand the dynamics of Brazilian society and its culture. This is particularly so given that, as pointed out in Chapter 1, the process of capitalist modernization in Brazil did not, as it did in Europe, entail the transformation of earlier social structures as a whole. Let us therefore examine some of the fundamental forms of social relations characteristic of peasant society in Brazil as it exists today.

The land is generally cultivated by the family unit either independently or as a tenant farmer on a large estate. Due to the rudimentary nature of agricultural techniques, families are forced to rely on each other for mutual assistance, coming together when required to form small cooperative groups known as *mutirões*.[71] There is little social differentiation in the *mutirão*; similar tasks are carried out jointly creating social bonds involving the person as a whole rather than as a representative of a social role.[72] Due to their semi-nomadic existence, families tend nevertheless to be small and fragmented and to live in considerable isolation from each other. This condition is compensated for by the institution of *compadrio* and by the many rituals and celebrations which characterize the popular Catholicism of the rural population. *Compadrio* entails establishing close ties between godparents and godchildren, godmothers and godfathers belonging to the same *bairro rural* or rural district; wealthy or influential people may be sought out as godparents in order to secure the future wellbeing of one's offspring in an insecure world. The importance of these relations of *compadrio* in reinforcing the collective identity of a rural district is reflected in the variety and number of rituals through which it is established. In June for example, during the festivities of São João, future *compadres* utter ritual formulae as they leap together over a bonfire.[73]

To the uninformed traveller the hinterland or *sertão* may appear

75

uninhabited; a closer look however will reveal a landscape dotted with a few humble houses, coloured bright blue, pink or yellow, located at the foot of a gently sloping hill crowned by a small chapel. Living at great distances from hospitals or schools, relying on primitive agricultural techniques and a precarious social network formed by the rural district, the *sertanejo* grows up immersed in the natural rhythms of the seasons. Appeals to the supernatural powers of the patron saint and the Virgin Mary, and knowledge of medicinal plants and magical practices which establish direct contact with the divine constitute the cultural devices through which nature is rendered pliable to human purpose. Oral transmission of the group's cultural traditions in the form of legends, teachings, stories, anecdotes and dance-dramas constitutes in an almost non-literate social group the means through which meaning is constructed. In this respect it could be maintained that in some aspects the social structure of peasant society in Brazil resembles that of societies once defined by anthropologists as 'primitive'. Practices belonging to different spheres in complex societies with an elaborate division of labour – such as farming, hunting, fishing, religious worship and aesthetic expression – form part of a single continuum of experience while art is embedded in a mythico-religious interpretation of the world.

Religious devotion in popular Catholicism manifests itself primarily in rituals and festivities which mark the seasons of the year, a person's life events such as birth, marriage and death, as well as in the yearly celebrations of the patron saint. As we saw earlier on, in contrast to official Catholicism with its hierarchy and elaborate belief systems, popular Catholicism is characterized by a sense of the immediate presence of the numinous in the visible world. Mysterious beings, saints, devils and souls of the dead inhabit everyday life. Priests, indispensable mediators of God in official Catholicism, are hence of no great relevance, since a festivity celebrating a patron saint and the procession or pilgrimages which accompany it can be carried out without their aid. Instead, the two figures of greatest importance are the *capelão*, a lay preacher, and the *festeiro* or sponsor of the festivity.[74] The lay preacher is familiar with the prayers and practices required for the worship of the saints as well as the rules governing the religious procession and the details of the non-religious festivities which take place simultaneously. This function can also be fulfilled by an elderly woman. In a semi-literate culture in which oral transmission is essential to guarantee the continuity of cultural tradition, the lay preachers represent the collective memory of the group. The sponsor of the feast on the other hand, usually chosen from the more prosperous families, is responsible for organizing the feast and providing food for the congregation's collective meal. A small group called the *folia*, which includes the sponsor, a few musicians and an individual bearing the flag of the patron saint, travel through the rural district, singing, dancing and collecting offerings for the festivity. The *folia* is received with fireworks by each peasant family, and before the offerings are handed over prayers are sung in front of the flag of the patron saint. On the day of the feast, the food is consumed collectively, followed by a procession. The patron saint or Virgin, erected on a small elaborately decorated platform, is carried on the shoulders of the faithful as the procession winds its way through the streets.

The patron saint acts as a kind of heavenly godparent bound to his godchildren by ties of mutual obligation. From his elevated position on the family altar, he accompanies their joys, trials and tribulations; his image carved in wood or clay is at one and the same time the manifestation of his divine presence. Endowed with supernatural powers his assistance is sought in cases of illness, lovers' disputes and family conflicts, or to protect his followers from droughts and the arbitrary power of landowners in cases of dispute over land-use.[75] Gratitude for a favour obtained often takes the form of a pilgrimage to a sacred city, where *ex-votos* are deposited in the church of the patron saint or of a revealed image of the Virgin. *Ex-votos* include images of parts of the body which have been healed: arms, heads, legs and hands of wood, clay or more recently polystyrene, made by local artisans; photographs bearing an inscription dedicated to the saint; a sheep in thanks for a good harvest; offers of money and lighted candles. Acts of penance such as following the stations of the cross, and above all the religious feast, comprise the devotional acts through which divine forces can be moved to act in favour of men and women.

Popular Catholicism is both instrumental and mythical. Like a mirror-image of the patronage system, the relationship between the saints and the faithful consists in an exchange, in this case of promises for divine intervention in difficult life circumstances. This is, however, understood in terms of a mythical cognitive framework which explains reality in terms of extraordinary and mysterious events not reducible to empirical reality. The social order is seen as part of a broader cosmic purpose rather than as a product of human practice open to historical transformation. Thus although the world vision underlying popular Catholicism has, as we have seen in our earlier discussion of Canudos, spawned messianic movements challenging the social order, this challenge does not arise out of a critical-problematizing attitude towards social reality. Indeed, in the sociology of peasant movements there has been some controversy about whether messianic movements such as

Canudos are, as the historian Eric Hobsbawm argues, an expression of pre-political forms of protest against the established rural order or whether, as Maria Isaura Pereira de Queiroz claims, they reproduce the structure of patronage and dependence on which it is based.[76]

An essential component of the religious celebrations in devotion to the patron saint are the cultural practices which take place simultaneously, and which, if they involve any of the forms of popular theatre, are performed in the public square, in front of the church or in an open space belonging to a farm or estate.

These popular theatre performances, defined by the poet and folklorist Mário de Andrade as dance-dramas (*danças dramáticas*), are constructed around a simple plot of secular or religious nature which is developed through song and dance. Originally the dramas stem from mediaeval Portuguese mystery plays or *autos* performed during the Christmas and Easter festivities and from songs in praise of the saints, during which scenes from their lives were represented.[77]

Transplanted to Brazil by Portuguese colonizers, the *autos* spread throughout the North and Northeast reaching as far south as Santa Catarina. They were frequently used by the Jesuits in the sixteenth century, who incorporated indigenous figures in their representations in order to facilitate their missionary undertaking of converting the heathen Indians to Christianity. In their migration to the tropics, however, the original European form was transformed and subverted by the introduction of pagan Indian and African elements and by the devotional rituals characteristic of popular Catholicism, crystallizing into original native dance-dramas.[78] Among them perhaps four stand out as genres which have retained their vitality, although even these, as will become apparent, are being modified by the dynamics of capitalist development. They comprise the *Pastoris*, the *Cheganças*, the *Congadas* and most importantly the *Reisados*. All the dance-dramas are divided into two parts: a *cortejo* or procession in which participants dance through the streets of a village or small town announcing the second part, the performance of the dramatic narrative, defined as an *embaixada* (embassy).

Like the majority of the dance-dramas the *Pastoris* are performed during the cycle of the Christmas festivities, lasting for twelve days from Christmas day to 6 January, when the Three Kings arrived in Bethlehem to present Christ with their gifts. Children and adolescents dressed like shepherds in white, wearing flowered hats and carrying baskets full of fruit, eggs and other offerings, accompanied by tambourines and a small stringed instrument called a *cavaquinho*, dance and sing a variety of hymns, waltzes, boleros and sambas written and composed for the occasion by literate individuals, against a backdrop of the manger at Bethlehem. A multitude of allegorical figures including winged angels, the seasons, human virtues such as Faith and Hope, the stars, Sun, Moon and Earth, the Samaritan, Cupid and an array of animals form part of the group proclaiming the birth of Christ.[79] The play reaches its climax when the Lost Shepherdess, also called 'Libertine' is tempted by Satan, whereupon she is saved from the Prince of Darkness by the Archangel Gabriel. Rural migration to the cities, the commercialization of Christmas and the widespread influence of North American Christmas motifs such as snow-sprinkled deer and Santa Claus, have to some extent reduced the practice of this *auto*. A *folia de Reis*, in which a small group of musicians and a harlequinesque fool go from house to house announcing the birth of Christ, is still common among migrants in the steel factories of São Paulo.

The *Chegança* is related to the maritime travels of the Portuguese. Represented on an allegorical caravel of the sixteenth century, usually in front of a church, this *auto* is constructed around the fate which befalls the crew of a boat assailed by a storm on the high seas. A captain, sailors, a priest, a cook and various naval officers accompanied by a small band of stringed instruments recount the events on board through song and forms of sung dialogue. Two events constitute the highlights of the play: as provisions run out, the crew draws lots to see which one of them will be devoured; and hidden within one of them is the devil, who has come for the captain's soul.

The *Congos* or *Congadas* are dramatizations centring around the theme of the battles of the warrior queen Ginga of Angola. More generally, they re-enact the coronation of the kings of Africa, narrating through song and dance events in African history retained in the collective memory of the descendants of slaves. Frequently, they are syncretically fused with devotional songs dedicated to the Catholic figures Our Lady of the Rosary, Saint Benedict and the Divine Spirit.

The *Reisado* called *Bumba-meu-Boi* is perhaps one of the richest, most extraordinary and lyrical of the dramatic dances, synthesizing in a hybrid form Indian, African and Iberian traditions. The term *reisado*, of Portuguese origin, refers to the enactment of a theme, contained in a popular song, on the eve and day of the Three Kings. In Brazil, it has been the custom to connect two or more *Reisados* in a manner based on the compositional principles character-istic of the musical suite, that is, linking fragments of other dramas, of disparate songs and poems, choreographic elements, popular characters, animal and supernatural creatures and sketches drawn from everyday life, in such a way that the main skeleton of the play – the death and resurrection of a dancing *boi*, or ox – forms only the nucleus to which the other elements are attached in a semi-arbitrary fashion.[80]

The play is thought to stem from various sources, so the presence of the ox and its death and resurrection contain multiple overlapping meanings. The burlesque figure of an ox made of a wooden frame covered with a coloured cotton cloth, to which a mask with horns is attached, was thought to have danced among the saints and angels which formed the pantheon of divine beings in the ancient religious processions of Portugal.[81] Usually performed around 6 January, it is related to the birth of Christ and constitutes a celebration of one of the animals witnessing the Nativity. The term *rancho* has been used to describe groups of dancers representing shepherds on their way to Bethlehem carrying a gift, in the form of a plant or animal; each group bore the name of an animal at Christ's manger: *ranchos* of the ox and donkey. This Christian tradition was also influenced by pagan totemistic practices of African and Indian origin, in which the death and resurrection of a totem is celebrated. In the *ranchos* of the horse, the jaguar, the deer and the serpent in the Amazon region, the animal designating the respective group dies and is brought to life again. Mário de Andrade points out that rites worshipping plants or animals and marking the return of the seasons – characteristic of primitive society – reveal a belief in a superior natural force, which needs to be appropriated through acts of exorcism and appeasement. This manifests itself particularly in symbols of the recurrent return of a positive element, which act as a defence against the fear of deprivation; in the notion of the 'death and resurrection of the land, the sun, the ox, the animal and the plant, of the God'.[82] Their continued presence, however, in contemporary rural culture ought not to be regarded merely as expressions of the 'survival' of African and Indian symbols. Instead, it is suggested that this is due, as pointed out earlier, to the specific nature of the process of colonization of the Brazilian countryside, which, owing to the low level of development of the forces of production connected with it, established a relationship between human beings and nature of the kind associated with 'primitive' society.

Moreover, the intense attachment to the ox revealed in the importance of the *Bumba-meu-Boi* is also connected to the essential role of the ox in the rural economy of Brazil, particularly during the colonial period when a *civilização do couro*,[83] a whole way of life based on the use of leather for clothing and in the household, emerged. In large parts of the hinterland, the life of the cattle-breeders or *vaqueiros* has been immortalized in songs and poems referred to by students of oral culture in Brazil as the *ciclo de vaqueiros*. This attachment is evident in the performance of the *Bumba-meu-Boi* in Maranhão during the religious festivities dedicated to São João. This saint, according to a prevalent legend, owned an ox who knew how to dance and whom he loved most dearly. On the eve of São João's birthday on 23 June, the ox, made of black velvet and elaborately embroidered with multicoloured sequins, portraying images of nature, Christ and the saints, is baptized before an altar encircled by candles and incense.

The phrase Bumba-meu-Boi relates to the refrain Eh Bumba and the beat of the drum which follows every twist and turn of the dancing ox. Defined by the participants as a brinquedo (a game or playful diversion), it lasts eight hours and sometimes, as in Maranhão, a number of days. Originally, the auto was seen and applauded by all classes; at present its actors and its audience are drawn from the peasantry and the working classes.

During the performance, sugarcane brandy flows freely among actors and spectators alike, and the latter actively participate in the action: they sing with the choir, applaud the choreography, mourn the death of the ox and rejoice when it resuscitates.[84] The interaction between audience and performers is also encouraged by music and dance, which in combination with the use of a great number of masks, destroys any pretence of realism. In many respects the Bumba is similar to the popular theatre of the commedia dell'arte, in that the play centres around a loosely structured soggetto (theme). The dramatic episodes are orally transmitted or recorded in manuscripts, but since the participants tend to be largely non-literate, the texts are subject to refabulation.[85] The dramatic power of the play therefore depends on the actor's skill in improvising dialogue and in perfecting his interpretation of a character through gesture, mime and dance. As in Elizabethan drama, the women are represented by men, except for the cantadeira or singer, who sits beside an orchestra consisting of a zabumba (drum) a ganzá (a cylindrical object containing pebbles), and a tambourine, and sings as the characters enter or leave the 'stage'.

The characters can be divided into three categories: human, animal and fantastic, the latter being taken from Indian mythology. One of the most important human characters, the capitão, also known as cavalo marinho, is the owner of the ox and represents a landowner or powerful political boss; speaking, whistling and singing, he commands the spectacle. This figure is made up of a frame in the shape of a horse with reigns, and the actor slips into it in such a way that he appears to be riding the horse. He is assisted by two vaqueiros or cowherds, Mateus and Sebastião, whose responsibility it is to look after the boi. Mateus is wicked and shrewd, while Sabestião, who is black, is portrayed as lazy and awkward. They are two clownlike figures, holding an animal bladder filled with air which they use to strike the characters at the end of each scene, chasing them off the 'stage'. Catirina, also black, enjoys dancing, drinking and behaving in an insolent manner. While these three represent popular characters, the engineer, the priest and the doctor appear as authority figures. The *burrinha* or little donkey mounted by a cowherd, a serpent and most importantly the ox comprise the animal figures. Like the ox, the fantastic characters wear masks attached to larger-than-life frames emphasizing their grotesque and frightening qualities. Among them are the *caipora*, a bad geni taken from Indian mythology and represented by an urchin with a loincloth; the fearful *babau*, an animal ghost in the form of a horse's skull, a two-headed creature called the 'Dead carrying the Living'; the Devil, who appears spitting fire, dressed in red with black wings and a tail. These and many other figures, distributed throughout the core narrative as well as the supplementary scenes, constitute the vehicles through which a satirical, burlesque and fantastic form of drama is created in which one scene blends into another with extraordinary imaginative freedom.

The core narrative unfolds in the following manner: the *capitão* riding his horse enters on the 'stage' formed by the circle of spectators and calls for his acolytes, Mateus and Sebastião, asking for the ox to be brought in. Mateus and Sebastião go off calling him by his name, which varies depending on the region in which the play is being performed. Announced by the choir, the ox enters dancing wildly, turning and swaying, attacking the public, the choir, and the *vaqueiros* indiscriminately. Suddenly, the beloved ox collapses and dies; fatigue, an arrow or a blow to the head have led to his death. The choir sings a melancholic song of lament:

> My poor ox is dead
> Dear God what will become of me now?
> I will go to find another one
> At the very far end of Piauí.[86]

The captain summons the doctor to cure the ox and the *capitão do mato* calls for the forest guard to arrest the aggressor responsible for his death. Always represented in a satirical manner, the doctor sometimes appears as a blind man: feeling the ox with his hands he mistakes it for a young woman. In some versions of the drama, the parts of the ox are distributed among known members of the public in a comical and farcical manner. Alternatively, wine representing the ox's blood takes the place of his flesh. Subsequently, the priest called to act as his confessor enters dancing and singing and blessing the crowd. Irreverently, he laments the dearth of sugarcane brandy and wondering why he feels so cold under his frock he asks: is it full of shit? In further comical scenes he marries Catirina and Mateus. After a lot of pleading and beatings on the head with the air-filled bladders, the doctor prescribes a cure, and to the collective joy of all present the ox is resuscitated. Ecstatic, choir, orchestra and actors sing as the brandy flows freely; the ox passes the hat round the audience to collect money; the actors file past and as dawn approaches, the *cantadeira* sings a mournful farewell song.[87]

The use of masks in the play facilitates the satirical parody of stock characters in traditional rural society. Irreverent scenes illuminating the shortcomings of the doctor, the clergyman and the captain invite the audience to a critical attitude towards authority figures, while laughter stimulates the release of repressed emotion. Although the figures representing 'the people'; such as Catirina, Mateus and Sebastião are portrayed stereotypically from the point of view of the dominant class, as drunken, irresponsible and roguish, this does not necessarily imply that the predominant function of the *auto* is to exercise social control by ridiculing those who do not behave according to the norms of hard work and good behaviour prescribed by society. The exalted and the humble are equally satirized and the audience and actors jointly participate in an event in which play and ambiguity, the use of distortion and indecent expressions, an emphasis on the fantastic and the body undermine the narrow seriousness through which the established social order forecloses possibilities which question its interpretation of reality. In this sense, it could be argued the *Bumba-meu-Boi* is grounded in the carnivalesque style of expression, which Bakhtin in his work on Rabelais suggests is characterized by the opposition to 'all that [is] ready-made and completed, to all pretence at immutability . . . . All the symbols of the carnival idiom are filled with the pathos of change and renewal, with the sense of the gay relativity of prevailing truths and authorities.'[88] The *Bumba-meu-Boi* could thus be regarded as a form of popular culture not only in the sense that it is performed and produced by 'the people', but also in the broader critical and emancipatory meaning of the term discussed in the Introduction.

With the advance of modernization and capitalist development during the last thirty years, the *Bumba* has undergone various changes. In some cases, this is manifested in the fact that it ceases to be a dance-drama in order to become a form of revelry or amusement in which the aesthetic element predominates over its critical function and mythico-religious meaning. In the *Bumba-meu-Boi* of Maranhão, for example, various processes have contributed to this transformation. It has been incorporated by the tourist industry into one of the attractions offered to an urban public, seeking to recover something of the aura of the sacred and the marvellous, absent from the standardized and mass-produced products of the culture industry. Gradually the *Boi*, originally defined as a *brincadeira*, relying on inventiveness and improvisory talent, is transformed into a self-conscious predictable show; the religious festivity is replaced by the spectacle; and since frequently it is financed by local politicians and commercial enterprises, the critical element of the drama is also suppressed. As the *Boi* becomes a commercially profitable product, the internal organization of the group changes. Expenses are no longer met by the *brincantes* as a whole, but by individuals able to secure a return on investment. The *Boi* ceases to belong collectively to a rural district or a village street in order to become the private property of investors and organizers. In Maranhão there is now an equivalent to the *Sambódromo*, where the yearly carnival processions in Rio take place, for the *Bumba-meu-Boi*. In addition, competition between different groups forces them to retain their best singers and dancers with the offer of high fees, locking them more firmly into the circle of production and consumption of the broader capitalist economy over which they have no control and which divorces the *Bumba* from its original source of inspiration.

However, although this may be an identifiable process, it is not inevitable and the relation between rural popular culture and the transnational culture irradiating from the modern sector of the economy varies, depending on the specific context in which the encounter takes place. In some cultural manifestations discussed below rural popular cultural forms become articulated with the modern sector in a way which allows them to survive and develop in ways which do not always or entirely entail their transformation into a standardized commodity.

Oral Poetry and the Art of Storytelling

Of all the rich traditions in Brazilian rural popular culture, one of the most important is the poetry written by the peasantry, paradoxically defined as 'oral literature'. Related to it, yet constituting a different genre of its own, is the poetry of the *cantadores* (travelling singers).

Both forms stem from a common European mediaeval and, to a lesser extent, Indian and African oral tradition which goes back to a multiplicity of sources: popular stories, myths and legends, mediaeval romances and Iberian picaresque narrative. It contains epic, satirical, burlesque and fantastic

elements, moral counsel, religious teachings and abundant critical commentary on everyday life and on historical and current events.[89]

This poetry in its written form emerged in the Northeast towards the end of
the nineteenth century. Originally transmitted orally by the *cantadores*, it
began to be sold on the outdoor markets and small bookselling shacks of the
Northeast in the form of small *folhetos* or pamphlets. (In Portugal, these
folhetos, recounting the heroic deeds and marvellous adventures of knights and
princesses, were defined as *literatura de cordel* (string literature) or *literatura do
cego* (literature of the blind), due to the fact that they were displayed on string
and sold by blind itinerant pedlars.)

In sevententh-century France the city of Troyes was the centre of a similar
form of literary production, the *literature de colportage*, which in Spain was
known as *pliegos sueltos* and in the Spanish colonies of Mexico, Peru and
Argentina acquired the name of *corridos*.[90]

In Europe in the nineteenth century this form of literature was in the
process of extinction. In the Northeast of Brazil, however, the slow
development of industry and trade in its urban centres and the concomitant
rise of a modest middle class stimulated the growth of small artisan printing
establishments. The abolition of slavery in 1889 and the expulsion of the
peasantry from the land due to the expansion of the sugar economy created a
mass of transient rural workers no longer capable of sustaining themselves
within a self-contained subsistence economy and hence increasingly dependent on a wage. The development of a wage economy in turn created a
consumer market in the *sertão* for the *literatura de cordel* produced in the cities.
Simultaneously, the introduction of salaried work gradually undermined the
traditional social relations underpinning rural society: an impersonal con-
tractual relationship based on a cash nexus partially replaced the personalized
distribution of patronage in exchange for services.[91] (Social upheaval,
impoverishment and insecurity, worsened by a particularly severe drought in
1879, thus gave rise to messianic movements which became central themes in
the imaginative universe of *literatura de cordel*.)

From the turn of the century until the late 1930s, there were a series of
rebellions by the poor in the hinterlands which in their violence and despair,
expressed in the apocalyptic vision of their prophetic leaders, bear witness to
the social injustice of the rural social order of the Northeast. These
movements were characterized by two different yet related reactions by the
peasantry to their condition: the congregation of followers around a religious
'prophet' with alleged miraculous powers, often involving the worship of a
sacred ox; and the formation of groups of bandits, defined as *cangaceiros* who

roamed the countryside, assaulting *fazendas* and engaging in armed conflict
with landowners and the state authorities. Prophets and *cangaceiros* became
central figures in the oral culture of the Northeast; in particular the *cangaceiros*
Antonio Silvino ('Lampião') and his companion Maria Bonita were renowned
for their courage, insolence and fierceness.) Many *folhetos* with a religious theme
are dedicated to Padre Cicero, a priest who is said to have had miraculous
healing powers and is still today worshipped like a saint [Plate 5]. The
'prophet' Antonio Conselheiro, whose messianic preachings announced the
day in which 'the waters of the Vasa-Barris would be transformed into milk
and its margins into bread of sweetcorn'[92] was, as mentioned in Chapter 1, the
spiritual leader of a community of believers established on an abandoned farm
called Canudos.

The *folheto* is made of cheap, brownish paper comprising either four, eight,
thirty-two or sixty-four pages. Although the number of pages is determined by
the poetic form, the fact that the pages are always in multiples of four is a
result of the printing techniques used, whereby one printed sheet is folded
into four pages. The epic narratives or romances and the *pelejas* describing
poetic duels between two *cantadores* tend to be the longest. There are also
many different ways of versifying: some poems take the form of ten verses as
in the *martelo agalopado* (the galloping hammer), but the most popular form is
the *sextilha* (six-step pattern) rhyming according to the pattern ABCBDB:
'Caro leitor, eu te peço/Para ler com atenção/Este livro até o fim/E grande a
satisfação/Se queres saber um pouco/Da vida de Lampião.'[93]

The vendor of the *folheto*, the *folheteiro*, usually displays his wares laid out in
the form of a fan in an open suitcase or on a small stall. In order to attract the
attention of his customers, a curious animal is also frequently exhibited. As
soon as a sufficient number of customers have gathered around him he
announces with a set phrase the type of *folheto* he is going to 'sing'. At the
moment of greatest suspense, he interrupts his recitation, exhorting his
listeners to buy the pamphlet if they want to know the outcome of the story.[94]
One of the most remarkable features of the *folheto* is its cover. Initially it was
illustrated with simple vignettes; these were gradually replaced by woodcuts
representing in simple, bold, expressionistic forms the contents of the poem.
Recently, and to the chagrin of many students and aficionados of *literatura de
cordel*, the covers produced by a large publishing house in São Paulo frequently
resemble the covers of comic-strip magazines. Multicoloured, realist
representations of Lampião and Maria Bonita with North American features,
in poses reminiscent of urban soft porn literature, replace the woodcut images
[Plate 12]. These covers are very popular among readers.[95] On the basis of our

interviews with migrant rural workers who purchased the *folhetos*, it seems that by contrast to the woodcuts, which reflect the poverty of the means of production, these technically sophisticated covers provide them with a sense of participating in the fruits of modernity. This raises one of the central theoretical problems raised in the Introduction: if we reject the above 'opinion poll' as well as an essentialist concept of the popular – as market ratings or an inherent quality of a text or artefact – and posit it as a concept denoting the relations of cultural power between dominant and subordinate groups, which of the covers is to be regarded as popular? As we look at the production and circulation of *literatura de cordel*, at its form and content and the alterations it has undergone as a result of capitalist development, we will hopefully come closer, if not to an answer, to an understanding of the complex considerations involved in trying to find one.

Until the 1960s, when campaigns to eradicate illiteracy were initiated by the then reformist, populist regime, more than 50 per cent of the population was illiterate. Of these, the majority were concentrated in the rural areas and in particular in the Northeast of Brazil. How is one to explain the widespread popularity of *literatura de cordel* in a largely oral culture?

The *folheto* is a cultural product which is used collectively. It is bought on one of the outdoor markets in the Northeast and read aloud by a literate individual to a family or a group of families in a rural district. The reciter of the *folheto* needs to master the art of narration and his reading is accompanied by the same rhythmic and melodic emphases which the *cantador* uses when reciting improvised poetry. Moreover, in the absence of adequate primary and secondary education the memorizing of *folhetos* read aloud acts as an aid through which listeners learn eventually to read. Mauro de Almeida in his research on *literatura de cordel* quotes one of the major poets, Manoel de Almeida Filho, as having told him the following story. As a child he used to go to the outdoor market to hear the *folheteiro* reciting the contents of his booklets to a group of listeners. On one occasion, touched by the beauty of what he heard, he bought one himself and gradually taught himself to read.[96] The role of the *folheteiro* in this apprenticeship is crucial, in that his art as public narrator and performer is replicated in the collective readings which take place in the domestic sphere, thus initiating future generations of poets into their craft.

While there are different categories of *folheteiros*, depending on the type of *folheto* being sold, most of them are poets themselves. Not owning the necessary capital to print his poetry, the *folheteiro* needs to sell it to an editor who thus acquires his copyright. In return, the poet receives a certain percentage of the printed *folhetos*, which, in order to make a living, he needs to sell.[97] The desire of every *folheteiro* is hence to become a publisher himself, in some cases to become the author-publisher-vendor. At each point in the circle of production, the poet – a peasant or rural worker part of the time – is present. His apprenticeship begins in infancy, listening to *cantadores* or *folheteiros* in the outdoor markets or at the collective readings in the domestic sphere. The aesthetic norms of rhyme and metre are imbibed early on in life at an unconscious level, becoming an integral part of the future poets' mental structures.[98] The poet is thus a more developed expression of a shared and largely oral culture, in which reality is apprehended through a narrative code and through the poetic use of language, and in which the process of becoming a poet is inseparable from the family and community life of the peasantry. As the poet João Cabeleira, living in São Paulo, explains: 'The *cordel* you see here was the beginning, I used to read romances, somebody would call me and I sang the poem. I am semi-illiterate, but *cordel* gave me a broad vision of the blessed things of this earth, I expanded, opened my mind to the more difficult words.'[99]

There is much controversy over the correct classification of the themes of string literature and even whether, given the changing social reality to which many of the poems refer, such a classification is possible.[100] We have therefore chosen to discuss a few of the genres of greater importance. The poems of mediaeval European origin, very popular and usually referred to as *folhetos de tradição* are for example: the 'Story of the Empress Porcina' and of the 'Princesse Magalona', 'Charlemagne and the Twelve Knights', 'The Forgiveness of Dulcineia'.[101] Related to these romances are the tales defined by some students of *cordel* as belonging to the *ciclo do maravilhoso*, in which the human world is rendered marvellous and extraordinary through the presence of a wide array of animals, of legendary beings such as mermaids, ogres, witches and werewolves, African deities and Indian and Greek mythological figures. The 'Mysterious Peacock', written in 1938 by José Camilo de Resende has become a classic poem of this genre in which the laws of nature are suspended through magical intervention.

Another genre often included among the *folhetos de tradição* is the poetry with mystical and religious themes. Innumerable *folhetos* contain visionary descriptions of religious experiences and of the exemplary lives of 'prophets', whose alleged miraculous powers and eschatological preachings inflamed the imagination of their followers with messianic hopes of redemption from hunger and destitution. In this sense, the poet of the *folhetos*, present not only in the Northeast of Brazil but also in other parts of Latin America such as

Colombia and Mexico, could be seen as a precursor, indeed as an important original source of magical realism. As Alejo Carpentier in his preface to *El reino de este mundo* (*The Kingdom of this World* 1949) points out, in the cultural universe of Latin America the prevalence of myth, magical practices and diverse cosmogonies facilitate the emergence of 'the marvellous' in every-day life – of which, as we shall see below, the poets of *cordel* are able chroniclers. He writes, 'the marvellous is only truly actualized' when it arises from an unexpected alteration of reality (the miracle), from a privileged revelation of reality, from a unique illumination which brings to light the unnoticed richness of reality'.[102]

Poems informing and commenting on everyday life, on past and present social events, on natural phenomena and important personages, frequently in a corrosive satirical manner, are usually referred to as *folhetos de época*. These *folhetos* are very popular perhaps because their biting, black humour and sensitivity to the absurd make a precarious existence more tolerable. On the death of the populist leader, Getúlio Vargas, for instance, 70,000 copies of a *folheto* recounting the circumstances of his death were sold. Moreover, in the absence of a literate public and popular newspapers, these pamphlets were, in the early part of this century, the rural population's main source of information. Even today, *folhetos* are still valued as vehicles through which everyday life is transfigured by the imagination, critical perception and interpretative depth of the poet. Leandro Gomes de Barros, one of the first and perhaps the greatest poet of string literature in Brazil, published and sold his own poetry, collecting material on his travels through the arid Northeast on the Great Western Railway, financed and administered by the British. This included the latest news on the war between *cangaceiros* and landowners, on the prophets and their followers, on changing customs and many ordinary and extraordinary events.

Of particular importance are the *folhetos de valentia*, epic poems recounting the courageous deeds and exploits of heroic individuals [Plate 13]. These narratives are closely linked to the mediaeval tales of the travelling knights. In the context of the *sertão*, however, the landowners have replaced the despotic kings of feudal Europe, while the errant knights have metamorphosed into *cangaceiros*. Their violent confrontations with the police and landowning clans, their astuteness in outwitting their persecutors, their contempt for death and astonishing capacity to rise above the limits of human endurance, have been recorded in verse by all the major poets of *cordel*. An interesting feature of these poems is that the *cangaceiros* are frequently seen as having a privileged relationship to the Devil. As such, it seems they partake of the ambiguous nature of the daemonic: they are portrayed as the perpetrators of evil but, like Lucifer, who defied the authority of God, they are rebels who challenge the power of the landowners and the state. Their mockery of authority, their fearlessness and, occasionally, their defence of the poor are immortalized in such works as 'Lampião, the Terror of the Northeast', and 'The ABC of Maria Bonita, Lampião and his Cangaceiros' by Rodolfo Coelho de Cavalcante.

The *folhetos de valentia* contain many tales about the intolerable working conditions of the rural labourers, which invariably lead to a confrontation between a virtuous and brave peasant and a rapacious landowner. This personal conflict mirrors a broader opposition between the *sertão*, representing the positively connotated, hard but independent life of the peasant in a subsistence economy, and the plantation, standing for the dehumanizing subjection of wage-labour. The drama which unfolds in the *folheto de valentia* thus also relates to a central element in the historical memory of the population of the Northeast: the condition of being a wandering people, condemned to seasonal work and migration. The *folhetos* contain eloquent verses denouncing the injustice of the prevalent social order and utopian visions of a reconciled humanity. This critical stance, however, is rooted in an idealization of the past, embodied in myths of a bygone Golden Age, in the mediaeval ideal of love between valiant knights and pure maidens, and particularly in the customs and values of traditional society, a world as yet untouched by the 'evils of progress'.

As pointed out earlier, the industrialization of Brazil went hand in hand with a severe economic and political crisis in the rural economy of the Northeast. As wage-labourers no longer protected by the patronage system, nor as yet by the new protective labour legislation of the 1930s, modernization brought few benefits to the peasantry. It is not surprising therefore that the prevalent social order is criticized from the standpoint of an idealized traditional past. This enables us to make sense of the coexistence of rebellious and submissive, irreverent and moralistic, critical and authoritarian elements in *literatura de cordel*. Many of the *folhetos*, particularly those containing comments on changing social customs, eulogize traditional values of filial respect, marital fidelity and religious faith.

Various narratives provide lurid accounts of how human beings are transformed into animals or strange monsters as a punishment for transgressing traditional social norms. In Rodolfo Coelho de Cavalcante's much-sold *folheto* 'The Girl who Beat her Mother and became a Dog', Helena, the rebellious daughter, is metamorphosed into a snarling canine with a human head and animal body. In 'This is Corruption' and 'The Scandalous Fashions of Today', readers are advised not to succumb to the immoral influence of such modern secular values as greed, promiscuity, ambition and dishonesty.

Women are almost invariably represented in stereotypical roles as highly idealized, virtuous maidens and self-sacrificing mothers, or alternatively, if their sexuality is not linked to marriage and procreation, as depraved creatures, allied to Satan, causing the downfall of men.[103] Given that *literatura de cordel* emerged within a patriarchal society in which the power of the word is considered a masculine domain, it is not surprising that there are few women poets. Those who transgressed gender boundaries frequently led a marginal life indulging in the masculine prerogatives of drinking and promiscuity, although with the advance of industrialization and growing opportunities for women to work outside the home, more women poets have emerged. In this sense it is interesting to note that the 'evils of progress' are often negatively associated with the decadence generated by the blurring of gender boundaries. In many *folhetos* women who defy traditional morality suffer at the hands of supernatural forces. In a 'Baby Devil appeared in São Paulo', a woman longing to enjoy the pleasures of the body, curses her pregnant belly and future child, which prevent her from joining in the Carnival festivities. On the following day she gives birth to a baby devil:

> And she saw that the baby was
> hairy with horns and tail
> and it snarled like a dog
> it was daring and fierce
> one needs to think no further
> it could only be the devil.

Swearing, cursing and creating havoc in the maternity hospital, in a church and in the city, the baby devil declares his allegiance to the modern world:

> I am the administrator
> of the new modern world
> false religions
> are recorded in my book
> they can follow their beliefs
> in the depths of hell.[104]

Social contradictions tend to be presented in mythical terms as a struggle between opposites: between virtue and vice, rich and poor, bandits and the police, God and the Devil – this Manicheistic world vision was elaborated in one of Glauber Rocha's most outstanding films, *Black God, White Devil* (*Deus e o diabo na terra do sol* 1963). The perennial conflict between peasant and landowner is rarely resolved within the narrative in such a way that oppression is transformed through the creation of an alternative social order. More often it is resolved at an individual level, through the substitution of the evil by a benevolent landowner or with the peasant's marriage to his daughter. In this sense it could be argued that one of the social functions of *cordel* is to relieve tensions created by social inequality, but without fundamentally challenging established relationships and institutions. There are, however, some exceptions to this pattern; during the 1960s, when a trade union movement emerged in the Northeast acting in defence of rural labourers, the liberation of the poor through social change began to appear as a theme in various *folhetos*. During the military dictatorship of 1964–85, poets were frequently arrested for propagating 'subversive' thoughts and in some *folhetos de época*, the poet lucidly unveils the social and economic mechanisms responsible for the people's falling standard of living. For instance, in 'Poverty dying of Hunger' José Costa Leite writes:

> If the poor didn't plant
> what would the rich do?
> They have money in their pockets
> but that doesn't produce food
> the man who walks barefoot
> is the one who produces
> in order to see Brazil grow.[105]

In the 1970s, *literatura de cordel* itself entered a critical phase due to the rising cost of paper, the spread of radio and television and the consequent privatization of leisure and closure of artisan printing presses. Various poets and *cantadores* with whom we spoke about this issue maintained that the other means of communication could not fully replace the *folheto*, because they did not possess the 'sweetness of verse' which their readers so cherished.[106] Nevertheless, in the last ten years there have been significant changes in the production, form and content of the *folhetos* as a result of rural migration to the cities and the expansion of the culture industry. This can be seen operating at various levels. First, a large publishing house, the Editora Luzeiro, located in the centre of the modern sector of the economy, in São Paulo, has taken over a large share of the market for string literature. Using more efficient, industrialized methods of production and distribution, it produces *folhetos* resembling the format of comic books. Second, as rural labourers and peasants from the Northeast join the ranks of the underemployed living in the shanty towns on the outskirts of the city, *cordel* is used in novel contexts and with new themes, explicitly addressing the question of hegemony; the relations of power between social classes become part of its poetic discourse. In the 'Life of a Northeasterner in São Paulo', the poet describes the journey of 'Norbertino' to São Paulo. Peasant life is depicted nostalgically as characterized by bonds of solidarity and a relationship of harmony with nature:

> Oh those beautiful oxen
> during sowing time
> the people joyfully
> plant corn and beans
> drink sugarcane brandy, make merry
> and dance with abandon.
>
> And then there was the *mutirão*
> in the barnhouse
> if one picked manioc
> the whole neighbourhood came
> we met, enjoyed ourselves and worked
> and there was plenty of food for all.

In São Paulo, in contrast, the individual is lost in the lonely crowd of wage-slaves rushing past each other in time to the inexorable rhythm of the clock:

> In each and every situation
> I saw fear and need
> lack of trust
> and information
> I looked at reality
> and said: in truth
> the abolition of slavery never took place.[107]

Norbertino experiences a moment of enlightenment as he gains understanding of the new social relationships of which he is part: forging new bonds of friendship with his fellow workers during a confrontation with management in the factory, he becomes aware of the importance of solidarity.

Many *folhetos* produced in São Paulo comment critically on the relationship between the use of nuclear energy, the external debt and the rising cost of living. In some cases, the themes of urbanized *cordel* have been linked to the the steelworkers' trade union movement out of which the Brazilian Workers Party, led by 'Lula' (Luis Ignacio da Silva, leader of the Workers Party and presidential candidate in 1990), himself of Northeastern origin, emerged in the 1970s. A *folheto* which has had considerable repercussions among workers in the construction industry – often unskilled rural migrants – was the didactic poem 'Accidents at Work in the Construction Industry'. On one particular occasion it was used in conjunction with a film shown by the construction workers' union; poetry from the booklet was sung to the accompaniment of images on a screen, followed by the distribution of the poem itself and a discussion of the dangers on the construction site. Here we see the coincidence of two concepts of the 'popular': the use of a traditional rural form, originating in an oral culture, in conjunction with a modern medium enlisted in the service of raising the political consciousness of a subordinate class and validating its needs and demands. Rural migrants to the city undergo a process of cultural loss, not only because the skills and values they bring with them are invalidated, but also because their incorporation in the urban context, as deskilled factory hands, denies them access to new forms of knowledge.[108] The above cultural practice, however, enables them to maintain a distinct identity and also to acquire tools to assume their urban existence. In this sense a more politicized, secularized vision informs this urbanized *cordel*. In the process, however, it has forfeited some of the lyrical and poetic qualities which characterized the classic texts. This development of forms of cultural resistance is clearly manifested in the practice of the *cantadores* who have migrated to São Paulo.

A performance (*cantoria*) of the travelling singers always involves two poets who engage in a dialogue, sometimes in a duel – a *desafio* – of poetic improvisation, to the accompaniment of a *viola*, a twelve-string guitar. The performance sometimes takes place in the outdoor market or, if in the city, on a public square. However, it is considered more appropriate to perform in a predetermined place: the home of a patron, a farmyard, a restaurant or a bar. The *cantadores* or *repentistas*, as they are also called, are formally invited by the proprietor of the establishment and remunerated by the public who leave their contributions on a platter placed in front of the two contenders. A *cantoria* lasts two hours or more and occasionally for several days, as in the famous poetic duel in 1870 between Inacio de Catingueira and Romano de Teixeira.[109] A good *cantador* masters various forms of poetic improvisation, characterized by definite patterns of rhyme and metre. The role of the guitar is to punctuate, to emphasize the rhythmic breaks in the poetic flow of words, which are enunciated loudly in a hoarse, nasal, liturgical tone.

At the beginning of a *cantoria*, the poets introduce themselves, extolling their poetic prowess and describing the qualities of their host and listeners with florid words of praise as well as ironic commentary on their appearance and social position. The participation of the public is crucial for the success of the performance since it is in the public's interaction with the poets that the process of poetic creation unfolds. A member of the public, who shares with the performers a narrative and poetic code, presents the duo with a *mote*, a theme on which they are asked to improvise in a given modality and which is phrased in the form of two verses of seven syllables per line. Every strophe has to end with the *mote* and the public's critical appraisal of the poets' performance hinges on the skill, imagination, knowledge and inventiveness with which – as they inspire and challenge each other – they are able to improvise on the given theme [Plate 10]. The way the poets focus on the theme depends on the social composition of the audience and on the breadth of knowledge and linguistic versatility of the poet. This knowledge, defined by the poets as *bagagem* or popular science gleaned from various traditional sources, is gradually accumulated over the years to be drawn on by the *cantadores* when they are required to meet the challenge of improvising on a theme.[110]

There are various texts which provide the poets not only with the content of their improvisations but also with new words and phrases to assist them in the difficult task of rhyming in accordance with a given modality. The *Lunário perpétuo* is a rich source of knowledge on the movement of the winds, the sun, the moon, rain, clouds, eclipses, hurricanes and astrological data. Dictionaries, in particular the *Dictionary of the Fable*, history, geography and grammar books, romances, anthologies, almanacs, encyclopaedias, newspapers, magazines, the Bible and Greek mythology constitute some of the main elements in the cultural archive of the *repentistas*. According to Mário de Andrade, who studied the compositional procedures of the *cantador* in depth, the act of improvisation relies on an initial process of simplification or 'reduction' to a lower level of complexity of a known poem or song (*desnivelamento*). In this way the singer fixes it in his memory by compressing it to a simple mnemonic structure. Then he improvises and elaborates on it, enriching it with associative images, raising it to a high level of complexity again (*nivelamento*). In his writings on the singer Chico Antonio, Mário de Andrade comments on how the melodic structure is raised from the 'lower' to the 'higher' level: 'Once the melody in its simple form is fixed schematically, the singer begins to sing in a "hot" style, phantasizing, recreating consciously, producing variations and embellishing. Until in full command again . . . he invents an entirely new song.'[111]

In the last twenty years *cantoria* records have been produced but as a result the quality of poetic improvisation has suffered. If played over the radio the records are interrupted by advertising and confined to the limited time-span of a radio programme. Also, as the poet João Quindingues comments, 'the poet when he sings needs time to improvise; the band of a record is four to five minutes but the poet needs freedom to become inspired and to sing what Art requires us to sing'.[112] Simultaneously the *cantador*, originally regarded as a teacher, now becomes a professional performer forced by the requirements of the market to produce sounds which, in the words of the poet Sebastiano Marinho, no longer allow for the rough atonality of 'roots singing' (*cantar raiz*). Nevertheless, in the large cities, the practice of the *cantadores* has been marked by its cultural resistance and, paradoxically, this has in part been due to the use which they have been able to make of the culture industry as a way of maintaining their cultural identity. The use of the media by the poets has led to the creation of a national community of listeners and producers, facilitating not only the professional development of the *cantadores* as a whole, but also creating a bulwark against the loss of cultural identity among the large population of Northeastern migrants spread throughout the country.[113] In the 1970s this was reinforced by the fact that elements of Northeastern music were taken up by the singers Caetano Veloso and Gilberto Gil and transformed into a new form of urban popular music, called *tropicalismo*, which helped to articulate a broad movement of opposition to the military government.[114]

There is also another way in which this oral popular poetry manifests itself as resistance, and this relates less to its content than to its form. In an article on the 'Storyteller and Artisan Cultures', Walter Benjamin draws a distinction between two forms of experience: *Erfahrung* which describes an integrated form of experience rooted in collective and individual tradition, the essence of which is manifested in the art of storytelling; and *Erlebnis*, a term which refers to the fragmented mode of experience characteristic of modern society typified in the notion of information.[115] Although Benjamin's distinction has somewhat romantic and anti-modern connotations, it is nevertheless useful. It allows us to understand how *cordel* and its capacity for *Erfahrung* enables it to transform fragmented reality into a meaningful whole through the interpretative and inventive power of narrative. Its continued vigour shows a capacity meaningfully to pattern not only peasant experience but also experience tied to a modern urban context. Thus this popular cultural practice sustains not only the capacity of the oppressed to dream of a better world, to defy society by playing with its language, but also functions as a reservoir from which original visions of reality spring.

II URBAN CONTEXTS

Moving to the City

It is no longer accurate to make sharp or fixed distinctions between rural and urban cultures in Latin America. This is the result partly of the massive increase in urbanization in recent decades, with 60 to 70 per cent of the population now living in cities, but more importantly of the fact that cultural codes, products and practices increasingly move between rural and urban areas and between different social strata, causing previously stable boundaries to lose their force. Almost all cultures in Latin America are now mediated to some extent by the city, both in the sense of its massification of social phenomena and of the communication technologies which it makes available. To see the city as a corrupting and contaminating force, in opposition to a pure and authentic culture rooted in the rural areas, is to indulge in nostalgia. On the other hand, the city is the place of entry of transnational culture, of TV programmes, comic-strip heroes and advertisements, whose references are to a different environment, that of the advanced capitalist countries. Is it possible, given the configuration sketched out here, to continue using the term 'popular culture' as designating a distinctive area? The answer given by actual usage is yes: the term popular culture, according to common usage in Latin America, evokes the possibility of alternatives to currently dominant cultural patterns. We address the political aspect of this issue elsewhere, in Chapter 3; for the present our concern is with the distinctive space of popular culture in a modern urban context.

To be of use, the term 'popular' must be distinguished from the products of the culture industry and the mass media. However, *Studies in Latin American*

Popular Culture, the only academic journal dedicated to popular culture in Latin America, defines the popular as solely pertaining to urban mass culture and the culture industry.[116] This is in line with the longer-established *Journal of Popular Culture*, which deals predominantly with the culture of the United States and Canada. In Latin America, the term is used more broadly, to include rural cultures, and has oppositional connotations. We prefer this latter usage.

Clarification of terms depends on establishing their history. Here the work of the Colombian scholar Jesús Martín-Barbero has made a significant contribution. Instead of taking the culture industry as that which produces mass society, he points out that massification arises not from a degradation of culture by the media but from the long slow process of prior establishment of mass cultural experiences, through the constitution of the single national market, the consolidation of the state and the making of unified national cultures. This happens where the state begins to supplant the dense network of local relationships, or where industrial working conditions and workers' struggles take on a mass character – beginning, approximately, in the 1880s. From these experiences, symbols and practices arise which start to become homogeneous over the whole territory.[117] This basis makes it possible for the culture industry to be built and for the mass media in their late-twentieth-century form to operate. Some of the key forms in the massification process are the *folletín* (newspaper or magazine serial), popular theatre, radio and cinema. On the one hand, the *folletín* served as a mediation between literature, consumed only by a small educated elite, and the masses. The time-structure of the serial, continually interrupted by the wait for the next instalment, generated a fragmented manner of reading, interrupted by everyday life and thus porous to its experiences.[118] The massive production of *criollista* (creolist) texts in Argentina between the late nineteenth and early twentieth centuries served a public which was in transition between the country and the city or who had recently entered Argentina as immigrants.[119] Popular urban *criollista* literature with its narratives of traditional rural types like the gaucho offered an identity and a way of negotiating the transitions.[120] The acquisition of literacy passed through the reading of *folletines*, bought not from bookshops but from kiosks or travelling salesmen, a more informal and approachable context.[121] The *folletines* included specialized women's serials, some of which reached a circulation of 200,000 copies.

At the same time, given that readers still belonged to a culture where the majority were illiterate, these serials were often read aloud to others; an experience of listening taken over by radio, which as a medium began to reach a mass audience in the 1930s. Major vehicles for the initial spread of radio were the tango and the bolero, while the radio was a major force in making them popular. Radio serials and popular theatre became models for the TV serials of the 1960s. The Mexican writer Carlos Monsiváis describes the essential formula of frivolous theatre in the 1920s as 'the combination of sex and politics': it sought to fuse together two types of excitement, 'that of the spectator amused by the merciless "humanization" of his leaders, and that of the spectator frustrated by the physical distance of his female idols'.[122] The Mexican actress Celia Montalván was one of the latter, and her image became familiar through the new medium of cheaply produced 'pin-up' photography. For Monsiváis, the photo-postcard, which circulates as a commodity, is something to be celebrated, not decried. It is modern in the sense of representing simulation and metamorphosis, of the rural girl become something else, dispersed into a 'gallery of archetypes of woman, according to the ideas prevalent in the 1920s': 'Girl with finger in the mouth, demure Indian girl, vamp, cocotte, . . . Mexican lady with sombrero and pigtails', and so on.

> Unlike Hollywood stars who incite universal redemption through luxury and insolence, a vedette, member of the procession of ordinary virgins, depends powerfully on the grace, the *humanity* of her face and on the voluptuousness which, as far as one can infer, does not call for the usual methods of home relief. What an intricate circumlocution for saying that to masturbate in front of these photos would be a sacrilege, an error![123]

Other mediations between the traditional and the modern, such as the *circo criollo* (creole circus) in Argentina and the popular circus in Brazil, as well as the popular music which arose with films, radio and the gramophone record, would need to be added to this greatly simplified account.[124] Our purpose here is to stress that the culture industry does not simply invade previously virgin ground.

The media have been vital to that consolidation of a single national identity which is necessary for the formation of the capitalist nation-state, particularly as regards the construction of a working-class identity. This can be exemplified by the role of cinema in the making of a mass national culture in Mexico after the Revolution: it is film, not writing, which creates, in Benedict Anderson's phrase, the 'imagined community' of the nation. 'El Indio' Fernández's film *Enamorada* restores and realigns the family torn apart by the Revolution: desire is bound by the increasingly inclusive contexts of family, church, *patria*. Fernández provides 'a powerful technique for shoring up the family (at least in theory) at a time when large numbers of immigrants were drifting into the city and finding themselves without the social censorship and the religious and political control that prevailed in the provinces'.[125] First language of the popular urban, cinema connects with 'the hunger of the masses to make themselves socially visible'.[126] Monsiváis sees a complicated action of simultaneous elevation and degradation: for the masses to recognize themselves on the screen, is 'a secret elevation'; but the images of the people as nation place nationality at *their* level, that is, low. So the national becomes 'irresponsibility, filial affection, laziness, drunkenness, sentimentality . . . the programmed humiliation of women, religious fanaticism, fetishistic respect for private property'.[127] For Monsiváis there are five main sources of popular urban culture in contemporary Mexico: film; the prints of José Guadalupe Posada which mix rural customs and iconographic styles with the urban world; the political theatre, similar to music hall; the comic strip, which played a major role in the extension of literacy, particularly in the 1930s; the musical style associated particularly with Agustín Lara and José Alfredo Jiménez, which transforms traditional rural songs, such as the *corrido*, into three-minute record tracks.[128]

The culture industry is a concept first elaborated by Adorno and Horkheimer in *Dialectic of Enlightenment*. The main burden of their argument is that unlike the genuine work of art, which demands concentrated and lucid attention, the industrialization of culture brings about mass deception and a consensus resting upon 'blind, opaque authority', rather than any rational principle.[129] While we do not accept this entirely negative view of its effects, we retain the term culture industry insofar as it marks technological and economic changes which involve the creation of a single national market for all cultural products. Its main vehicle in Latin America has been television. In order to explore its implications, let us consider the history of a specific culture industry, taking Brazil as an example and drawing on Renato Ortiz's study, *A moderna tradição brasileira*.[130]

The consolidation of a cultural market in Brazil begins in the mid 1960s. Previously there had been too much localism (radio stations, for instance, reached only regional audiences) for the establishment of a culture industry. The main agency for the attempt to create a homogeneous national identity was the state. The existence of a national television network became possible through the following stages: the state, specifically an authoritarian military state (1964–85), as main user of the publicity industry, enabled the latter to grow, and to become in turn the main motor of television expansion. Television integrated the market in a context of 'political integration of consciousness brought about by the state', until finally the national became identified with the market.[131] Television thus presided over the achievement of modernity and in fact became its main sign. In the 'advanced' countries, by contrast, the integration of the market occurred well before television. Currently, the size of the television audience in Brazil, the seventh largest in the world, is not very different from that of Britain or France, giving the Brazilian market an international dimension. Surprisingly, at least for those who deduce the loss of national identity from modernization, the proportion of foreign programmes diminished from 60 per cent in 1972 to 30 per cent in 1983. At the same time, the Brazilian culture industry exports a considerable proportion of what it produces, so that, as Ortiz puts it, the export of the international popular has displaced the defence of the national popular.[132] In other words, with the globalization of the media, the popular as marker of the national becomes problematic. The modern in Brazil has effectively become a norm, a tradition, whereas up to now the term tradition has brought to mind above all the idea of folklore. The situation thus described, where all symbolic materials are affected by the market for cultural goods, pertains in varying degrees in the different countries. Similarly, transnationalization, whereby cultural goods produced by media conglomerates increasingly cross cultural boundaries, varies in its impact, but is nowhere absent. Nor can its results be assumed simply to consist in a homogenization destructive of memory and differences.

The transitions from local pre-capitalist forms to late-twentieth-century international ones can be traced in the history of salsa. In the Spanish Caribbean, during the colonial period, there arose a counter plantation culture, made up of escaped slaves, Indians from the large estates and Andalusian Spaniards discriminated against by the Castilian nobility. The meeting of these three elements occurred outside state jurisdiction. The polyphonic Afro rhythms, which later became a key element of salsa, derive from the escaped slave population.[133] It was the *artesano* class of Puerto Rico, a group which undermined the boundaries of social hierarchy, who first transformed these rhythms into a national urban dance form, the *merengue*, which brought rural and urban experiences together at a time of peasant migration to the cities. This occurred in the latter part of the nineteenth century. In the twentieth century, after the imposition of a capitalist economy and the creation of an urban working class, the musical tradition of opposition to the state and the social order shifted to the sphere of intimate personal emotion, as in these words from a famous bolero, 'Lamento borincano' ('Borinquen lament' – Borinquen is the indigenous name of Puerto Rico):

Borinquen, my land of eden
which the great Gauthier
called 'pearl of the seas'.
Now that you are dying
with my sufferings
let me sing to you also.[134]

Salsa, which by the 1970s had become the main dance form both in the Spanish Caribbean and in New York and other US cities with large Hispanic populations, embraces a wide range of social attitudes, from cynical acceptance to defiant, though possibly confused, rebellion. An expression of the latter – and not a confused one – is Eddie Palmieri's song 'La libertad – ¡logico!' ('Freedom – of course!'), included in a record whose title, 'Vamos pa'l monte' ('Let's go to the forest'), recalls escape from slavery:

Freedom, sir
Don't you take it from me . . .

But look I'm human too
And I was born here . . .

Economically,
Economically your slave . . .

Your slave, sir
But what of it, you don't fool me
You don't fool me
You don't fool me.[135]

It is necessary at this point to consider the distinctive features of the urbanization process in Latin America. As we have indicated, during the past forty years there occurred throughout the subcontinent a massive change from rural to predominantly urban societies. The cultural migrations, instabilities and reconfigurations flowing from it continue to occur. The main form of urban growth has been through the erection of shanty towns, usually encircling the cities and usually on land which had first to be invaded or squatted. Dwellings are initially put together from whatever materials are to hand, including cardboard, polythene, woven matting and bamboo. Invasions have to be coordinated; they often require the planned action of thousands of people and may involve confrontations with police and army and the risk of death. Later stages include the erection of more permanent types of dwelling and the establishment of services such as water, electricity, sewage and transport. This process reflects the failure of industry to absorb the peasantry or to create an adequate urban infrastructure. The material needs for housing and services are not supplied by the state as an obligation to the settlers, but have to be fought for and paid for in large part by residents in a long, slow accumulation of resources. These organized mass migrations constitute incipient forms of sociality which challenge the hierarchies of the society as a whole. Urban space begins to be refashioned, older parts of the city invaded, fashionable beaches 'taken over', and so on. Every Sunday in São Paulo, for instance, the Praça de Sé is invaded by immigrants from the Northeast, who come in from the *favelas* to play and listen to traditional music or to watch rural spectacles re-enacted in the city. Over the past twenty years Lima's Plaza San Martín and the streets around it have filled with *ambulantes*, itinerant vendors selling everything from individual cigarettes to shoes, clothing and pirated tapes. And as the semicircle of *pueblos jóvenes* expanded northwards, the Ancón beach, previously a redoubt of the bourgeoisie, changed hands. In recent years, some Peruvian intellectuals have begun to speak of the 'psychosis' of the middle classes who find their sense of the city under threat from the mass of Andean peasant migrants with their different culture.[136]

New arrivals to the city seek out the areas inhabited by migrants from their region, and a patchwork of relocated territorialities comes into being whose boundaries are much more fluid than in the original rural context. In the city, it is the *pedaço*, the *barrio*, the *sector*, which provide a relatively stable space, created by a network of relationships of neighbourhood, extended family and rural origin.[137] The recent tendency throughout the subcontinent for struggles in the poorer urban districts to be mediated less and less by the traditional political organizations – such as political parties and trades unions – is reflected in the increasing importance of the mobilizations of *pobladores* (inhabitants of shanty towns) around demands for water, light, sewage, and so on. Recently in Mexico City, a figure who calls himself *Superbarrio* has appeared at the front of demonstrations: the popular struggle is raised to epic level within an imagination shaped by the comic strip. First appearing in popular mobilizations for housing after the 1985 earthquake, *Superbarrio* wears a mask and a uniform with the letter S, appropriating Superman symbolism for new uses. On one occasion *Superbarrio* challenged the Chamber of Deputies to wrestle with him and take off his mask [Plate 8].

The debt crisis and subsequent economic austerity measures here brought about an increase in the structural violence suffered by the majority of urban populations, in the form of malnutrition and high infant mortality. Chronically semi- or mal-employed as well as unemployed, these populations are largely dysfunctional to the needs of national and transnational capitalism; yet they are still inside the net of television reception, the ownership of a television set being among the first priorities after basic shelter and food. In fact the contrast between strong cultural presence and weak economic power is a main feature of their lives. As the debt crisis makes social mobility less and less possible, cultural mobility becomes the only one available. In this connection it is worth noting that the idea of the culture of poverty, made popular in the 1960s by Oscar Lewis's books, has been discredited.[138] A projection of the United States ideology of self-improvement, it was an attempt to explain what it produced: the static lives of families in Mexico City, caught in a circle of poverty and low expectations. Lewis edited out of the books, which were based on taped interviews, examples of breaking with the family and/or the past. And recent interviews show that the families currently living in the distinctive *casas de vecindad* with their communal courtyards, supposedly examples of a spirit of collectivity, not only hate the lack of privacy but would prefer the buildings to be called condominiums.

However, there is no question of simply copying or 'catching up with' the cities of the advanced countries. The rapid and multiple cultural transitions and juxtapositions brought about by the urbanization process produce a unique mixing, or perhaps more accurately simultaneity, of forms. In the Praça de Sé it is possible to see *capoeira* (a form of self-defence originally practised by slaves, transformed into dance), rock music played on electric guitars, and poetic duals between *cantadores*. The intense faces and extra-ordinary verbal prowess of the latter hold their particular audience in thrall, while thirty yards away the rock music generates a different mode of intensity. People move from one group to another in the densely filled square. On one occasion, on the cathedral steps above the square, a group of fifteen to twenty people watched the slow dance of a man who drank from a large plastic bottle labelled 'Industrial Alcohol'. Was it a kind of public suicide?

The juxtaposition of technology and tradition is now a main feature of living space: television sets sit beside religious images and framed photographs of parents and grandparents [Plate 1]. Symbols and objects associated with rural tradition, bearers of memory, become refunctionalized in new settings, while, simultaneously, modern symbols and materials become resemanti-cized. In Brazilian *favelas*, for example, rooms are painted in pink to recall rural dwellings, while the fridge and the television become domestic altars, new focuses of traditional religious sensibility. When rural festivals become urban festivals, they establish a more variegated space, where formerly rural symbols such as the grotesque masks of dancers have become elements within a representation of national rather than local identity.[139] Or materials such as tin cans are used to make handicraft objects with traditional rural styles. Another feature of the ferment of old and new in the contemporary urban centres is the multiplication of new religions and religious sects, particularly in Brazil.[140]

The process we are describing constitutes a new stage of cultural exchange, as important as that of the sixteenth century, one which moreover reopens in popular memories the traumas of that first invasion. This is nowhere better shown than in the later work of the bicultural Peruvian writer José María Arguedas, which traces the counter-invasion of the city by the peasants. Arguedas imagines an alternative modernity, where modern industrial technology comes together with magic, a pre-capitalist form of technology. The key feature of Arguedas's view of the process is that the pre-modern cultural archive does not have to be destroyed: it is capable of confronting the modern technological universe, both transforming and transformed.

Resistance and conformity are terms which have been much used in debates about popular culture, but it is risky to let them become an exclusive paradigm. A complex cultural field becomes reduced to two poles, while cultural practices are subjected to ideological readings according to which of the two poles they are taken to represent. As Marilena Chauí shows in her study, *Conformismo e resistencia*, popular culture is best seen as a dispersed set of practices occurring inside a given social system. This is well exemplified in an important strike which occurred in Brazil in the 1970s. In the national steel industry, which had been declared a 'national security zone', all forms of organization were forbidden. In order to gain the right to organize and negotiate, the workers invented a new form of action.

> Under the existing conditions of discipline and surveillance, without a place for exchanging ideas and information, without their own press and unable to trust the official union, ... the COSIPA workers created their own information network ...: the doors of the toilets were converted into clandestine newspapers, which were erased by the last workers to use the toilet at the end of each shift. ... On the *Day of Amnesia* all the workers suffered a sudden loss of memory: they all left their identification documents at home. This meant that a long and meticulous examination was needed for each worker to be admitted to the factory. Queues thousands long formed outside the gates. ...[141]

Once memory is defined in terms of official information, then amnesia becomes subversive. The terms reverse if one considers how, deprived of their own collective memory by social amnesia, human groups become subject to manipulation and domination. It has been claimed that the mass media do provoke a form of amnesia by destroying the collective memory characteristic of peasant life. José Jorge de Carvalho has argued strongly that the mass media, because of what he sees as their immediacy and apparent transparency, exclude the possibility of collective memory. The culture industry 'is essentially amnesic: it offers the illusion of total and immediate participation between producer and consumer . . . but without the possibility of accumulation. It lacks an interpretative dimension' whereby everyday life can be transformed into experience.[142] By contrast, the products of folklore continue to offer that interpretative power, and in fact continue to be the predominant source of symbols for communality.[143] The rituals and symbolism of harvest would no doubt exemplify what de Carvalho has in mind.

While it is useful to contrast the different interpretative modes of rural and urban cultures, the problem with de Carvalho's position is that it leaves out of count how the mass media are actually received and used by their audiences, and fails to allow for the multi-layered, ambiguous and irreverent responses of popular audiences. Consider, for instance, what Carlos Monsiváis reports of the Otomí Indians of the state of Hidalgo: when the government decided to give them technology to help them organize themselves, it transpired that there was more interest in watching the videotapes of their meetings than in attending the meetings themselves: the whole community came to watch the tape.[144] Or there's the case of the Otomí women who had worked in the USA and whom people called 'Marías': they were asked 'why their daughters were called Jeanette, Yvonne, Deborah, Pamela instead of traditional Mexican names. The answer was that this was the only way they wouldn't be called "Marías", which they'd had enough of, and this was why they looked for the most unfamiliar names in order to make sure their daughters were seen as individuals.' This makes plain how far certain features of popular rural cultures have been made into fixed images which no longer correspond to reality.[145]

The *Telenovela*: From Melodrama to Farce

Media are technologies which alter the cultural field they enter: this is the manner in which they mediate.[146] Therefore resistance, where it occurs, cannot be resistance to new media as such, but only to their control and reception. Discussion of the media in Latin America in the 1970s was dominated by the concept of cultural dependency, the classic text of this debate being Dorfman and Mattelart's *How to Read Donald Duck*.[147] While being a very valuable study which brings out the blatantly imperialist tenor and hardly less blatant social chauvinism masked by the innocence of the characters of the Disney Corporation, it nevertheless makes a closed circuit between the ideological messages and their reception. The gap between ideology and everyday life also tends to be short-circuited in Mattelart's studies of the media in Chile in the early 1970s. He points, for instance, to the alienating effect of advertisements for consumer goods which the majority of Chileans could never hope to purchase. Nevertheless, he seems to assume that the receivers of these images have no choice but to receive them passively, that they have no alternative representations available to them. Here social modelling and ideology have been collapsed into each other, as if people were unconscious of the disjunctures or had no way of negotiating them. The novels of Manuel Puig, which will be discussed in more detail in Chapter 4, tell a different story. Puig's characters are addicted to the stereotyping of radio serials and films, but actively collude in being manipulated, and know very well how to negotiate the gaps between the ideal and the actual: the responsibility is not solely that of the media. Puig's novels introduce desire into the equation.

In the light of this, the notion of a distinctively popular urban culture requires investigation in three main directions. In the first place, there is the question of how far earlier forms of mass culture have left traces in the contemporary culture industry, and therefore how far the latter does include a dimension of social memory. Second, there is the issue of the receiving public as actively participant in the constitution of messages, and therefore of the messages themselves as not univocal, not imposing a single or fixed interpretative key. Third, the popular is perhaps above all a space of resignification, in that the culture industry's products are received by people who are living the actual conflicts of a society and who bring the strategies with which they handle those conflicts into the act of reception. We will explore these possibilities in terms of the most famous Latin American form of mass culture, the *telenovela*. This is also the form which most extensively crosses national boundaries.

There have been many negative judgements of the *telenovela*, but one example will be enough. In his essay 'Be Happy Because Your Father Isn't Your Father: An Analysis of Colombian *Telenovelas*', Azriel Bibliowicz discusses *Manuela*, whose plot combines romantic intrigue with a social message about the nineteenth-century peasant–landlord struggles. He calls it a 'Manicheistic construction' on the grounds that 'the "notables" who have "bad intentions" are cruel to the peasants while the mayor who is from the same social class as the "notables" has "good intentions" and wants to help them. The *telenovela* offers a simplistic analysis of the problem which is posited on the character of certain individuals and not the socio-economic reality of the country which is the real issue.'[148] But foregrounding the ethical and the emotional is precisely a characteristic of the popular forms (the melodramatic tradition in the theatre and the *folletín*) which historically passed into the *telenovela*. It is also a characteristic of the nineteenth-century novels, such as *Aves sin nido* (*Birds Without a Nest* 1889) which have been used for *telenovelas*. The fact that emphasis on the moral and emotional levels is a popular tradition clashes with Bibliowicz's univocal ideological reading.

We will look first at some of the relationships between the form of the *telenovela* and history, drawing mainly on Martín-Barbero's argument. The first *telenovela* in both Mexico and Brazil, the two main producing countries, was *El derecho de nacer* (*The Right to Be Born*). Transferred to television in the mid 1960s, it had originally been a radio serial produced in Cuba in 1948. The plot concerns a young lawyer trying to find out who his parents were. Melodrama involves a drama of recognition: of son by father, mother by son. Playing a major part in the intrigue is the struggle against a world of appearances and evil actions which prevents true identity being recognized. When melodrama emphasizes recognition of kinship as social being, by the same token it ignores the idea of society as a 'social pact' between rulers and ruled, that goal of liberal regimes from Bolívar onwards. 'Is there not a secret connection here between melodrama and the history of this subcontinent? Certainly melodrama's non-recognition of the "social contract" speaks loudly of the weight which that other *primordial sociality* of kinship, neighbourhood solidarity and friendship, holds for those who recognize themselves in melodrama. Must there not be some sense in raising the question how far the success of melodrama in these countries speaks of the failure of political institutions which have given no recognition to the weight of that other sociality?'[149]

Between the time of history, time of the great agglomerations such as the Nation, and the existential time of the individual life, family time enters as a mediation, deploying the markers of generations and differing degrees of affiliation within the extended family. The time of the family is already anachronistic, given the regulation of everyday life by work and the market ('time is money'). Nevertheless this memory of another time is essential to the reception of the *telenovela* in Latin America, since it charges plot intrigue with a sense of the social in opposition to the dominant.[150] As well as its links with the *folletín*, the television melodrama also retains connections with the narrative mode of folktales, Brazilian *cordel* literature, and the chronicle of events in *corrido* and Colombian *vallenato* songs: these connections have to do with a constantly elongated narrative flow and a porousness to what is going on outside the text. A Brazilian critic has taken these claims further, with the suggestion that melodrama is a carnivalesque genre, in which author, reader and characters constantly exchange positions.[151]

Interviewed for a British television programme about their attitude to *telenovelas*, a group of women in Mexico City said they preferred to watch the lives of rich people, because rich people have less problems. These viewers were obviously quite aware of the distance between everyday life and the world on the screen. It is also worth mentioning that one of the older Mexican *telenovelas* was called *Los ricos también lloran (The Rich Also Cry)*, an indication of how the classic 'rags to riches' plots, which engage a desire to resolve economic problems, combine with an effect of emotional democracy.[152] So although there is an undoubted emotional self-indulgence in *telenovelas*, they have another, potentially more political, side. The dynamics of popular uses of the *telenovela* are sketched out as follows by Monsiváis:

> collectivities without political power or social representation... sexualize melodrama, extract satirical threads from black humour, enjoy themselves and are moved emotionally without changing ideologically.... The subaltern classes accept, because they have no alternative, a vulgar and pedestrian industry, and indisputably transform it into self-indulgence and degradation, but also into joyful and combative identity.[153]

To this should be added the pleasures of memory, and of sharing that memory with others – since television is not received in silence or a rapture of total possession – in the face of extraordinarily complicated plots.[154]

Popular reception thus already implies a tendency to resignification, which by mobilizing popular experiences and memories produces a margin of control, not over the ownership of media (this is the province of alternative media), but over their social meanings. One type of reappropriation is indicated by the *barrio* circuses in Brazil, where television characters are incorporated into older forms of entertainment which include burlesque, conjuring and acrobatic display. But mostly forms of entertainment other than television are increasingly unavailable, and it is in the changing styles of the *telenovelas* themselves that the pressures of changing contemporary social history are manifest.

Let us consider two recent productions by Televisa, the Mexican national television monopoly.[155] *The Strange Return of Diana Salazar*, broadcast in 1988, has as its basic plot the reincarnation in 1988 of a seventeenth-century aristocratic woman, burnt by the Inquisition as a witch. It includes the customary elements of good and evil and their misrecognition, plus a love story, but it also has the special powers of the heroine transferred to computers, thus acknowledging the growing fetishism of information technology but reappropriating it into the erotics of melodrama. This is a more complex and modern plot than the usual ones inviting the poorer sections of society to watch the moral and emotional dramas of the rich. The double historical identity of the heroine and hero, both modern and seventeenth-century, can be taken as a device to reglamourize the bourgeoisie, whose aura has drastically faded in the past decade. Monsiváis stresses that 'the current move of the *telenovela* towards the spectacle of the degradation of the bourgeoisie is connected with the impossibility of continuing to base plots on the credibility of honour and family sentiments'.[156] The shift reaches an extreme in *Cuna de lobos* (*Cradle of Wolves*), whose heroine is the incarnation of evil. She wears a black patch over one eye and ruthlessly murders those who get in her way, for instance by putting sugar in an aeroplane engine. But the outlandishness is a way of doing commerce with reality, with a social crisis in the real world marked by a lack of confidence in authority and higher values: in one of the murders she puts a whole phial of digitalis in a glass of orange juice, exactly the way in which the last Pope is reputed to have been murdered.

Until the early 1980s, the expanding Mexican economy had been able to offer a prospect of more or less continuous social mobility. The devastating economic crash of 1982, whose effects were compounded by the very serious earthquake which hit Mexico City in 1985, unleashed profound changes whose impact can be seen in the form taken by recent *telenovelas*. These changes have to do with increased social violence, sharpened perception of official corruption, and the crisis of the political populism which had ruled Mexico for fifty years. 'The populist State is no longer able to respond to the excessive popular demands, and is abandoning attempts to represent them. . . . Social struggles and movements no longer find a way out by looking upwards', as Sergio Zermeño puts it, in an article entitled 'The End of Mexican Populism'.[157] The Director of *Cradle of Wolves* comments that in the current crisis 'people want to identify with someone decisive with a will of iron; this is what produced the strange phenomenon whereby people identified themselves with evil, not with good'.[158] It was watched by the largest audience ever known for a *telenovela* – 40 million people, that is, half the population. When the last episode was shown, the city came to a standstill; the underground drivers refused to work and everyone stayed at home. According to *Cuna de lobos*'s writer, Carlos Olmos, 'melodrama is now a farce, we can't take seriously any more the melodramatic contrasts of good and evil'. For Monsiváis, it marks a change of perception: anger at class relationships has displaced the old moral thrill, and the only future possibility is parody of the genre.[159] The only other thing that remains from the old *telenovela* is the pleasure in unravelling a baroque plot.

Before leaving the *telenovela* it is worth enumerating the variety of threads which converge in the process of its reception. There is the ethical emphasis, characteristic, it has been argued, of popular aesthetics. Then there is the democratic world of the emotions, where everyone is capable of the same intensity and in this sense class distinctions disappear. The emotions provide motivations for plots based on the drama of recognition. The complicated plots require considerable prowess of memory, one of the response mechanisms which is exchanged in the shared experience of viewing. Finally, the episodic structure, drawn out over several months or more, generates an interplay of completion and distension. Each episode offers a promise of the kind of finality and completeness which is lacking in actual life, a sensation heightened by the fact that the viewer knows that some inevitable alteration will occur in the next episode. In these senses, it is an error to separate out the Manichean moral element as if it were the one controlling level.

We have already seen how the *folletín* passed into the *radionovela* and later the *telenovela*. The most widely read material in the contemporary context is the *fotonovela* (photoromance) and the *historieta* (comic), sometimes published in editions of more than two million a week. Like the *folletín*, this material corresponds to situations of fragmented reading time and limited literacy. However, its immediate affiliation, in style of imagery, is not with radio or television but with cinema. Cornelia Butler Flora distinguishes three main types of *fotonovela*: the *rosa* (pink), whose themes are of the middle-, upper-middle-class or old-fashioned variety, which offers Cinderella-type plots; the *suave* (soft), whose theme is middle- and upper-middle-class life; and the *roja* (red), distinguished by its violent subject matter, such as rape or incest. Throughout, however, a particular outlook tends to predominate: 'the individualization of problems and their solution is the overwhelming message presented'.[160] The suggestion, in other words, is that the demands of integration into a modern capitalist economy are being articulated through plots which nevertheless allow the reader the expected ingredients of the genre.[161]

Comics are less affected by the transnational culture industry (for example, Disney) than might be expected. In Mexico, for instance, some 80 per cent of production is national. One particular variety is the *libros semanales* (comic-strip novels) and these raise the question of how women negotiate the transition between traditional and modern structures. Unglamorous in comparison with the older types of escapist romantic fiction (such as the Corín Tellado novels), they are 'clearly intended for women who are integrated or about to be integrated into the work place', as Jean Franco argues; they 'require a different kind of modernization plot, one that cannot simply hold out the carrot of consumption'.[162] The process of modernization requires a readjustment of attitudes to the family, that nexus of controls of the present by the past.

> Mexican postrevolutionary policy had encouraged the secularization of public life while leaving the traditional patriarchal family untouched and absorbing machismo into its national image. The Mexican family is thus an extremely complex institution, not only a source of considerable tensions, especially among the poor, but a source of support and daily communication that the state and its institutions cannot replace.[163]

The stories in the *novelas semanales* include an invitation to women to distance themselves from the traditionally male-dominated family: 'women are invited to see themselves as victims of a plot, the plot of old Mexico that has passed on the tradition of machismo and thus harmed them. If, instead of reading themselves into the plot as helpless victims, they turn their resentment against the older generation of men and separate themselves from this influence, they can expect to succeed.'[164]

Here is a summary of the plot of *Una mujer insatisfecha* (*An Unsatisfied Woman*), an example dating from 1984:

> the heroine is married to a boring and impotent businessman who believes in patriarchy and the traditional values of family life. Luisa is repelled by his puritanical attitude to marital relations and quarrels with her Italian mother-in-law, whose ideas on marriage are strictly traditional. She sets up her own consultancy as a designer and meets another man but refuses to enter into a relationship that promises to be as oppressive as the one with her husband. Back in her mother's home, she hangs up the telephone when her new lover calls, feeling 'free, happy and without ties'.[165]

Once again, as with the *telenovela*, the family emerges as a crucial mediator of reception. As far as we know, no one has yet written a comprehensive history of the family in Latin America.[166]

Another key effect of the modern urban environment is the disconnection of social classes and cultural strata. Increasingly, all social groups have at their disposal the same cultural repertory. As opposed to a minority being able to understand literature or art, now everyone is able to draw on a stock of recognitions which make up the ability to decode the media. Television series use an archive of allusions from film and television, and these are now part of a common culture in the same way that the great works of literature were previously.

> The different repertories become mixed in such a way that it is no longer possible to be educated [culto] by knowing the great artistic works or to be popular because of being able to understand the meaning of the objects and messages generated by a more or less closed community [ethnic group, barrio, class]. Nowadays these collections are unstable, they renew their composition and their hierarchy as fashions change, they intersect all the time, and above all every user can make their own collection.[167]

This situation, the so-called postmodern, is important for present purposes because it prevents one from equating the deterritorialization of cultural practices with their degradation, and from proffering nostalgic returns to a time when membership of a social elite could be equated with some guardianship of culture (or vice versa). The latter attitude is in fact more typical in Western Europe than in Latin America, where the utopianization of rural authenticity has more symbolic power. The increasing migration of rural cultures and their retransmission through new urban-based channels mean that popular cannot mean purity nor the culture industry its loss. A different definition of the popular becomes necessary, in terms of the possibility of a counter-hegemony.

Alternative Media

Alternative media represent a deliberate attempt to give a counter-hegemonic force to mass communication practices, by exploring the use of media technology outside the control of the culture industry. Alternative media embrace audiotape, radio, television and video, film, and newspapers. We will refer only to radio, but the issues that emerge have a bearing on the whole range of media. Certain characteristics facilitate the use of radio as a medium for popular reappropriation: relatively low cost, wide outreach, and the accessibility of recording technology. Rosa María Alfaro's account of the experiences of *Calandria,* a group dedicated to radical social communication, in the Peruvian shanty town Pamplona Alta, exemplifies some of the possibilities and problems of popular radio. The project began as an idea for a local newspaper. The main problems here were the difficulty of finding a written language which could convey the oral world of the inhabitants without doing violence to it, and the fact that the organization of the newspaper did not mesh with the actual life of those it was addressed to: 'the everyday life [*vida cotidiana*] of the people flowed by silently, at the margins of the organization, through other communication practices'.[168] This everyday cultural world was a complex and confusing one for those entering from outside: a coexistence of 'the Sacred Heart of Jesus and the Venezuelan *telenovela,* the folk-music radio programme and salsa and disco music'. The newspaper project failed to engage with the popular imaginary.

The second phase of the project involved inventing alternative uses for the public address system in the local market. The initial format, consisting of local news programmes, was not well received: the mere denunciation of problems was not felt to be adequate, given they had no short-term solution. At the same time, 95 per cent of the buyers and sellers in the market were women and they felt insecure about their own ability to 'speak well' vis à vis the haughty (*engolado*) style of voice associated with professional announcers. However, once they were invited to put together programmes of folklore from the rural regions they came from, their lack of confidence evaporated. The programmes included interviews, each woman speaking about her place of origin. These developed into a *radionovela,* whose plot was the story of the woman who comes from the country to the city, elaborated from the real experiences of one of the women: it drew on mass media formats without copying them. The scenes were recorded on a portable recorder at the market stalls, in full interplay with real events: 'the actrices improvise, moving between the imaginary fiction of a better reality and a harsh realistic description of the violence of the city'.[169] In her conclusion, Alfaro stresses the importance of everyday life as a matrix of communication: creating alternative media is not just a matter of technology.

Although not broadcast over the airwaves, these experiments in popular radio developed a process of production predicted on the exploration of a particular social memory. This respect for local difference continues in the radio programmes broadcast for the peasantry. Although the transmitters and studios are located in the urban centres, the receivers are scattered over wide areas of countryside, sometimes at several days' walk from a road. In the case of the Peruvian programmes *Tierra Fecunda* and *Mosoq Allpa,* beamed from

Lima and Cusco respectively, a main part of programme material consists of tapes sent in by peasant communities, with music and accounts of *costumbres* (customs), such as house-thatching rituals, narrated by the peasants themselves. The urban–rural interchange includes legal and technical advice. Although the professional programme-makers are urban-based, they spend a considerable amount of time travelling in order to collect material, and must be competent in both Quechua and Spanish, since the programmes are bilingual. Sometimes the material collected is a fictional narrative, combining humour, the supernatural and political denunciation, which will be broadcast with a minimum of editing. Other types of programme are broadcasts of peasant assemblies, or of speeches from a *cabildo abierto,* an open council meeting in which all citizens may speak. In the latter instance, instead of seeking 'balance', the idea that the truth must lie somewhere in the middle, the programmes are edited so as to show that both sides cannot be right, leaving it to the listeners to make their own decisions. As well as generating urban–rural flows which are both reciprocal and oriented to the needs of the peasantry, this type of radio also facilitates transverse intercommunication between peasant communities in widely separated geographical areas.

One particularly revealing way in which the struggle for the services and infrastructural amenities of urban life in the peripheries of Latin American cities involves the formation of new identities is exemplified in the history of Vila Aparecida, an area on the outskirts of São Paulo inhabited mainly by rural migrants. The journey from the centre of São Paulo to Vila Aparecida takes roughly two hours by bus, the journey terminating in front of a bar/bakery – one of the main meeting points which sustains the broad network of informal social relations of the area. For the inhabitants of the *periferia* this network is essential for their physical and psychological survival; here the anonymity and fragmentation they experience in factories, offices and crowded buses is counter-balanced by the sense of identity derived from belonging to the area.

Crossing the football field one reaches the main pathway of the Vila. Ramshackle houses, shops and bars painted in the lively blues, yellows and pinks characteristic of rural dwellings line the pathway. Children and dogs playing, open sewers, the sound of television and record-players, inhabitants standing in the doorways or carrying parcels and talking to each other constitute the typical landscape of everyday life on the *periferia*. Turning left one reaches the church built in the early 1980s when, with assistance of lay preachers and workers of the Catholic Church connected to liberation theology, the Vila began to organize itself and demand land, running water, a sewage system, electricity and improvements in health, education and transport.

Since the majority of the inhabitants of the Vila were illiterate, the community group set up a 'People's Radio' (*Radio do Povo*) in the hope that an oral means of communication would facilitate the process of mobilization. The main objectives of the People's Radio were: to 'recover the voice of the people, its history, religiosity and culture, tradition and legends'; to 'provide basic information, to support the organization of the struggles of the community and to communicate the hopes and problems of the people'; to 'promote the transformation of society through tasks undertaken in common'; to 'support popular artists as well as music and festivities'; and to 'encourage participation at every level and engage in the formation of new community leaders'.[170] The radio's weekly programme – which could be changed in response to demands made by the community – included: readings from the Bible adapted to and interpreted in the light of the experience of the inhabitants of Vila Aparecida; the presentation of 'socio-dramas' invented and presented by members of the area, dramatizing in a critical manner the problems and aspirations of the inhabitants; announcements relating to the organization of community groups and a variety of courses; discussion of current political issues; information on the price of food, employment opportunities and public services; and the transmission of urban and rural music.

One of the community leaders and organizers of the People's Radio commented on its role:

> the work of the Radio is part of something broader which is the economic situation of the country and the struggle for the land in this area. We try to take people beyond thinking only of their problems. People begin to see that we alone will not be in a position to solve the housing problem, that it is only by participating in the Movement for those without Land [*Movimento Sem Terra*] at regional level that steps forward can be taken.[171]

Intertwined with the everyday life of the inhabitants of the Vila, the People's Radio has developed a form of political mobilization which transcends the confines of class and political parties, in the process resemanticizing rural symbols which become bearers of a new collective memory. In the following example an element of the religious processions of popular Catholicism acquires a new meaning. One of the members of the People's Radio recounts:

> In the Popular Movements of the area we often take the Radio out on the streets. When we are waiting to speak to the government authorities in front of their

offices, people come and sing and talk and here in the Vila we do something similar. Since it is not possible to pass through our streets with the radio-van (the streets are narrow and of mud), we use the Radio like a litter carried by people. In the processions and celebrations, the litter with the Saint goes in front of the litter with the Radio behind. This year we organized a pilgrimage in favour of peace related to the question of the condition of blacks and to violence. And the Radio was present.[172]

The relationship between the personal and the political established by the People's Radio is revealed in many testimonies of the women of Vila Aparecida, who are also some of the principal organizers and leaders of the community groups: 'the Radio plays a different kind of music, it tells the story of unemployment, it talks of bread, flour and the rise in prices and it is all so true – I think it is good – people like it.... The music they play is about what we go through: one day you go to the supermarket and the milk has gone up, it talks about bread, flour, salaries, I think that is important. And then who fixes these prices?'[173]

To celebrate the creation of the People's Radio an annual festival of music and poetry is organized in the Vila. It consolidates the network of social relations in the area and stimulates the emergence of small bands which play throughout the year at birthdays, weddings and demonstrations. The festival itself consists of a mixed repertoire of rural and urban music, of poems and songs created by the inhabitants of the Vila, the most popular presentations being imitations of current 'hits' and trios playing music of rural origin.

One of the most noteworthy aspects of this and other uses of alternative media is the fact that the structure of the communicative field is based on the reciprocity between receivers and broadcasters.[174] It is in this sense above all that, in contrast to the culture industry, projects like the People's Radio can be regarded as popular. The media of the culture industry replace the concrete social world made up of social divisions and differences with an imaginary, homogeneous, yet privatized community of television viewers. They create the illusion of participation and undisturbed communication while legitimating a particular social hierarchy. The effect of this structure in a community of rural migrants is one of cultural invalidation.[175] Integrated in the urban context as unskilled cheap labour subject to repetitive monotonous tasks, rural migrants lose the knowledge and skills they previously mastered, without acquiring the material and intellectual means necessary to participate in the urban context. In the People's Radio the cultural product is a more approximate reflection of a communicative act which has not been distorted by violence and domination. Moreover, as we saw from the testimonies of the inhabitants of the Vila, the Radio is a vehicle through which they express their social conditions, in which they recognize themselves. This facilitates a critical cognitive grasp of their marginalized status. The Radio thus simultaneously validates the migrants' rural cultural identity, while also promoting their participation in the urban context, their access to modernity in the role of producers and knowers.

Another type of alternative communication can be seen in the groups which produce popular theatre in peasant communities and shanty towns. Many of the latter have achieved a high level of organization, not visible in most European television films about urban Latin America which tend to go in for a voyeurism of poverty. For instance, Villa El Salvador, which lies to the south of Lima, has created a Centre of Popular Communication and Culture, which includes theatre, cinema and video workshops. The Director of the Theatre Workshop, César Escuza, speaks of their experience as follows:

> we began with works about concrete problems, such as health, transport, education, housing.... More recently, we began to work with authored texts. But the population were asking for something different.... 'Written works are alright, they have important themes, social emotion, all of that, but why don't you tell us about Villa El Salvador? How did it only take fourteen years to become organized into districts and achieve the category of a city, when other places haven't got that far in a hundred years or more?'[176]

As a result, a decision was taken to present the history of Villa El Salvador. Two parallel methods of preparation were used: improvisations which set up a dialogue with the collective memory of the population, and the study of documentation in the form of sociological monographs and interviews with older members of the community. It should be stressed that the members of the workshop are all self-taught and most of them are under twenty years old. The result of the preparatory work was the play *Diálogo entre zorros (Dialogue Between Foxes)*, whose title acknowledges José María Arguedas's vision of a creative breaking of boundaries between Andean and modern urban Peru in *El zorro de arriba y el zorro de abajo (The Fox from Above and the Fox From Below* 1971). The play begins in an epic mode, showing the invasion of the land, the struggles with the police, the death of one of the inhabitants. It then moves to comical and satirical methods, and uses a variety of mediations of knowledge and memory, such as the format of the school lesson, to present information. One scene shows people waiting for a bus and endlessly pushing in front of each other: the failure to form a queue serves to reveal the need for the invention from scratch of an ethics and thence the creation of forms of democratic organization [Plate 7].

However, it is important to stress that there is no automatic translation of cultural resistance into political change. As Alfaro puts it, 'if peasants question hegemonic power and do not participate in the symbolic consensus, thus deepening the political crisis, nevertheless they do not see themselves as subjects of an alternative political project.'[177] This prompts the reflection that to give to cultural difference an automatic connotation of oppositional politics is to indulge in romanticism or populism, as is the case with much fashionable discourse about ethnic minorities. The other side of the coin is the fact that

> the space of politics has stagnated. We lack concrete modern alternatives in which the people are subjects and protagonists of their own liberation; there are only utopian statements. The peasant and urban movement is expressing itself violently, appropriating the city, inundating the radio waves with coastal *cumbias,* Andean tropical folklore and the so-called vernacular as symbolic expression and enjoyment of a different power, desired but not yet constructed.[178]

In the very different cultural environment of Nicaragua, discussed more fully in Chapter 3, the promotion of popular culture as a vehicle for a new national identity was a major part of government policy. However, the fact that the actual content of the first lessons in the extraordinarily successful literacy campaign concerned Sandinismo, makes the specific use of literacy, in relation to popular culture, problematic. On the other hand, the government-sponsored poetry workshops invited participants, including those who had newly come to literacy, to bring without ideological constraint their experience into poetry as written record. These poems contribute to the formation of a written popular memory without documentary emphasis: the aim was to locate emotion precisely in time and place, in the vernacular, and using a modern open poetics rather than trying to imitate prestigious poetic forms of the past.

There are conditions under which massive erasure of memory can occur. A study, began in 1985, of *villas miserias* (shanty towns) in Córdoba, Argentina, has revealed an absence of memory of the period of military government (1976–85), as compared with the years preceding it. This silence is not the result of fear: informants were not hesitant with information about their activities in the preceding period, details of which could equally be considered 'subversive'. Nor does it indicate lack of knowledge, since the issue was what they remembered not about the country or the government but about their own lives.[170] What it showed was that during the time of military totalitarianism there was a lack of any 'discourse about the collective sphere', and that this related to 'the lack of any space in which together with other people one could act upon reality'.[180] All of this amounts to the lack of a place for the articulation of memory, its former location in everyday life having been suppressed. While there was no fundamental change at the economic level, the report indicated that the life of the *villeros* changed at a level which affected symbolic processes: 'people no longer gathered together for anything, not even to play cards or to talk about football at a street corner.... There was no longer a search for collective responses to local needs. In the schools, pupils were no longer allowed to have meetings during break-time....' This suppression was not government surveillance – the regime would not have been able to control life at this 'capillary' level – but rather self-surveillance.[181] What the authors of the report describe, therefore, is a type of imposed communality which suppresses social memory. This may seem a paradoxical statement, since what we are dealing with is, at first sight, the regime's destruction of 'community'. However, the ideological charge of this word makes its descriptive use more or less untenable.

Given that social amnesia, as we noted earlier, is an effect which some critics ascribe to the culture industry as such, it is important to draw attention once again to the social and political contexts of reception. The situation of Chilean shanty towns in the 1980s – also a period of totalitarian military rule – nevertheless has different characteristics, and these have allowed the preservation of local memory and to some degree its transmission by the culture industry. During the Pinochet regime the gulf between the city and its peripheral shanty towns increased, to the extent that the latter can perhaps be compared with the South African 'homelands'. Some 150,000 persons have been 'eradicated', a newspeak term for relocation in the periphery of those urban poor who previously lived in upmarket areas.[182] The new attitude of the capitalist class in Chile is a repetition of the archaic social relations of the period of primary accumulation, that is, of the early stages of capitalism: 'it is a question of nothing other than a refusal to accept the cost of the reproduction of an important section of the workforce, which, when need arises, the capitalists want to be able to make use of like water or air'.[183] Part of the process has been the mercantilization of services such as health, education, housing and social security. One form of popular response has taken the form of mass social expropriations for subsistence needs, such as land invasions, *colgados* (illegal tapping) of electrical power lines and diversion of drinking water supplies. The *colgados* have to be regulated by the local community so as not to burn out the cables. Extra policing is needed to prevent assaults on shops and supermarkets – a phenomenon occurring, in fact, throughout most of Latin America. A simultaneous effect is the resurgence of locally generated communality, which 'rejects the type of modernization promoted by the regime and compensates for the vacuum left by the ending of the [Allende government's] model of "popular promotion" '.[184]

This is the context in which a new type of rock music began to be produced. Broadly, two types of rock have appeared in Latin America: an imitation of British and United States bands, often sung in English, for middle-class consumption: and 'rock nacional' or 'rock subterráneo', sung in Spanish and produced in the urban periphery. Instead of using imported music as a repeatable format, sound and textual motifs are resemanticized in terms of the local. For instance Los Prisioneros (The Prisoners) deploy a crude aggressive sound, with elements of punk–reggae fusion, against the nostalgic and 'pure' sounds of the 'new song' style, whose typical singer is referred to in one of their songs as 'a bad copy of a gringo hippie', and whose 'famous protest' is contradicted by 'your beautiful elaborate harmonies'. 'You're an artist not a guerrilla,/You pretend to fight and you're just a trendy shit', the song continues.[185] As the Peruvian critic Oscar Malca has said, in an article on similar Peruvian groups in the 1980s, protest and rebellion are now 'the toboggans that all artists and writers must acquire in order to slide to the rosy parnassus of prestige and commercial success'.[186] There is also, particularly in the Chilean case, the issue of changes in the political culture, whereby the appeal to the conscience of others implicit in protest has been replaced by more autonomous forms of organization. The song 'I Demand to be a Hero' breaks with the polarity of heroism or sell-out, the old protagonism of vanguard politics: 'Monday, Tuesday... The streets seen from the windows/Are all the same./Kicking stones, getting money,/I'm just a listener.' The ambiguous lines, 'Life is too expensive and boring/To take it as sold out', imply ironically that the only possible politics derive from the way time is spent living. The 1980s, with their 'atmosphere/Saturated with boredom', change the way in which memory is to be framed. By the mid 1980s, Los Prisioneros had moved from an attitude of rejection of all organized politics to become spokesmen of a new wave of anti-government actions in the shanty towns the Left had tended to abandon. At that time they also began to sell more records than any other group, a mass mediation made possible by the culture industry.

In Peru chicha music became in the past decade the most widely listened to in the whole country (the word chicha refers to Andean maize beer, a drink associated with ceremonial and ritual occasions). A fusion of Andean and tropical (Afro-Hispanic) elements, it reflects mass Andean immigration to the coastal cities and resignifies both traditions. The *chicha* group Los Shapis sold more records in the 1980s than any other group in Peru. Their fusion of the Andean and the modern urban occurs at every level: they wear specially design-ed white trousers and T-shirts, with the Andean rainbow motif across the knees and shoulders. Their lyrics seek to define the morality of new situations and to register experiences of survival and migration. The song 'Hombre casado' ('Married Man') begins with the words, 'I don't know what has happened to me/I'm a married man/It's impossible to keep silent/It should be told', sung by a male voice. A female voice then enters, repeating each verse. After the man says, 'I fell in love.../With someone who isn't my wife', the female voice replies, 'Yes, but you must forget her/And very soon.' Another song 'Ambulante soy' ('I'm a Street Vendor') is based on the childhood experiences of Jaime Moreyra, one of the members of the group, when his mother used to take him to provincial fairs.[187] The electric guitars and tropicalized rhythm (with elements of cumbia and salsa) are combined with attenuated versions of the rhythm and melodic line of the Andean *huayno*. Seen from above, as a mere mixture, *chicha* can seem like an impoverishment of the traditions it deploys, but to examine it horizontally is to become aware of the historicity of its different elements, of its importance as a site for storing and processing memory.

If the dimension of memory is suppressed, there remains only a pragmatic acceptance of existing power relations. Such inevitability is characteristic of the destructive modernization advocated by the spokespeople of accultura-tion in the 1950s and of neo-liberalism in the 1980s. The cultural politics of the New Right in Latin America leaves no place for remembering the social cost of the types of modernization policy imposed by the IMF and transnational corporations.[188] Without memory, people can be made to accept the otherwise intolerable. The resources of the culture industry have been used in attempts to eradicate popular memory, but their products have also had to respond to the pressures of that memory.

From Slavery to Samba

The vital importance of memory for the formulation of cultural identity is particularly apparent if we look at the development of African culture in Brazil, where music and the body were to become the repository of a black identity and the cradle of urban popular music in the 1920s. However, in order to understand how this came about, it is necessary to focus briefly on the formative influence of African religion and the institution of slavery. Two preliminary considerations need to be raised in order to elucidate the forms the black cultures of Africa took in their new and hostile environment. First, in traditional African cultures music did not exist as an autonomous practice separate from the religious life of the community, which also expressed itself through dance, myth, ritual and sacred objects. Second, dance and music were interwoven in the sense that musical form developed as a function of dance, and dance itself was a visual correlate of musical form; and both in conjunction served the purpose of religious communication between humans and with the natural and supernatural world. [189] Thus the body caught in the motion of dance also became one of the means by which resistance to reduction of the body to a productive machine was expressed. We will focus on three of the main devices through which black cultures survived and reconstituted themselves in Brazil before the twentieth century in order to understand how this occurred.

On the early colonial plantations with their large number of slaves, forms of dance were practised which, despite their diversity, were generally subsumed by the Portuguese chroniclers of the period under the Angolan term of *batuque*. To the sound of a tall drum (the *atabaque*) dancers form a small circle singing and clapping hands. All the participants enter the circle in turn; when the dancer in the middle is ready to leave the centre he or she chooses the next one to enter the circle with a forward nudge of the pelvis. Since this contact was said to take place between the navels – or to use the Portuguese term *umbigos* – of the respective dancers, this *batuque* was also described as *umbigada* or, using the Angolan term for navel, as *semba*. Slightly modified to 'samba' this subsequently became the general term for various forms of song and dance of African origin. According to white chroniclers of the period, this particular highly sensual, and in their view lascivious, form of dance, which often lasted deep into the tropical night was, in contrast to religious practices, fomented by plantation owners. Due to its erotic quality, it was considered a stimulus to reproduction and hence a cost-free way of acquiring additional labour. Moreover, because of their rhythmic nature and cathartic qualities, these dance rituals, practised during moments of leisure, seemed also to replenish the exhausted energies of the slave population and thus to sustain their productivity. However, since there was little interest among the colonizers in the culture of the Africans and their descendants in Brazil, the *batuques,* far from being secular forms of leisure, were unbeknown to their masters also used by slaves as a means for maintaining their religious

123

traditions by enacting through dance myths relating to African deities, the *orixás*.[190]

A further Portuguese government policy designed to forestall insurrection entailed dividing blacks into their respective 'nations' of origin, thus encouraging rivalries between them. However, this procedure also had the effect of preserving cultural traditions otherwise threatened by the levelling effect of slavery; in particular it facilitated the development of cultural resistance in the cities. In contrast to the rural areas where blacks were more integrated in the patriarchal family, the anonymity of urban life and the greater concentration of blacks working for their masters outside the house and hence not under their direct control strengthened the bonds of ethnic solidarity between members of African 'nations'. Moreover, the cities, where the institutions of official culture and the centres of government and administration were located, were a stronghold of white European culture.[191] It is thus in the cities that greater class segregation and anatagonism between black and white culture prevailed, and that Afro-Brazilian religions were to flourish with the establishment of the first Afro-Brazilian temples in Bahia in the late nineteenth century.[192]

The fusion of African and Catholic elements in Afro-Brazilian religions is generally described as a form of syncretism, a combination of divergent or incompatible beliefs. Abdias do Nascimento, in his critical survey of race relations in Brazil, makes the point that the use of this term to describe the amalgamation of African divinities with Catholic saints – characteristic of Afro-Brazilian religions – has led to the widely accepted but false presupposition that they are the product of an equal exchange between Catholic and African religious traditions.[193] In fact, however, as with the *batuque,* religious syncretism also reveals a double duality of resistance and accommodation to white civilization.

One of the main institutions in which these new hybrid religious creations emerged were the black brotherhoods or *confrarias* (in particular the brotherhoods of Nossa Senhora do Rosário and São Benedito) created by the Catholic Church to secure the salvation of the blacks' pagan souls. Many African customs not in direct conflict with Catholicism were tolerated in these black brotherhoods. Their elected leaders or kings were crowned as in the mother country, and religious processions in honour of the black patron saint São Benedito or the black Virgin Nossa Senhora do Rosário – defined because of their bantu origin as *Congos* or *Congadas* – dramatized inter-ethnic battles for the crown worn by an African queen. While ostensibly these brotherhoods became characteristic of black Catholicism, they also unwittingly served to perpetrate African religion or *Candomblé*. Among the Afro-American cults, *Candomblé* has perhaps been the most studied by anthropologists and a considerable body of knowledge about it exists. In Cuba it is referred to as *Santería*, in Haiti as *Vodun* and in other parts of Brazil as *Shangô* (Recife) or *'Tambor de Mina'* (Maranhão). Although these cults are not identical, we will look at *Candomblé* as one of the most significant.

The core of the *Candomblé* cults is constructed around the personal relationship between their followers and the gods that make up the pantheon of African divinities, referred to as *orixás* or saints. Each divinity has a definite personality, a preference for particular colours and foods and is called forth by music and dance which express its personality and current mood. This relationship is first established when a divinity (also known as a *santo*) reveals him- or herself to a future member of a cult through a sign; after this the elect leaves the profane and enters the sacred dimension of existence by joining the cult.[194] One of the most important ways the mystical communication between the believer and his or her god is established is through rituals of possession in which the *orixá* becomes embodied in the person of his chosen son or daughter. By contrast to Christian mysticism, where the soul leaves the body to commune with God, here the divine is manifested through the body itself, which to the accompaniment of music expresses the character of the specific god. Whereas in Christian theology the body is regarded as the repository of evil, in *Candomblé* it is the vehicle through which the divine reveals itself to humans. Indeed the extent to which the *orixá* has become incarnated in his son or daughter is manifested in the degree to which he or she expresses the god's qualities through mimicry and dance. It is thus that the body becomes inscribed with multiple layers of meaning.

The gods of the African pantheon have masculine and feminine identities and are related to each other through ties of kinship. *Candomblé* has been described as a religion of participation. For instance, a necklace of shells which corresponds to a specific deity is bathed in animal blood and herbs and is left on the stone embodying the deity. In this way the necklace participates in its divine essence. Existence in African religion is not as in Western philosophy defined in terms of either being or nothingness; instead there are believed to be different levels of existence, where evil, in the form of illness, poverty or unhappiness, appears as a diminished form. It is thus possible for a person to exist in greater or lesser degree, depending on the degree of participation in a deity, which through its power infuses the community of believers with *axé*. *Axé* signifies vital energy which gives life to all beings and is generated through ritual in order to increase the degree of existence – the physical and spiritual health and happiness – of its members.[195] In the course of the development of Afro-American cults, the deities and mythology of different African nations intermixed and were amalgamated with Amerindian spirits and Catholic saints and rituals. Gradually complex syncretic configurations emerged in which every African deity had a corresponding Catholic saint – and in some Afro-Brazilian cults such as *Umbanda* also a corresponding Amerindian deity.[196]

In Yoruba mythology, the goddess Yemanjá and her brother Aganju gave birth to a son who, overcome by lust, pursued his mother who then fell to the ground and died. As she lay prostrate her body began to swell, emitting water from her breasts; her womb became a lake and from it a multitude of gods emerged, only some of which survived in Brazil. The father and chief among gods is Oxalá or Orixalá. He is a calm and benign figure dressed in white and his Catholic equivalent is Jesus Christ. Xangô, the son of Orixalá, is lively and temperamental and this is reflected in the fact that he is the god of thunder and lightning. The female divinities are almost all connected with water in some way. Yemanjá, variously called siren of the sea or mother of the water (*sereia do mar, mãe d'agua*) is perhaps the most venerated of them. Offerings to her in the form of combs, soap, mirrors and above all flowers are cast into the sea [Plate 4].

Possession through trance occurs during the ceremonies in honour of the gods. Ritual offerings are made, including animal sacrifice. Following a propitiatory song invoking Exu, intermediary between gods and humans, a fixed repertoire of particular rhythmic structures is played on percussion instruments, themselves regarded as intermediaries of the divine. As the repertoire is sung the sons and daughters of a given *orixá* fall into a trance and are led into an adjacent room from which they return dressed in the clothes appropriate to their respective gods.

During this state of trance the legendary past of the deity is enacted, with the son or daughter of an *orixá* taking on the personality of the god [Plate 2]. It is possible for a man to be possessed by a feminine *orixá*, and vice versa, and frequently the dramatization of a god's personality may be in conflict with the individual's social and gender role outside the community. Indeed the way in which masculine and feminine characteristics are distributed within the *Candomblé* community does not necessarily correspond to their biological sex or the gender roles of men and women in society at large: many members of the cult – including married members with children – are openly bisexual or homosexual.[197]

The Afro-Brazilian cults thus offer the dispossessed, whose development is limited by their subordinate position within society, a symbolic universe through which to transcend these limitations. It is a widely held view that, like other forms of religion, these cults are mere 'opium for the people'; which in offering the popular classes the compensation of being transformed into a god and of acquiring positions of prestige within the *Candomblé* community, depoliticize them and thus contribute to the maintenance of social inequality. However, such arguments fail to recognize that the *Candomblé* cults that emerged towards the end of the nineteenth century helped maintain African traditions and forms of group solidarity, protecting blacks from the disintegrative effect of urbanization and the abolition of slavery.

As slaves fled from the plantations to the cities after abolition, they congregated in shanty towns on the hills and outskirts. While they were no longer integrated in the hierarchy of the patriarchal family, they were also not in a favourable position to compete on the labour market of the emerging urban industrial society. The *Candomblé* cults offered the slaves, transformed into an urban proletariat, refuge and support: they became the main means by which the communal structure and emotional bonds based on reciprocity characteristic of the African village were reconstructed in the cities of Bahia and Rio de Janeiro, thus protecting blacks from the dehumanizing and atomizing effects of the city.[198] *Candomblé* thus offered its members not only a form of refuge but also possibilities for creative expression to which, given their disadvantaged position in society, they would not otherwise have had access. As de Carvalho and Segato point out, the worship of the *orixás,* which has flourished with the growth of the *Candomblé* cults in the twentieth century, brings with it knowledge of a rich symbolic universe, of various forms of dance, song, polyrhythmic structures and percussion instruments, the ability to prepare sophisticated dishes to offer the gods and to design and elaborate forms of clothing. Thus in the organization of all ritual events, of the objects and space associated with ritual, the *Candomblé* cults reveal the extent to which in Afro-Brazilian religion worship of the deities is connected to aesthetic practices.[199]

To turn our attention now to the development of black popular culture in Brazil, it is at the turn of the twentieth century that the cultural practices connected to *Candomblé* transcend the boundaries of the religious cult house and give rise to secular forms of dance and music, in particular samba.

Carnival and Black Identity

With the advance of modernization and industrialization in the 1920s the preconditions for the emergence of specifically urban forms of popular culture were in place. São Paulo, where the wealth created by coffee and the influx of immigrants had stimulated industrial development, became the most powerful regional centre, but it was in Rio de Janeiro that the greater mobility and diversity of urban life would lead to the emergence of a tradition of urban popular music and dance. Paradoxically, this was due to the fact that, although large parts of colonial Rio had been demolished and replaced with an architecture intended to reflect Brazil's new modern identity, it retained many traditional features. This would lead to an extremely fruitful fusion between African musical forms, originally tied to the slave quarters and the *latifundio,* and European music. Radio, the record industry and the greater density of the urban population following the abolition of slavery amplified the repercussions of this process of amalgamation. At the same time a new stratum of free men emerged who were no longer tied to slave-labour and reliance on *favor* – the patronage of the powerful – to sustain them in the absence of regular work. This stratum, which furnished the composers and public of new urban music, was made up of public servants, small businessmen, former soldiers and a host of vagrants and loafers with no fixed address or occupation, masters in the art of surviving in a twilight zone between the established order and a bohemian underworld of dissolute-ness.[200]

The theme of work becomes central to this music, but not as a positive value. Rather, it is the opposite to a life of pleasure, idleness and subterfuge, as expressed in the image of the *malandro,* the charming rogue who embodies what the literary critic Antonio Candido has called the 'dialectic of *malandragem',* present as a theme and literary device not only in popular music but also in literature.[201] Essentially this dialectic consists in using the institutions, representatives and upholders of the established order to pursue illicit interests, avoiding the punishment of work, often in connivance with that same order, so that the very opposition between order and disorder becomes ambiguous. Reflected in it also is the process of capitalist development in Brazil. Urbanization and industrialization were insufficient to absorb the freed slaves who migrated to the cities, while the continued prevalence of the *latifundio* hampered the development of an internal market and a rise in the population's standard of living. Discriminated against at work and in education, blacks became a reserve army of labour for whom work evoked not only the oppressive memory of slavery but also the present equally oppressive experience of exploitation tied to the process of primitive accumulation of capital. Engaging in the dialectic of *malandragem* 'becomes the only means of survival in a society with a social structure which reduces the working man to an economically marginal status, more impoverished day by day'.[202] And black music, subsequently defined as samba, with its bitter-sweet eulogy of life on the margins of society and its syncopated rhythm, becomes the matrix of an urban music genre with a formative influence not only on composers in the 1930s but on a whole tradition of popular music represented today by contemporary composers such as Gilberto Gil and Chico Buarque de Holanda.

One of the many sites in which the samba as a specifically urban musical form was born was the house of Tia Ciata, who held an important position in the *Candomblé* community and in whose home many parties and reunions were held where music, dance and the discussion of religious themes intermingled. Muniz Sodré suggests that Tia Ciata's house could be seen as a 'living metaphor' of the manner in which the black population, by reformulating its musical traditions, negotiated its incorporation into urban life and thus tried to impose its presence as a collectivity. The house contained various rooms and in each a different musical/dance form was practised. These formed a continuum of decreasing social respectability: the front rooms, more exposed to the public eye, were reserved for socially acceptable forms of music, which included European waltzes and polkas; in the back rooms, sambas were played; and in the *terreiro* closest to the ritual space of *Candomblé*, the percussive rhythms of the original *batuque*, or *batucada* as it was now called, could be heard.[203] In this sense Tia Ciata's house represented a microcosm of the newly stratified social order and the new forms of leisure associated with it.

Among the public servants, artisans and unskilled workers who constituted the world of samba was the figure of the *batuqueiro* or *bamba*. Proficient in the art of *capoeira*, a form of self-defence developed by fugitive slaves and disguised as a form of dance, he was not only a good fighter but also a gifted improviser of solos to which other *bambas* formed in a circle around him responded with a refrain accompanied by tambourines and *cavaquinhos* (small guitars).[204] Dressed in clothes parodying the stereotyped outfit of the bourgeoisie – a white linen suit, a silk shirt, a scarf, a straw hat and two-tone shoes – these *bambas*, also known as *malandros* or rogues, were key figures in the articulation of the world of samba and its ethos. This ethos expressed on the one hand the social organization and religious inheritance of the

Candomblé cults, and on the other it constituted a kind of counter-culture of play and leisure from which the petty-bourgeois values of work and respect for money and authority were excluded.[205] Musically it was manifested in a collective form of composition and in the emphasis on a syncopated rhythm, which in the *Candomblé* cults functioned as the privileged transmitter of *axé* – the vital energy underlying existence. But rhythm as a way of structuring time is also a way of seeing and experiencing reality – it is constitutive of consciousness, not as an abstraction but as a physical force affecting all the organs of the body. Muniz Sodré points out that in contrast to Western music, African syncopated rhythm is characterized by a homogeneous mythical time, in that the end of every rhythmic sequence returns to the beginning in a cyclical movement which is endlessly repeated. He suggests that because this movement is cyclical it manifests itself musically as an affirmation of life in which death, the terminal point of a linear sequence, is elided; thus 'to sing, to dance, to enter into the rhythm is like listening to one's heartbeat – it is to feel life without allowing for the symbolic inscription of death'.[206] This form of syncopation moreover was a result of a fusion of European melodic structures and African rhythms generating a rhythmic–melodic synthesis which in its language revealed 'the way in which blacks made use of the European tonal system while simultaneously destabilizing it rhythmically through syncopa-tion – a compromise solution'.[207]

The multiple and varied cultural exchanges between classes and ethnic groups in Latin America accelerated by the process of urbanization produced 'miscegenated' or hybrid musical forms manifesting within their very form the struggle for predominance between musical elements connected to their respective social classes or ethnic groups of origin. Nowhere is this more apparent than in the vicissitudes of this syncopated melodic–rhythmic structure, which during the first decades of the twentieth century left the confines of the Rio de Janeiro hilltops in which the poor black population was concentrated to descend into the valley and infiltrate the forms of dance and music practised by the growing middle-class public of the city.

The original *batuque* with its characteristic pelvic nudge was transformed by the mulatto population through the introduction of an elaborate choreography into a form of dance or song called the *lundu*. This, fused with the equally lively European polka, was danced in the proliferating cafés, bars and theatres of Rio, and when deprived of its more explicitly 'savage' elements, it was sung in the salons of the urban elite. As the *batuque-samba* rose in the social hierarchy to meet with the polkas and mazurkas imported from Europe, so equally the latter made their way to the proletarian areas. There they were transformed by the clarinets, guitars and oboes of popular orchestras, the *chorões*, and the gestural language of the *samba-lundus*, into a new form of dance, the *maxixe*.[208] The *maxixe* travelled to Europe where, known as the *tango brésilien*, it was enthusiastically received in the café society of the French Belle Époque. In Brazil, however, excepting the masked balls during Carnival, it was largely rejected by the middle classes due to its sensual movements and proletarian origin.

Carnival has its origins in the saturnalia and Bacchanalia of Ancient Greece and Rome, during which in Dionysian rituals involving the use of masks and disguises, sexual orgies and much drinking and eating, singing and dancing, the established social values and hierarchies that governed everyday life were temporarily inverted.[209] In Brazil until quite recently, Carnival had been a somewhat violent and uncouth affair. The *entrudo* – as it was called since the seventeenth century when it became a common practice inherited from Portugal – consisted of street festivities during which the 'common' populace bombarded each other with flour while from the houses above homemade wax projectiles in the form of lemons and oranges filled with water were thrown on the revellers below.[210] While the chaotic battles of water and flour raged in the streets, excessive eating and drinking took place in the private quarters of otherwise respectable families.[211] Although gradually forbidden, aspects of the popular *entrudo* persisted in more sublimated forms well into the twentieth century, but as the process of class formation advanced with urbanization, it was overshadowed by other carnivalesque practices, which now involved both dance and music. As a result, the samba, in a complex process of cultural appropriation by the middle classes and the state, would become elevated to a national symbol.

Two different forms of carnivalesque entertainment emerged. In the private hotels and theatres, masked balls imitating the European carnivals of Venice and Paris were introduced by the middle classes, who danced to the sound of polkas, tangos, waltzes and the risqué *maxixe*. The *sociedades carnavalescas*, literary–musical associations organized by minor businessmen and shopkeepers, paraded down the main streets with sumptuous allegorical floats inspired by progressive and republican ideals. So-called *cordões* or cordons made up of blacks and poorer whites danced down the streets to the syncopated rhythm of the samba disguised as clowns, devils, kings, queens, bats, death and in the characteristic dress of the *Candomblé* follower, the *baianas*. The symbols that characterized the *cordões* related to nature or to religious themes and were known by such names as the 'Goddess of the Sea', 'Children of the Lightning of the New World', 'Silver Rain', 'Lovers of Saint

Teresa', 'Club for the Recreation of Angels'. The clowns or frequently the *capoeiras* cleared the way through the massed spectators for the King and Queen of the Gods, for the devils and gypsies accompanied by their royal entourage – a variety of butterflies and devils. Partly under the influence of black families who had migrated from Bahia – among them the family of Tia Caita – these *cordões* fused with the *ranchos*, described earlier. The *ranchos*, originally organized to celebrate the Nativity, joined the street festivities bearing on banners in totemistic fashion the name of an animal or plant by which their group was known. Dressed in vivid clothes they danced through the streets accompanied by guitars and the *ganzá* (a cylindrical rattle filled with pebbles), dramatizing the death and resurrection of their totem, or as they developed into more sophisticated carnivalesque organizations, narrating in allegorical form stories frequently of mythological character. In addition to the *ranchos, blocos* made up of casual *sambistas,* followed in spontaneous formation one or other masked figure. One of the major carnivalesque innovations introduced by the *cordões* and *ranchos* was the organization of their parade through the streets according to the form characteristic of the religious processions of popular Catholicism. In other words these were 'paganized' religious processions, which during the days of Carnival invaded the urban landscape of Rio, transgressing the geographical boundaries imposed by class divisions.

This process by which the subaltern classes made themselves visible, demanding social recognition, was partly aided by support from the radio and a growing urban press, in particular the newspapers published by the Carnival Associations. In Brazil, as in many other Latin American countries poor in representative civic institutions, these associations undertook the task of announcing the festivities, discussing stylistic innovations and promoting competitions between *ranchos, blocos* and *cordões,* transforming the clanic rivalry characteristic of totemistic organizations into modern forms of competition.[212]

These popular Carnival Associations, which congregated on a square in Rio, the Praça Onze, close to the proletarian areas, gave rise to the *Escolas de Samba* (samba schools) whose parade gradually became the predominant form of street Carnival. Originally, the *blocos* and *cordões* were persecuted by the authorities and their redefinition as samba schools was designed to shroud them with a veil of respectability. This is hard to believe given the fact that today they exist as veritable modern urban-industrial enterprises. In another sense, however, the initial successful attempt at obtaining social recognition could be seen as a first step in a long process of cultural transformation. It is notable for the manner in which it renders visible the struggle for cultural hegemony and the way in which cultural forms change in their journey from one cultural register to another. Let us look at the vicissitudes of this struggle first in terms of a particular form of samba, the *samba-malandro* and secondly the development of the samba schools.

Carnival is characterized by the fact that for a brief few days, the rules governing social behaviour, which uphold the hierarchical organization of society are suspended, transgressed or inverted. Individuals, divested of their customary social roles, relate to each other in a free and familiar manner; as princes, deaths, devils, fairies or fools, their interaction is based on equality and expressive freedom. This is reinforced by the atmosphere of collective joy and communion, which stands in sharp contrast to the inequality and suffering of everyday life. Announcing the 'gay relativity of prevailing truths and authorities',[213] Carnival festivities enact a form of ritual dethroning and rethroning: the absolute is relativized and the sacred profaned; the fool is king and all that is serious laughed at. But the essence of Carnival is that while it temporarily inverts the social order, this inversion itself is also relativized. All negations are themselves open to negation; thus ambiguity permeates the language and symbolism of Carnival.[214] Moreover this ambiguity is manifested in the fact that it brings together through the use of mask and disguise the most disparate elements: devils as gods, men dressed as women, humans as animals.

According to Claudia Matos in her insightful work on the development of different forms of samba, this structure of the carnivalesque experience constitutes the very nature of a particular genre of samba, the *samba-malandro*, or rogue samba. Many *sambistas* were *malandros* par excellence. Poor yet elegantly dressed in a dapper white linen suit, the *malandro* wore a mask not only during Carnival but throughout the year; living on the margin of society, he actualized the ambivalent mode of existence characteristic of Carnival. By rejecting routinized forms of work and leading a bohemian existence in the world of samba, the *malandro* dethrones the sacred values of thrift and hard work underpinning petty-bourgeois existence. He is in a sense the most highly developed expression of this world, in that within the pleasurable universe of samba, the hierarchical order of society is negated, giving rise to a particular poetics, that of *malandragem*, contained in privileged form in the *samba-malandro*. Using Bakhtin's work on the poetics of Dostoyevsky, Claudia Matos points out that the *samba-malandro* is based on a 'carnivalized discourse' in which the inversion and relativization of values, the ambiguity of Carnival, is expressed in literary form through an inner polyphony, or dialogue between opposing elements. Since this dialogue is constant and never resolved in any definitive affirmation or negation, the structure of the *samba-malandro* could be termed 'dialogic'. In contrast to other forms of samba which emerged in the late 1930s, patriotically exalting the nation or discoursing on love, and to Carnival songs which optimistically extol the pleasure of living, the *samba-malandro* is neither optimistic nor pessimistic. Like the anti-hero *malandro* himself, it exists on the margin, dethroning in its lyrics the society in which blacks occupy a subordinate position, while simultaneously questioning the alternative reality of the world of samba. In Matos's view this is expressed with clarity in the samba 'Que Rei sou eu?' ('What King am I?') which addresses the idea that the *malandro* is king in the world of samba while pointing in an inverse movement of negation to the reality of poverty which underlies this kingdom:

> Without a kingdom or a crown
> Without a castle or a queen
> What sort of king am I?
> My kingdom is small and confined
> I reign only in my area
> Because the king there has died
>
> I have no servant in livery
> Nor carriages or butlers
> Nobody kisses my feet
> My blue blood
> Is devoid of royalty
> The samba is my nobility
> But after all what sort of King am I?
> What sort of King am I?[215]

With the development of radio and the record industry in the early 1920s, the samba is transferred to a new cultural register. As composers of the *ranchos* and *escolas* become professional musicians, the samba, in becoming the work of specific authors producing for a new cultural market, loses its improvisatory character thus introducing a rift between producers and consumers. When it was an integral element of the world of samba, it was composed collectively and remained, as it circulated with the black community, an 'unfinished work', intimately connected to dance. As samba becomes a closed, finished piece belonging to a single composer, these links between the community and the composer, who is now self-consciously defined as an 'artist', are severed.[216] Gradually, samba becomes a 'popular' and profitable form of entertainment transmitted together with commercial advertisements by radio stations which had until then only used educational texts or 'classical' music. Under Getúlio Vargas, the state regulates the production of samba through measures which are both protective and repressive. Composers are legally entitled to higher salaries from radio stations; their music however is enlisted in support of the broader project of national development and required by the censors to be patriotic and educative. Gradually the theme of *malandragem* appears in a more coded form or gives way to lyrics extolling the virtues of work.[217]

In Muniz Sodré's view, the logic of capitalist production also leaves traces in the temporality of samba. In its early phase, the presence of the gestural language of the body was more evident in that any object – hands, plates, tins, matchboxes – could become instruments of percussion. The need to expand the music market with new products means that songs follow each other in quick succession, while the intricate and playfully sensual steps of samba during the Carnival parade tend to be replaced by acrobatic and often stereotypically erotic performances.

Although these judgements on the fate of contemporary samba may appear excessively negative, it is certainly arguable that the transition from one cultural register to another had ambiguous effects. The samba was transformed into a 'popular' massified genre and an exportable symbol of national identity. While this appropriation by the media may have eroded the socializing function of samba within the black community, it also created the preconditions for the emergence in the 1960s and 1970s of the counter-cultural music of Gilberto Gil, Chico Buarque de Holanda and Cateano Veloso. Of middle-class origin and deploying new harmonics, these singers developed the capacity for the duplicitous play on words, ambiguous poetic construction and irreverent satire characteristic of the *malandro*, combining it frequently with critical commentary on Brazilian society. During the military dictatorship (1964–85) their music became one of the main vehicles by which not only opposition but also an acute awareness of the calamitous changes taking place during this period was expressed. To return to the concept of 'mediation', the history of the *samba-malandro* illustrates clearly the way in which media are technologies that alter the field they enter. A further illuminating example of the way in which they have entered and transformed the cultural field to which samba belongs, can be seen if we look briefly at the changes undergone by the samba schools since the 1920s.

The samba schools are associations which exist not only during the three days of Carnival but throughout the year. During the year, they rehearse for the coming Carnival, and take part in social and recreational activities funded by the Carnival Parade, which is open to the public. A samba school is also present at birthdays, weddings, funerals and religious events celebrating the patron saint of its neighbourhood.

Essentially, a samba school is made up of various *alas* or wings, of *sambistas* and shepherdesses (a figure derived from the religious processions of the Nativity). They dress alike in a costume through which the story or theme of the procession is narrated in conjunction with the allegorical floats. Some dancers are singled out for their agility and virtuosity, while the *ritmistas* make up the percussionists who rhythmically structure the procession. Important also are the *Mestre Sala* (master of ceremony) and the *Porta-Bandereira*, who carries the banner with the insignia of the school. Dressed in the royal attire of the eighteenth century, including fans and lace handkerchiefs, the couple elegantly greet the spectators as they perform their duo. The *samba-de-enredo*, the song sung during the procession, narrates the story represented by the school and invented and developed by the *carnavalesco*, who is also in charge of designing the allegorical floats and costumes of the partici-pants.[218]

In the 1930s the procession of the samba schools was officially organized by the state authorities in the form of competition for monetary prizes. Meanwhile their gradual transformation into tourist attractions put in motion a process of social differentiation not only of the composer from the black community, but of the school itself. As it became recognized by official white society, it became a vehicle for social mobility subject to the pressures of the 'ideology of whitening'. Until the early 1960s, the processions of the schools could be seen and applauded by all; subsequently they could only be watched from temporary stalls, access to which is paid and where the best view is reserved for the most expensive seats.

Their increase in size and importance (a school now consists of up to 4,000 members) has had various consequences. Frequently professional artists, drawn from the middle classes and sharing the criteria of the officially appointed judges of the competition, are invited by the school to design not only the costumes and theme but also to select from the many sambas produced by the composers the one which best fits the theme. Originally the *samba-enredo* for the procession was selected during rehearsals according to the degree of enthusiasm a given melody evoked in the wings. The organizational requirements and the need for capital investment in musical instruments and costumes has led to a rationalization of the schools. As a result they have had to introduce a stricter division of labour, involving a host of people – lawyers, accountants, administrators – external to the world of samba. This has led to the paradoxical situation of 'trying aprioristically to imprison an activity the essence of which consists in spontaneous creativity, informal commitment and in the autonomy of the agents which participate in it.'[219] Moreover, with the growth in television popularity, the schools have to some extent become a means of self-promotion not only for composers seeking to become economically independent by increasing the record sales of their sambas, but also for the new media elite created by the extraordinary expansion of the culture industry in Brazil in the 1970s and 1980s. Well-known actors and actresses from the *telenovelas*, almost invariably with white Aryan features, adorn the allegorical floats in positions of prominence.

Thus while samba has been affected by the process of massification which accompanied the formation of the state and a national market of symbolic goods, on which the expansion of the media is predicated, it cannot be said that this quantitative expansion has led to a significant qualitative improvement in the social condition or cultural status of the black population in Brazil as a whole. As do Nascimento points out, although Brazil is the second largest black country in the world, blacks are discriminated against in education, work and housing. Only 0.6 per cent of the black population go to university and 'blacks are not represented in any body with decision-making power'.[220] In recent years, the extraordinary time of Carnival, the atmosphere of communion and liberation from established norms and conventions, has been used to voice criticisms of the legacy of the military dictatorship, the external debt, the destruction of the Amazon and to proclaim the solidarity of African peoples. The subordinate status of black culture can, however, only be ameliorated insofar as the ideology of whitening loses its legitimacy. This in turn depends on the extent to which the collective psyche of Brazilian society as a whole ceases to be divided between (devalued) African symbols and (idealized) Western institutions and cultural forms.[221] Signs that this may be happening can be seen in the fact that, despite the cultural expropriation of samba, particularly of the Carnival procession itself, the samba schools, the *Candomblé* cults and the *capoeira* groups continue to function as neighbourhood organizations which sustain a black identity and the beginnings of a black consciousness movement. In that sense, it is suggested, the samba schools are sites for the articulation of a form of 'unofficial citizenship' not encompassed by the state. This function is also fulfilled by another popular cultural form crucial for an understanding of Latin America: football. Once again, however, the state has not been slow to recognize its potential as a form of social control.

Football and the Political Significance of Style

Football was originally introduced to Brazil, Argentina and Uruguay by the English at the end of the nineteenth century. While Britain was still the major imperial power in the world, the British not only invested capital in mining, banks, commerce, telegraph and railway networks; they also created, along with cricket grounds and squash courts, the first football clubs of Latin America. During this early phase of its history in Latin America, football was an elite sport, played on impeccable lawns by amateurs whose conspicuous use of English terms such as 'full-back', 'inside-right' and 'I'm sorry' when a player was hurt, distinguished them as 'gentlemen'.[222]

Gradually the sport was taken up by the popular classes in Brazil as in other Latin American countries, above all by the semi- and unemployed former slaves and rural migrants who populated the streets of Rio and São Paulo. It required little equipment and could be played on empty plots cleared by the demolition of Rio's colonial architecture to allow space for government buildings, cafés, offices, cinemas and automobiles. At the same time, successive strikes and urban riots against the expulsion of the poor from the city centre, led by immigrant anarchists and agile capoeiras, prompted the authorities and factory owners to construct football grounds. The practice of an energetic and disciplined sport, it was thought, would harness to more constructive purposes the energies of the unruly people living in dangerous promiscuity on the streets and emerging shanty towns. Gradually, as the sport became popular it also became professionalized – few could afford to play as amateurs.

In this process of popularization in which blacks and mulattoes formed the ranks of the best players, football changed in style. In contrast to the earlier emphasis on discipline and technique, the new style, identified by Gilberto Freyre as 'Dionysian', placed the emphasis on the element of play, on improvisation, aggressive daring, agility and elegance.[223] While Freyre may regard this 'Dionysian' style of play as a product of Brazil's racially mixed civilization, it is suggested that in fact it reflects a complex of attitudes learnt in the practice of survival by the popular classes and sedimented in the language of the body. As was seen in our discussion of the samba-malandro, the development of capitalism in Brazil entailed the formation of a black subculture whose response to the harsh reality of discrimination and exploitation led to a rejection of the work ethic and to a counter-cultural idealization of idleness and of the body as a source of pleasure rather than as an instrument of work. Contained within the popular imaginary is the memory of the art of surviving on the margins of the established order and achieving success through qualities associated with the picaresque trickster: astuteness, intuition and duplicity, the capacity to deal with an insecure and ambiguous reality, and confounding agility in outwitting opponents.

This can be clearly illustrated by one of the many anecdotal accounts of Mane Garrincha's style of play. During a game in Costa Rica, Garrincha dribbled past his opponents. As he arrived in front of the goal he pretended to shoot, but instead in an ironical gesture he dribbled around the goalkeeper. Finally he shot the ball through the goalie's legs. However, as the ball entered the net, the final whistle was blown and Garrincha's shot was disqualified. When his exasperated colleagues asked why he had not scored earlier, he replied: 'Well, the goalie didn't open his legs earlier!' This incident reveals not only Garrincha's mastery of the art of the trickster, but also a gratuitous pleasure in the perfect shot for its own sake – in itself more important than victory or compliance with the rules of the game.

Characterized in the late 1940s by an identifiable national style and disseminated beyond local and regional boundaries through inter- and intra-city games, Brazilian football became a vehicle through which class, ethnic and neighbourhood allegiances were articulated, while also integrating them within a broader emergent national identity. Radio and the press contributed to this process by promulgating shared images and a new form of knowledge without connotations of class privilege. Like samba schools, football clubs bear the name of the area in which they are located; both constitute voluntary organizations offering a degree of grassroots democracy not otherwise possible in a highly unequal and hierarchical society in which the state and political parties have only limited legitimacy. As such they could be considered one of the few organizations in which a popular sociality, popular aspirations and experience acquire form. However, it is precisely for this reason that they become important for the achievement of political hegemony. This is clearly evident if we consider the relationship between the state and football at two different moments in Brazilian history.

In 1950 the populist leader Getúlio Vargas returned to power with a programme based on state-led industrialization, nationalism and labourism. The programme entailed considerable popular mobilization and this was reflected in government promotion of football: regional federations were created, and the Pacaembú stadium in São Paulo and the Maracaña in Rio, the world's largest stadium, were constructed. Getulio, whose popularity as 'father of the poor' was rivalled only by that of the black player Leonidas da Silva (the 'Black Diamond'), had a preference for addressing 'the people' in football stadiums, where in 1954 shortly before his suicide, he declared to them: 'Today you are with the government. Tomorrow you will be the government.'[224]

The period of populist democracy which ended in 1964 with the right-wing military coup is generally regarded as the high-point of Brazilian football. The promotion of popular culture as the basis of national identity facilitated the transformation of football into a ritual in which the new social relations of a developing nation with popular – although limited and controlled – participation are dramatized. Notwithstanding this, football players, elevated to the status of national heroes, have suffered considerable exploitation. Having interrupted their previous activity, they frequently find themselves poor and unemployed at the age of thirty, with no pension rights or insurance against illness.[225] Fausto, the Black Marvel of the 1930s, and Garrincha in the 1960s died in poverty. Pelé is one of the few to have escaped this fate.

In Argentina, where football had to some extent a parallel history, the national-labourist period under Perón witnessed the defeat of England by the Argentine team; this is often referred to as the day on which not only the railways but also football was nationalized. In contrast to Brazil, however, the commercialization of football here led to the formation of a trade union of football players and to strikes in the 1940s protesting against the exploitation of players as cheap commodities.

The second important moment in the relations between football and the state occurred in the 1970s during the most repressive period of the military government. Encapsulated in the motto 'security and development', the model of development adopted by the military regime was based on accelerated economic growth through the importing of foreign capital in the form of technology and loans and drastic cuts in salaries. This was underpinned by a legal and political framework which entailed the virtual abolition of civil liberties, the suppression of trade unions and most political parties, and the torture and persecution of dissenters.

The 1970 victory of the Brazilian team in the World Cup contest for the third time was used by the government to legitimate its version of nationalism and development. When the triumphant Brazilian team returned from Mexico, it was personally received by President Médici, and there were special Carnival celebrations. The team anthem 'Pra Frente Brazil' ('Forward Brazil') became a theme song of the regime and was played on radio, television and by army bands. It conveyed the message that, as in football, Brazil was progressing ineluctably towards modernity, fulfilling its promise of becoming a major world power.[226]

Nevertheless, despite the success of the Brazilian team, the military regime considered it necessary to 'modernize' football as well. This entailed appointing a military official as head of the Brazilian Confederation of Sports with the responsibility of developing a style of play based on discipline, technique and training. Since then Brazilian football is said to have deteriorated while also becoming predominantly 'white' again.

Reflecting on these two moments in the relationship between football and the state, one is inevitably led to the conclusion that the main function of this form of popular culture has been to promote social integration, and to further the hegemonic interests of the government in power and the respective model of development it sought to actualize. In his article 'Sócrates, Corinthians and Questions of Democracy and Citizenship', Matthew Shirts offers a valuable and more complex analysis.[227] In 1982, during the first years of political liberalization which would eventually lead to a return to civilian government, the competition for the presidency within the Corinthians football club in São Paulo was won by the 'Corinthians Democracy Movement'. This movement not only sought to replace the authoritarian and personalist organization of the club with greater fan and player participation, but also to reinstate the pre-military style of play defined by Sócrates, a Corinthian and international football star, as a struggle 'for freedom, for respect of human beings, for equality' as well as for the preservation of the 'ludic, joyous and pleasurable nature of the activity'.[228] In 1984, the movement transcended the boundaries of the club, organizing fans to rally in favour of free elections. In this instance football had clearly mobilized counter-hegemonic forces. As Shirts points out, this mobilization was organized around a matrix of popular cultural identity, as it manifested itself in a given style of play. This cultural struggle over style, he argues, reflects a much deeper rift in Brazilian society between the state and civil society, whereby the samba schools and football clubs articulate a more genuine although 'unofficial' citizenship than the formal institutions modelled on European and United States paradigms. And in crucial moments, such as the early 1980s when the military regime was suffering a severe crisis of legitimacy, popular cultural organizations can potentially become vehicles for the legitimation of this 'unofficial citizenship' and of a political culture which connects the serious and universalistic values of freedom and equality with the particular identity-forming aesthetic, with the celebratory and irreverent elements of popular culture.

The clash between popular and dominant styles was also manifested in the events surrounding the death of Tancredo Neves. On the day Neves, the first civilian president after twenty-one years of military dictatorship, was supposed to assume the presidency, he fell seriously ill. He was transported in a critical state to a hospital in São Paulo where he spent several weeks on the brink of death while the nation agonized over its future and Tancredo was transformed into an icon of hope by the popular classes. Festive musical vigils as well as religious ceremonies were held in front of the hospital and promises to God and various saints were offered in return for his recovery. The press, which presented itself as the voice of objectivity and rationality, interpreted this fusion of civic mobilization, popular religiosity and festivity as another unfortunate manifestation of 'archaic' Brazil rather than the modernity the leading political parties were promising.[229]

The state's view of its own people as an unruly mass in need of 'modernization' is reminiscent of the nineteenth-century positivist obsession with imposing order and progress – with 'civilizing' the 'barbaric' religious fanatics of Canudos. In this sense it could be argued that Socrates's version of a football rooted in popular tradition and the military's attempt to subordinate it to a systematizing rationality, Neves's death and the attitude of the press express a broader trend in the relations between the state and popular culture.

Notes

1. The claim to represent an alternative civilization would find its nearest comparison in the Maya culture of Mesoamerica.

2. The proposition that the Great Rebellion enshrined an alternative political vision and project is not uncontroversial. For some recent discussion, see Steve Stern, ed., *Resistance, Rebellion and Consciousness in the Andean Peasant World, 18th to 20th Centuries*, Madison 1987, and Jan Szeminski, *La utopía tupamarista*, Lima 1983.

3. La Habana 1986. Flores, among others, has seen a connection between Andean utopianism and the contemporary phenomenon of the Sendero Luminoso (Shining Path) guerrilla movement.

4. Louis Baudin, *L'Empire socialiste des Inka*, Paris 1928.

5. Inca Garcilaso de la Vega, *Royal Commentaries of the Incas and General History of Peru*, Austin 1966.

6. We are indebted to Olivia Harris for this point. For an example of Indian politics, see the periodical *Pueblo Indio* (Lima).

7. Olivia Harris, 'De la fin du monde: notes depuis le Nord-Potosí,' *Cahiers des Amériques Latines*, 1987, p. 101.

8. See José María Arguedas, *Los ríos profundos*, Buenos Aires 1958, pp. 62–4.

9. See Walter Ong, *Orality and Literacy*, London 1982, and R.T. Zuidema, *The Ceque System of Cusco*, Leiden 1964.

10. Rosaleen Howard-Malverde, personal communication.

11. There is an important debate about the extent to which the *quipu*, a complicated system of knotted strings, was able to convey information in the manner of a script.

12. See Rolena Adorno, ed., *From Oral to Written Expression: Native Andean Chronicles of the Early Colonial Period*, New York 1982.

13. Tristan Platt, 'The Andean Soldiers of Christ. Confraternity Organisation, the Mass of the Sun and Regenerative Warfare in Rural Potosí (18th–20th Centuries)', *Journal de la Société des Américanistes*, LXIII, pp. 156, 167, 173.

14. Platt, pp. 169, 172–3; Harris, p. 187.

15. Platt, p. 169.

16. Edmundo Bendezú, *La literatura quechua*, Caracas 1980, pp. 284–5.

17. Harris, *passim*; Platt, pp. 171–3.

18. T. Bouysse-Cassagne and Olivia Harris, 'Pacha: en torno al pensamiento aymara', in *Tres reflexiones sobre el pensamiento andino*, La Paz 1987.

19. Henrique Urbano, 'Discurso mítico y discurso utópico en los Andes', *Allpanchis*, X, pp. 3–14.

20. See Harris, p. 111 and Platt p. 172.

21. Nathan Wachtel, *The Vision of the Vanquished*, Hassocks 1977, p. 35.

22. Ibid., pp. 36–7.

23. See John Hemming, *The Conquest of the Incas*, Harmondsworth 1983, pp. 317–32.

24. A. Flores Galindo, *Buscando un Inca: identidad y utopía en los Andes*, La Habana 1986, pp. 74–81.

25. Ibid., p. 294.

26. We are grateful to Yanet Orós, Rosaleen Howard-Malverde and Penny Harvey for help with transcription and translation.

27. See Thomas Turino, 'Somos el Perú [We Are Peru]: "Cumbia Andina" and the Children of Andean Migrants in Lima', *Studies in Latin American Popular Culture*, Vol. 9, pp. 15–37.

28. José María Arguedas, 'La soledad cósmica en la poesía quechua', *Idea*, Nos. 48–9, pp. 1–2.

29. C. Lévi-Strauss, *The Savage Mind*, London 1966, Chapter 1 and p. 268.

30. 'Vicuñitay waylla ichu', a *huayno* widely known in the Cusco region, has been recorded by the Conjunto Condemayta de Acomayo.

31. José María Arguedas, 'Oda al jet', *Obras completas*, Vol. V, Lima 1983, p. 243.

32. Harris, p. 112.

33. We have drawn here on a talk given by Henry Stobart at the Institute of Latin American Studies, London, 16 January 1989, and on Peter Gose, *Work, Class and Culture in Huaquirca, a Village in the Southern Peruvian Andes*, PhD Thesis, London School of Economics 1986.

34. See Arguedas, *Obras completas*, Vol. II, pp. 11–45.

35. Harris, pp. 110–11.

36. Platt, p. 143 and passim.

37. See Gose, p. 29; J. Nash, *We Eat the Mines and the Mines Eat Us*, New York 1979, and T. Platt, 'Conciencia andina y conciencia proletaria', *Revista Latinoamericana de Historia Económica y Social*, II, pp. 47–73.

38. Platt, 'Conciencia andina y conciencia proletaria', pp. 57, 59.

39. P. Gose, 'Sacrifice and the Commodity Form in the Andes', *MAN*, vol. 21, no. 2, pp. 296–310.

40. Bouysse-Cassagne and Harris, p. 49.

41. Mexico 1982.

42. García Canclini, p. 102.

43. Ibid., pp. 93-4.

44. We are grateful to Peter Gow for this point.

45. García Canclini, p. 168; see also Néstor García Canclini, 'Culture and Power, the State of Research', *Media, Culture and Society*, 10, pp. 489-90. Laredo is in Texas.

46. García Canclini, *Las culturas populares*, p. 172.

47. José María Arguedas, 'Notas elementales sobre el arte popular religioso y la cultura mestiza de Huamanga', in *Formación de una cultura nacional indoamericana*, Mexico 1975.

48. Mirko Lauer, *Crítica de la artesanía*, Lima 1982, p. 150.

49. Ibid., p. 154.

50. We are grateful to Allen Fisher for this suggestion.

51. See Carmen Bernand and Serge Gruzinski, *De l'idolatrie: Une archéologie des sciences religieuses*, Paris 1988.

52. Nathan Wachtel, *The Vision of the Vanquished*, Hassocks 1977, pp. 154, 260. Our translation.

53. See H.E. Hinds, ed., *Handbook of Latin American Popular Culture*, Westport 1985, p. 52.

54. G. Giménez, *Cultura popular y religión en el Anahuac*, Mexico 1978, p. 201.

55. See Octavio Paz, *El laberinto de la soledad*, Mexico 1950, Chapter 3, and García Canclini, *Las culturas populares*, pp. 78-9.

56. See Carlos Fuentes, *La región más transparente* (1958) and *Cambio de piel* (1967).

57. Laurette Séjourné, *Pensamiento y religión en el México antiguo*, Mexico 1957.

58. Giménez, p. 49.

59. Ibid., pp. 149, 73.

60. J. Ingham, *Mary, Michael and Lucifer: Folk Catholicism in Central Mexico*, Austin 1986, p. 8.

61. Ibid., pp. 9, 48, 180, 192-3.

62. L. Margolies, 'José Gregorio Hernández: the Historical Development of a Venezuelan Popular Saint', *Studies in Latin American Popular Culture*, No. 3, p. 32.

63. Ibid., pp. 33, 39.

64. Dawn Ades, *Art in Latin America*, London 1989, p. 293.

65. Michael Taussig, *The Devil and Commodity Fetishism in Latin America*, North Carolina 1980, p. 92.

66. Ibid., pp. 94-95, 101.

67. Ibid., p. 139.

68. Lauer, p. 155.

69. García Canclini, *Las culturas populares*, p. 160.

70. Eunice Durham, *A caminho da cidade*, São Paulo, 1973. See also Antonio Candido, *Os parceiros do Rio Bonito*, São Paulo 1987.

71. In the shanty towns on the outskirts of the cities, inhabited mainly by dispossessed peasants and rural workers, the *mutirão* is one of the main forms of cooperation used by migrants in order to provide services lacking in the community.

72. Durham, pp. 75-80.

73. Maria Isaura Pereira de Queiroz, *O campesinato brasileiro*, Petropolis 1973, p. 91.

74. Ibid., p. 86.

75. Ibid., p. 84.

76. See Eric Hobsbawm, *Primitive Rebels*, Manchester 1971; Maria Isaura Pereira de Queiroz, *La guerre sainte au Bresil*, São Paulo 1957 and *Mouvements messianiques et développement économique au Brésil* in Archives de Sociologie des Religions, 8 (16), 109-21.

77. See Luis da Camara Cascudo, *Dicionário do folclore brasileiro*, Rio de Janeiro 1969.

78. Mário de Andrade, *Danças dramáticas do Brasil*, São Paulo n.d.

79. Edison Carneiro, *Folguedos tradicionais*, Rio de Janeiro 1982, pp. 129–49.

80. De Andrade, pp. 1–56.

81. Maria Isaura Pereira de Queiroz, 'O Bumba-meu-Boi, manifestação de teatro popular' in *O campesinato brasileiro*.

82. De Andrade, p. 22.

83. Manuel Correia de Andrade, *A terra e o homem no nordeste*, Rio de Janeiro 1973.

84. Marlise Meyer, 'Le merveilleux dans une forme de théatre brésilien: le "Bumba-meu-Boi"' in *Revue de Théatre*, 1963 pp. 94–101.

85. See Hermilio Borba Filho, *Espectáculos populares do nordeste*, São Paulo 1966.

86. Quoted in Marlise Meyer, p. 97.

87. See Hermilio Borba Filho.

88. Mikhail Bakhtin, *Rabelais and His World*, translated by Helene Isnolsky, Bloomington 1984, p. 11.

89. Eduardo Diathay Bezerra de Menezes, 'Para uma leitura sociológica da literatura de cordel' in *Revista de Ciencias Sociais*, Vol III, Nos. 1 & 2, 1977.

90. Mark Curran, *A literatura de cordel*, Recife 1973; Sebastião Nunes Batista, *Antologia da literatura de cordel*, Fortaleza 1977.

91. See Ruth Terra *Memórias de luta: literatura de folhetos no nordeste (1893–1930)*, São Paulo 1983.

92. Rui Facó, *Cangaceiros e fanáticos*, p. 88.

93. 'Dear reader, I ask you/to read with care/This book until the end/great will be your satisfaction/if you want to know something/of the life of Lampião.' João de Barros, *Lampião e Maria Bonita no Paraíso*, Ed. Luzeiro, São Paulo 1980.

94. See Antonio Augusto Arantes, *O trabalho e a fala*, São Paulo 1981.

95. See Joseph Maria Luyten, *A literatura de cordel em São Paulo*, São Paulo 1981.

96. Mauro William Barbosa de Almeida, 'Folhetos', unpublished Masters thesis, University of São Paulo.

97. See Mark Curran, *A literatura de cordel*, and Antonio Augusto Arantes, *O trabalho e a fala*.

98. See Gustavo Barroso, *Ao som da viola*, 1921, n.p., Franklin Maxado, *A literatura de cordel*, São Paulo, 1980; Sebastião Nunes Batista, *Poética popular do nordeste*, Rio de Janeiro, 1982.

99. Interview with poet João Cabeleira in São Paulo, 11 September 1988.

100. See for an excellent account of oral poetry, its history and contemporary relevance, Maria Inez Novaes Ayala, *No arranco do grito, aspectos da cantoria nordestina*, São Paulo 1988, p. 101.

101. For an account of the origins of these romances, see Luis da Camara Cascudo, *A literatura oral no Brasil*, Belo Horizonte 1984.

102. Translation from Alejo Carpentier, Preface to *El reino de este mundo*, Barcelona 1979.

103. For an interesting development of this theme, see Nicolau Sevcenko, 'Amor, desejo e punição em tradição popular', in Geruza Pires Correa, ed., *O obsceno, jornadas impertinentes*, São Paulo 1986.

104. 'Pois viu que o bebê é/felpudo com chifres e rabo/e rosna como cachorro/é audacioso e brabo/não tem mais o que saber/só pode ser o diabo', in João de Barros, *Bebê diabo apareceu em São Paulo*, São Paulo, n.d.

105. 'Se o pobre não plantasse/rico o que ia fazer/tem o dinheiro no bolso/mas não presta pra comer/o homem de pé no chão/é quem faz a produção/pra ver o Brasil crescer!'

106. For this idea see Mauro B. de Almeida, 'Folhetos'.

107. E aqueles bois bonitos/dos tempos de plantação/onde o povo alegre/plantando milho

e feijão/tomava muita cachaça/comia e fazia graça/sambava com devoção. E ainda o mutirão/lá na casa de farinha/se um arrancava mandioca/toda vizinhança vinha/a gente se encontraval/divertia e trabalhava/comida pra todos tinha'.

'Via em cada situação/o mêde e a precisão/a falta de confiança/e tambem de informação/ Olhava a realidade/e dizia: Na verdade/nunca houve abolição.' Julio Gomes Almeida in *A vida do nordestino que veio para São Paulo*, Edições Cordel, São Paulo, n.d.

108. Marilena Chauí, *Conformismo e resistência*, São Paulo 1987, pp. 57–9.

109. See Graciliano Ramos, *Viventes de Alagoas*, São Paulo 1970.

110. A *mote* given to the poet João Cabeleira playing in a square in the city centre of São Paulo on the day following a new devaluation of the currency to control inflation was: 'The three zeros of the *cruzado* [Brazilian currency at the time] are gone/to make life tough for the Brazilian ('Vai sair os tres zeros do cruzado/pra acabar de lascar o brasileiro.')

See also M.I. Novaes Ayala, *No arranco do grito*; Luis da Camara Cascudo, *Vaqueiros e cantadores*, São Paulo, 1984, pp. 115–119.

111. Mário de Andrade, 'Notas sobre o cantador nordestino' in *Mundo musical folha da manhã*, São Paulo 1944.

112. Interview with poet João Quindingues, São Paulo 15 October 1988.

113. M.I. Novaes Ayala, *No arranco do grito*, p. 21.

114. See, for an excellent account of this transformation, Mundicarmo M.R. Ferreti, *Zedantas e Luis Gonzaga*, Rio de Janeiro 1988.

115. Walter Benjamin, 'The Storyteller and Artisan Cultures' in *Critical Sociology*, London 1976.

116. 'By popular culture we generally do not mean *"cultura popular"*, which traditionally has been translated into English as folk culture, and also more recently has been rendered as that culture produced by the impoverished marginalized sectors of society.' *Studies in Latin American Popular Culture*, Vol. IX, p. vii.

117. Jesús Martín-Barbero, *De los medios a las mediaciones*, Barcelona 1987, pp. 95–7.

118. Ibid., pp. 143–9.

119. The term creole originally referred to Spaniards born in Latin America, and viewed as inferior by the colonial administration. See Chapter 1, pp. 22–3. *Criollismo*, from the end of the nineteenth century to the first decades of the twentieth, referred to a type of cultural nationalism.

120. See Adolfo Prieto, *El discurso criollista en la formación de la Argentina moderna*, Buenos Aires, 1988, Introduction and Chapter 3.

121. Beatriz Sarlo, *El imperio de los sentimientos*, Buenos Aires 1985, pp. 19, 21, 23.

122. Carlos Monsiváis, *Escenas de pudor y liviandad*, Mexico 1988, p. 41.

123. Ibid., p. 43.

124. Martín-Barbero, p. 183.

125. Jean Franco, *Plotting Women*, London 1989, p. 152.

126. Martín-Barbero, p. 181.

127. Carlos Monsiváis, 'Notas sobre la cultura mexicana en el siglo XX', in *Historia general de México*, Vol. IV, p. 446.

128. Isaac León and Ricardo Bedoya, 'Cultura popular y cultura masiva en el Mexico contemporáneo: conversaciones con Carlos Monsiváis', *Contratexto*, No. 3, July 1988, pp. 71–2.

129. T. Adorno and M. Horkheimer, *Dialectic of Enlightenment*, London 1973. See also T. Adorno, 'The Culture Industry Reconsidered', *New German Critique*, 6 (1975), pp. 12–19.

130. Renato Ortiz, *A moderna tradição brasileira*, São Paulo 1988.

131. Ortiz, pp. 118–9; see also pp. 8, 48–9, 51, 113–4, 128, 165.

132. Ortiz, pp. 199–207. For a discussion of Gramsci's idea of the national popular, see Chapter 3, below.

133. See Angel Qintero Rivera, 'La cimarronería como herencia y utopía (II): Bases populares de una cultura democrática alternativa en el Caribe'. (occasional paper), Centro de Investigaciones Sociales Universidad de Puerto Rico, 1984, for a more detailed exposition. On the history of salsa see César Miguel Rondón, *El libro de la salsa, crónica de la música del Caribe urbano*, Caracas 1980.

134. Quoted by Quintero Rivera, p. 21.

135. Ibid., p. 25.

136. For instance Max Hernández, in a talk at Brandeis University, 27 April 1988.

137. Marilena Chauí, *Conformismo e resistencia*, São Paulo 1986, p. 69.

138. See *The Children of Sánchez*, New York 1963, and Jean Franco, *Plotting Women*, pp. 159–63.

139. The famous devil-masks used in Puno, Peru, and Oruro, Bolivia are examples.

140. See Carlos Rodrigues Brandão, *Os deuses do povo*, São Paulo 1980.

141. Chauí, pp. 44–5.

142. José Jorge de Carvalho, 'O lugar da cultura tradicional na sociedade moderna', unpublished paper, p. 22.

143. Ibid., pp. 23–4.

144. Isaac León and Ricardo Bedoya, p. 153.

145. Ibid., p. 153.

146. See Marshall McLuhan, *Understanding Media: The Extensions of Man*, London 1964.

147. Ariel Dorfman and Armand Mattelart, *How to Read Donald Duck: Imperialist Ideology in the Disney Comic*, New York 1975.

148. 'Be Happy Because your Father Isn't Your Father: an Analysis of Colombian Telenovelas', *Journal of Popular Culture*, Vol. 14, No. 3, Winter 1980. pp. 476–85.

149. Martín-Barbero, p. 244.

150. Ibid., p. 245.

151. Ibid., p. 246. Carnivalesque here refers to Bakhtin's work.

152. Sarlo, p. 16.

153. Quoted in Martín-Barbero, p. 213.

154. See Carlos Monsiváis, '*Contratexto* pregunta a Carlos Monsiváis', *Contratexto*, No. 3, julio 1988, p. 149.

155. These were featured in the third of the BBC's *Made in Latin America* series, directed by Mike Dibb.

156. Monsiváis, '*Contratexto*', p. 149.

157. Sergio Zermeño, 'El fin del populismo mexicano', *Nexos*, No. 113, mayo 1987, p. 35.

158. BBC series *Made in Latin America*.

159. Monsiváis, '*Contratexto*', p. 149.

160. Cornelia Butler Flora, 'The fotonovela in America', *Studies in Latin American Popular Culture*, No. 1, 1982, pp. 15–26. See also Jane H. Hill, 'Murder in *Valled de lágrimas*', *Studies in Latin American Popular Culture*, No. 4, pp. 67–83, which studies the 'vernacular theories around which Mexicans organize their understandings of and reactions to violence'.

161. See Jean Franco, 'Plotting Women: Popular Narratives', in Bell Gale Chevigny, ed., *Reinventing the Americas*, Cambridge 1986, p. 259.

162. Ibid., p. 259.

163. Ibid., p. 261.

164. Ibid., p. 263.

165. Ibid., pp. 263–4.

166. Mark Szuchman's *Order, Family and Community in Buenos Aires 1810–1860*, Stanford 1988, is a pioneering work.

167. Néstor García Canclini, '¿Modernismo sin modernización?', unpublished paper, p. 34.

168. Rosa María Alfaro, 'Del periódico al parlante', *Materiales para la comunicación popular*, No. 1, nov. 1983, pp. 5, 7.

169. Alfaro, p. 10.

170. *Radio do Povo*, unpublished document from Centro de Comunicação e Educação Popular de São Miguel, São Paulo.

171. Interview with community leader of Vila Aparecida, 30 September 1989.

172. Ibid.

173. Interview with inhabitant of Vila Aparecida, 24 October 1989.

174. M. Chauí, *Conformismo e resistência*, pp. 31-5.

175. Ibid.

176. Historia de Villa El Salvador en 'Diálogo entre zorros', *La República*, 7 feb. 1986, p. 23. We are also grateful to Jaime Presentación, of the Taller de Comunicación Popular, for making available to us his account of the founding and development of Villa El Salvador. See also for the theory and practice of popular theatre in Latin America, Augusto Boal, *Theatre of the Oppressed*, London 1979.

177. Alfaro, pp. 210-11.

178. Ibid., p. 211.

179. María Cristina Mata et al., in Néstor García Canclini, ed., *Cultura transnacional y culturas populares*, Lima 1988, p. 238.

180. Ibid., p. 239.

181. Ibid., pp. 241-2.

182. Eugenio Tironi, 'La revuelta de los pobladores: integración social y democracia', *Nueva Sociedad*, No. 83, may-jun. 1986, p. 31.

183. Alberto Bastías and Leopoldo Benavides, 'La rebeldía primitiva de los hambrientos', *Nueva Sociedad*, No. 82, mar.-abr. 1986, p. 72.

184. Tironi, p. 30.

185. We are grateful to Catherine Boyle for this material.

186. Oscar Malca, 'Leuzemia y Delpueblo', *La República*, 10 nov 1984, p. 9.

187. 'Los Shapis', *El Diario*, 9 nov. 1985, p. 20.

188. See Mario Vargas Llosa, *Contra viento y marea*, Vol. II, Barcelona 1986, and Francisco Durand, 'Mario Vargas Llosa o la nueva derecha peruana', paper presented at the meeting of the Latin American Studies Association, Puerto Rico, September 1989.

189. Muniz Sodré, *Samba o dono do corpo*, Rio de Janeiro, 1929.

190. See Roger Bastide, *Estudos afro-brasileiros*, São Paulo 1973.

191. Roger Bastide, *As religiões africanas no Brasil*, São Paulo pp. 70-100.

192. See Edson Carneiro, *Candomblés da Bahia*, Bahia 1948; Artur Ramos, *O negro na civilização brasileira*, n.p. 1971.

193. Abdias do Nascimento, *O genocídio do negro brasileiro*, São Paulo 1978.

194. Bastide, *Estudos afro-brasileiros*.

195. Ibid., p. 372.

196. *Umbanda* is like *Candomblé* a cult of possession. It differs however quite considerably from *Candombé* in that the pantheon of deities in *Umbanda* also includes non-African spiritual beings; spirits of light (spirits of children and of old slaves) and of darkness. *Umbanda* is a fusion of African religion, Catholicism, the spiritism of Alain Kardec, and some Amerindian elements. *Umbanda* practises homoeopathy and faith-healing. *Umbandistas* have been concerned with grounding their religion in scientific principles in order to distinguish it from what they see as the 'superstitious' elements of *Candomblé*. Animal sacrifices are also forbidden. While in *Candomblé* there is no division between the spheres of good and evil, *Umbanda*'s religious

universe is characterized by a conflict between good and evil spirits in a manner much closer to Catholicism. See Renato Ortiz, 'Ogum and the Umbandista Religion' in *Africa's Ogum*, Bloomington, Indianapolis 1989.

197. Rita Segato, 'Inventando a natureza: família, sexo e gênero no Xangô do Recife', *Anuário Antropológico* 85, Rio de Janeiro 1986.

198. Bastide, *As religiões africanas no Brasil*, p. 236.

199. José Jorge de Carvalho and Rita Segato, *Los cultos de shangó en Recife*, Caracas 1987.

200. Gilberto Vasconelos and Matinas Suzuki Jr., 'A malandragem e a formação da música popular brasileira' in Boris Fausto, ed., *História geral da civilização brasileira. Tome III, O Brasil contemporâneo, Vol. 4, Economia e cultura (1930–1964)*, São Paulo 1984.

201. Antonio Candido, 'Dialética da malandragem' in *Revista de Estudos Brasileiros*, No. 8, São Paulo 1970.

202. Quoted in Vasconcelos and Suzuki, p. 511.

203. Muniz Sodré, p. 20.

204. Ari Aráujo, 'As Escolas de Samba' in *Expressões da cultura popular*, n.p. 1978.

205. See for an excellent analysis of samba, Claudia Mattos, *Acertei no milhar, samba e malandragem no tempo de Getúlio*, Rio de Janeiro 1982.

206. Muniz Sodré, p. 24.

207. Ibid., p. 25.

208. The *chorões* (a noun derived from the term *chorar* to cry) with their melancholic and languid music were contemporary inheritors of what in the seventeenth century was defined as 'music of the slave-quarters'. This music was played by small bands of black slaves on the plantations or in the cities where it was known as 'barber's music' since the musicians were freed slaves employed as barbers. José Ramos Tinhorão, *Pequena história da música popular brasileira*, São Paulo, 1986, p. 60.

209. See Roberto da Matta, *Carnavais, malandros e heróis*, Rio de Janeiro 1987.

210. See Eneida, *História do carnaval carioca*, Rio de Janeiro 1987.

211. See Artur Ramos, *O folclore negro no Brasil*, São Paulo 1958.

212. It is interesting to note that, due to the patrimonial structure of Brazilian society, political parties representing the interests of the popular classes were poorly developed, the organization of 'the people' thus being accomplished often by associations such as the *ranchos, cordões* and carnival associations.

213. M. Bakhtin, p. 11.

214. C. Matos, p. 49.

215. Ibid., pp. 65–7.

216. The first recorded samba by the composer Donga, one of the *sambistas* who frequented Tia Ciata's house, was called 'Pelo Telefone'. The lyrics in which the police inform the underworld of *malandros* where a gambling session is taking place, reveal clearly the interaction between the spheres of order and disorder.

217. C. Matos, p. 91.

218. For a detailed description of the samba schools and the rules governing the procession see M. Rector, 'The Code and Message of Carnival: Escolas de Samba' in T. Sebok, *Carnival!*, Berlin 1984; Sergio Cabral, *As escolas de samba*, Rio de Janeiro 1974; Luis Gardel, *As escolas de samba*, Rio de Janeiro 1967.

219. José Savio Leopoldi, *Escola de samba, ritual e sociedade*, Petropolis 1978, p. 63.

220. A. do Nascimento, *O genocídio*, p. 87.

221. José Jorge de Carvalho, 'Mestiçagem e segregação in *Humanidades*, 1988, Ano V, 17.

222. Joel Rufino dos Santos, *História política do futebol brasileiro*, São Paulo 1981, p. 13.

223. See Gilberto Freyre, Preface to Mario Filho, *O negro no futebol brasileiro*, n.p. 1964.

224. J.R. dos Santos, *História política do futebol brasileiro*, p. 60.

225. See Janet Lever, *Soccer Madness*, Chicago 1983.

226. Ibid.

227. Matthew Shirts, 'Socrates, Corinthians and Questions of Democracy and Citizenship' in Joseph L. Arbena, ed., *Sport and Society in Latin America*, Connecticut 1988.

228. Ibid., p. 700.

229. M. Mayer and M.L. Montes, *Redescobrindo o Brasil: a festa na política*, n.d.

PLATE 1   A seamstress works on a dress for a *Candomblé* ceremony. Christian and Afro-Brazilian religious objects share the home-made shrine set up beside the television.

PLATE 2   An initiation ritual in *Candomblé* dedicated to *Ogun*, a warrior god. His colours are gold and blue; his fierce personality is impersonated in the expression of a *Candomblé* follower.

PLATE 3   Bolivian schoolchildren performing under the direction of a
schoolteacher: an example of folklorization.

PLATE 4   The day of Yemanjá on 2 February is
celebrated with an offering of flowers, perfume, combs,
mirrors, champagne and soap cast into the sea.

PLATE 5   Religious images are brought to the High Mass in order to receive the benediction of Friar 'Damião', a contemporary 'prophet' in the northeast of Brazil.

PLATE 6   Offering to the saints and the *pachamama*, San Pedro de Buenavista, Northern Potosí, Bolivia.

PLATE 7   Theatre workshop in Villa El Salvador, presenting the
history of the shanty town.

PLATE 8   *Superbarrio*, also called *Superbloque*, acts in support of a
teachers' strike in Mexico city.

PLATE 9   A Chilean *arpillera* depicting mothers, wives and daughters of the 'disappeared' chaining themselves to the railings of the National Congress.

PLATE 10   Two *cantadores*, Azulão and João Cabeleira, in a poetic duel on the Largo São Bento in São Paulo.

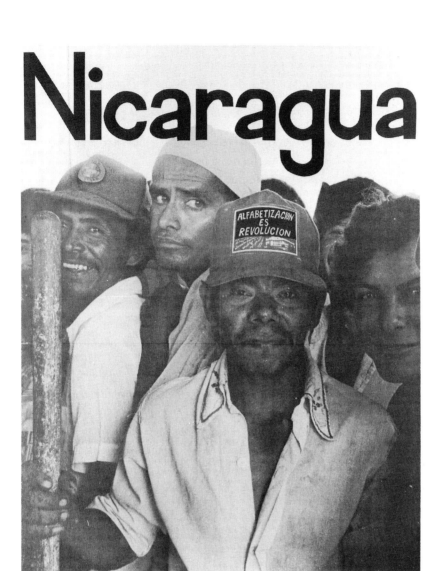

PLATE 11   A literacy poster, Nicaragua.

PLATE 12 Two different covers of the same *folheto*: 'Lampião and Maria Bonita in Paradise'.

PLATE 13 A *folheto* on two different heroes: the bandit Lampião, and Tancredo Neves, the first civilian president in Brazil after the end of the right-wing military dictatorship in 1985.

THREE

Popular Culture
and Politics

The Myth of the People

The main theme of this chapter is populism, as it has been the principal deployment of the idea of the people as controlling political power. With populism, the need to gain the loyalty of the masses becomes a programme which, at an imaginary level, places the masses – the people – at the centre of the nation and the state. Our aim is to look at ways in which *el pueblo/o povo* has been constructed discursively, using populism not as a strict analytical category but in order to refer broadly to the political use of the popular as a definition of national identity.[1]

Although the Latin American states were founded in the nineteenth century, populism is a twentieth-century phenomenon. In the nineteenth century, the rural and urban subaltern classes were a more powerful force than official history allows. Nevertheless this force took the form of pre-capitalist types of political organization, above all the paternalist institution of *caciquismo* and *coronelismo*. The Venezuelan *llaneros*, a rural population of cattle-herders under the leadership of Páez, whom Bolívar failed to incorporate within the liberal republic, are a pertinent example. Their dissension became a key factor in the breakup of La Gran Colombia into Venezuela, Colombia and Ecuador. It should also be pointed out, as a corrective to liberal versions of history, that many of the dictatorships deplored by liberals as 'barbarous' were more expressive of the culture and interests of rural and regional populations than were the liberal-democratic regimes modelled on those of European nation-states and expressing the interests of the coastal capital cities.[2] Populism arose in the early twentieth century, in a context of forms of mass mobilization based on the labouring class, which had begun to be built from the late nineteenth century. The problem generated by capitalism was how to discipline the mass workforce it had brought into being. When the traditional ruling oligarchies were unable to retain sufficient control over the new urban populations, new types of politics came into being.

These conditions are similar to those discussed by Gramsci in the *Prison Notebooks*, especially in 'The Modern Prince', where he considers the failure of the Italian bourgeoisie to obtain leadership over the masses in the process of forming the nation-state, and the consequences this had for twentieth-century politics in Italy, including fascism. The term he uses for the realization of such leadership is hegemony. It is a key concept for us because it includes culture as a main strategic factor in the gaining and maintenance of state power, in the sense that cultural allegiances are an essential factor of social power.[3] The first major debate in Latin America on the issue of hegemony took place in the late 1920s and laid the ground for what was to follow. It took place in Peru, in the context of the growing influence of Marxism on the labour movement and of competing paradigms for new mass political parties. Three main options were in play: Apra (an acronym for Alianza Popular Revolucionaria Americana – American Popular Revolutionary Alliance), a populist organization; the Peruvian Socialist Party, founded by José Carlos Mariátegui; and the Comintern, by the late 1920s seeking to establish Stalinist parties throughout Latin America.

The achievement, after a campaign of strikes and mobilizations, of the right to an eight-hour working day (1918), and an anti-clerical mass demonstration against the dedication of Peru, by President Leguía, to the Sacred Heart of Jesus (1923) showed the growing capacity of the working-class movement to challenge the state. A leading figure in the demonstration was Haya de la Torre, a young provincial intellectual from northern Peru, who also led a campaign for the foundation of popular universities, designed to intervene in the cultural life of the working class. Haya founded Apra in Mexico in 1924 as a continental organization against United States imperialism, in 'solidarity with all oppressed peoples and classes of the world'.[4] Apra ideology was 'the first organic theoretical "corpus" of the populist nationalism in Latin America'.[5] It was elaborated against the conceptions of the Communist Third International which saw the struggle against imperialism in Latin America as part of an international struggle against capitalism and in defence of the Soviet Revolution. Haya elaborated a theory of the independent historical needs of

Latin America, which he defined as achieving a sufficient degree of capitalist development to carry out the equivalent of the French Revolution, that is, a bourgeois revolution. This would depend on exploiting the mutual interests of Latin America and the USA ('we need the USA as much as they need us')[6] in such a way as to retain national control over US investment. During the election campaign Haya reassured the United States ambassador that Apra would not simply expropriate US interests. Haya obtained 35 per cent of the vote, insufficient to become president but enough to make Apra a major force in Peruvian politics, which it has continued to be until the regime of Alán García (1985–90), which almost certainly marks its demise as a party capable of bidding for power.

From its foundation Apra rejected the notion of the proletariat as a leading force for a social revolution, and based itself instead on an alliance led by the middle class. León Bieber puts it succinctly: 'a nationalist ideology . . . which sought to mould together the supposedly common interests of peasants, workers and middle classes under the hegemony of the latter'.[7] The iconography of one of Haya's election posters gives an idea of how the hegemony was supposed to work: reaching upwards from naked shoulders a mass of hands is shown, none higher than the cuff of Haya's left arm, which is held at waist height. His figure rises above them, depicted at double their scale, his face raised, with the eyes sighted upwards along the raised right arm which points upward and to the left. He sees (above and outside the frame) what the people cannot see. Below are the words 'Vote for Haya de la Torre', above to the right, 'Only Aprismo will save Peru!', and above the words is a pre-Columbian sun god symbol.[8] The invitation to religious sentiment and identification with the charismatic leader are clear enough. As Steve Stein comments, 'aware of the limited interest exhibited by the popular masses in his movement's ideology, Haya urged those who did not understand the doctrine to "feel" it'.[9] The political mechanisms involved making use of traditional forms of political clientelism going back to the colonial period, particularly those pertaining between the provincial aristocracy upon whom the local petty bourgeoisie and peasantry depended. Stein's critical comments bring out the way in which populism tends to take away the autonomy of those it uses: 'Mass political culture in Peru in 1931 may be defined as the politics of personal dependence. The political behaviour of . . . Apristas revealed that they held their own political competence, either as individuals or as a group, in low regard. . . . Real or imagined ties of personal dependence to these leaders were the major motivation in most cases for entering politics'; the result was 'the political massification of paternalism'.[10]

The criticism of Apra that it sought to control the masses rather than lead them to power is of little use unless placed inside the problem of what alternatives were available. In this connection, the writings of José Carlos Mariátegui, who founded the Peruvian Socialist Party in opposition to Apra, bring out the key issues. Mariátegui found himself increasingly in conflict with the Third International. The crux of his differences with the Comintern was his conviction that a socialist revolution was necessary and possible in Peru, without having to fulfil a previous bourgeois–capitalist stage. In practical terms, the dispute hinged above all on the role of the indigenous peasantry. The Comintern came up with the idea of 'Quechua and Aymara nations', to be granted separate national rights, a rigid repetition of the formula adopted for the Soviet Union. For Mariátegui, Peru itself was not yet a nation in any true sense of the word, and would not become so until the cultural and social divisions initiated by the Spanish Conquest were overcome. In this connection, he took very seriously the political ferment occurring among Indians in the 1920s, manifest in the rebellions mentioned in Chapter 2. He attended a Congress of the Indian Race and made contact with some of the leaders involved in the spate of rebellions. He also allied himself with the Indigenist groups in Cusco and Puno: these were provincial intellectuals who sought to translate on to a national scale the messianism expressed in the Indian uprisings. One of the key ideas was that of a neo-Inca state. Among these intellectuals was Luis Valcárcel, whose book *Tempestad en los Andes (Storm in the Andes)* spoke of the need for the Indian to find his Lenin. Mariátegui wrote a prologue to the book.

Mariátegui conceived the Indians as a proletariat in the Marxian sense, that is, as a social group whose self-liberation, achieved in alliance with the working class, would bring about the liberation of the whole society. This meant that the Andean peasantry were a revolutionary force, and not victims of feudalism to be delivered from bondage by a bourgeois revolution – a position shared by the Comintern (somewhat inconsistently with its formulae on the nationalities question) and Apra. The peasant's prime contribution to the transformation of Peru by socialism would come from the fact that the collectivism of the peasant community (*comunidad campesina*) was a form of already existing communism.[11]

Given that socialism vindicated ancient [*viejas*] national traditions, its task was to solve not only the problem of backwardness and poverty in Peru but also to achieve a vitally necessary settling of accounts with the Spanish Conquest, so that Peru would cease to be a defeated and frustrated society: defeated from the time of the implantation of colonialism, frustrated by the failure of the anticolonial projects after Independence. Socialism, by liberating us from these burdens of the past would be the indispensable tool for constructing the nation.[12]

These words are from Alberto Flores Galindo's outstanding book, *La agonía de Mariátegui*, which argues that Mariátegui's project remained essentially unfinished, given the defeat of his position by the Comintern and his early death in 1930. Mariátegui's originality lies in his conception of a socialist revolution growing out of the peculiarities of national culture. Flores puts the issues clearly: 'unlike the Apristas or the orthodox communists [who followed the Comintern], the problem [for Mariátegui] was not how to develop capitalism (and repeat the history of Europe in Latin America) but how to follow an autonomous path'.[13] Gramsci's idea of the national-popular needs introducing here, since it is vital to the discussion in hand. A 'national-popular collective will' is, as distinct from bourgeois nationalism, a necessary basis for the successful foundation of a modern socialist nation-state. It entails a bloc of social forces, cutting across the lines of class division.[14] In other words, it implies a process of hegemony. And the role played in it by intellectual leadership must be one in which an intelligentsia maintains 'its sentimental and historical links with its own people',[15] rather than merely importing the latest foreign ideas.

Mariátegui's willingness to confront the problem of how a new mass socialist politics can work makes his writing particularly interesting. The key point of transmission is between intellectuals and the masses, and it involves the more general and theoretical issue of the relationship between ideas and human beings. For Mariátegui, the socialist will to change needs the force of myth: 'bourgeois civilisation suffers from the lack of a myth, a faith, a hope';[16] traditional religions, including the positivist religion of progress, so important to the nineteenth-century bourgeoisie, have been overtaken by scepticism. At the same time the relativism of truth, as understood by modern philosophy, is insufficient to move the mass of human beings: a new myth is needed, since 'without a myth the existence of human beings has no historical meaning'. What are the characteristics of myth for Mariátegui? It fulfils a need for transcendence, a 'need for the infinite' ('*necesidad de infinito*'), and offers the 'deep self' ('*yo profundo*') an identity as subject. If the bourgeoisie lacks a myth, the proletariat has at its disposal the 'multitudinarious myth' of the social revolution.[17] This revolution is not a matter of 'science', of social engineering, but of 'faith, passion and will': these give revolutionaries their strength. Their force is a religious one, 'the force of Myth', but one where 'the religious motives have shifted from heaven to the earth'.

Mariátegui's thought was developed some forty years later by José María Arguedas, whose novel *Todas las sangres* (*All Bloods* 1964) shows a group of Andean Indians making use of modern industrial technology within their traditions of reciprocity and mutual aid as an alternative model to the distorted and oppressive forms of capitalist development imposed since the Second World War. The Indians do not need to be controlled by social engineering of the Fordist type; they are able to bring about a more creative intervention, in which the mobilizing resources of traditional Andean religion are transferred 'from heaven to the earth'. At the time of its publication, the novel received very negative criticism from left sociologists, who claimed it was not an accurate reflection of the peasantry.[18] At issue here is the Left's tendency to consider itself as the bearer of enlightenment, without understanding Andean thought, a problem which goes back to the failure of liberal and then socialist intellectuals in Peru to achieve a genuine national-popular programme.

A major difficulty needs to be confronted: not all the terms defining myth as conversion of popular will into political force exclude fascism. The difficulty relates to the need to distinguish populism from the national-popular and fascist from socialist uses of popular culture. These issues are implicit in much of the discussion which follows and will be taken up more specifically in connection with Peronism. At one point in 'The Modern Prince', Gramsci writes of myth as 'a creation of concrete phantasy which acts on a dispersed and shattered people to arouse and organize its collective will',[19] a statement which might apply to fascism. Yet, a few pages later on, he sharpens his definition, arguing that when a myth has become incarnated in an individual person, it is not suitable for the long-term task of social transformation: 'it cannot have a long-term and organic character. It will in almost all cases be appropriate to restoration and reorganization.'[20] The crucial word here is 'organic', a term much used by Gramsci when writing of the need for close connection between the party, the intellectuals, ideas and the people. As a biological metaphor, the term itself covers mythically any gaps between theory and practice, part and whole, and would seem to be a case of that mystification of politics he elsewhere condemns. Nevertheless, the term clearly arises from Gramsci's own acknowledged need for a utopian mythical language, one which produces images of desired connections. Reactionary parties could of course be organic, so the question arises: what would be the difference between socialist and fascist uses of myth? One difference, according to Mariátegui, would be that fascism attempts to resuscitate past myths: in the case of Italian fascism, which he is referring to, mediaeval and archaic Catholic myths.[21] Socialism, in this sense, would be concerned with creating new myths of a utopian kind. Another distinction, of a different order, is brought out by Gramsci when arguing that a socialist hegemony gives a particular content to the idea of democracy: 'in the hegemonic system, there exists democracy between the "leading" group and the groups which are "led", in so far as the development of the economy and thus the legislation which expresses such development favour the (molecular) passage from the "led" groups to the "leading" group.'[22] While Apra played a crucial part in constructing 'the people' as a political force, its conception of politics remained based in clientelist and verticalist forms of organization, which made use of the colonial inheritance. Mariátegui's project, on the other hand, sought to realize the potential of existing forms of mutual aid and collective property among the Indians in order to break entirely with existing power structures. For this to be carried through, myth was needed as a utopian and unifying force. A final point should also be made: the capacity of myth to mobilize populations over long periods of time can also become a liability, an obstacle to re-evaluation and change.

Mexican Schoolgirls in Greek Togas

Resistance to change has certainly been a characteristic of the apparatus of Mexican populism. Haya de la Torre stated in the late 1920s that Peruvians needed 'our Mexican Revolution',[23] and there can be no doubt that Mexico has afforded the most stable and enduring model of populist cultural politics in Latin America. Here we can only highlight three main features of the consolidation of the Mexican state: the mechanisms of power in the political culture, the role of education in gaining the allegiance of the popular classes, and the notion of cultural identity in connection with its elaboration by intellectuals. First, however, some brief comments should be made on the military phase of the Revolution and on the rural revolt, known as the Cristero War, which took place over ten years later.

Murals, films and photography tend to present that phase of the Mexican Revolution which consisted in battles fought by peasant armies as an entry of the masses into history; this was the version fostered by the post-revolutionary state, which abrogated to itself revolutionary continuity. However, given that history entails interpretation by writing or image, the question must be asked: whose history is referred to? – in the sense of who recorded it and controlled its meanings. The broad answer would be that the meanings were controlled by the same groups who formed the leadership during the military phase of the Revolution; this consisted largely in 'the rural microbourgeoisie, *rancheros*, schoolteachers, pharmacists, lawyers and priests'. These people became the core of the future political class, organizing themselves 'in masonic lodges, in clubs, in military *casinos*, which were much more effective cells of sociability than all the trade unions, leagues and parties': this continued until Calles and Cárdenas created a state revolutionary party which absorbed this leadership.[24]

Before the state achieved that degree of consolidation, an episode occurred which when properly examined serves as a corrective to the fiction of revolutionary continuity. This was the Cristero War, in which some 90,000 combatants died in conflicts between the government and the peasantry. The issue was state secularization in opposition to traditional Catholicism, which constituted the framework through which peasants' rights and their world view were articulated. The war brought about the end of an autonomous rural culture – a necessary step for the unification of the nation. Jean Meyer writes that the historian 'must be mindful of the fact that he is involved with a popular culture whose lively traditions derived from the Middle Ages and the sixteenth century',[25] a useful reminder of the slowness of change in pre-capitalist popular culture. A novel by José Revueltas, *El luto humano* (*Human Grief* 1943), also uses the Cristero period as a critical historical touchstone. Here the war is described as arising from the struggle of the peasantry to be 'owners of something, of God, the Church, the stones, of something one had never owned, the earth, truth, light or who knows what magnificent and powerful thing'.[26] As an episode revealing the cost to a traditional rural population of the creation of a modern nation-state, the Cristero War may be compared with the Canudos rebellion in Brazil, referred to in Chapter 1. A further instance of the way in which the Mexican Revolution did not resolve the problems of the peasantry but imposed a new dominant order is the unfulfilled – or cynically manipulated – programme of land expropriation and redistribution by the state, an issue highlighted in the experiences of the peasant leader Zapata and which continues into present times.[27]

During the post-military phase of the Mexican Revolution, which for the party of government constitutes its legitimating referent, as opposed to the disorder of peasant armies wandering through the countryside, the peasantry now supplied an imagery of honest fruitful toilers, receiving education from the state and producing handicrafts and folk motifs within a new programme of national identity. An examination of the characteristics of the political culture in Mexico will help to elucidate the workings of this populist project.

The establishment of a party to represent the nation passed through various stages. In the 1920s, Calles founded the Partido Nacional Revolucionario as the party of the state. In the next decade, Cárdenas established the Partido de la Revolución Mexicana; it included peasant and worker 'sectors', with the result that it absorbed all the main popular organizations. The final version was the PRI (Partido Revolucionario Institucional), which is still in power, though possibly for the last time. Founded in 1946, the PRI reflected the pressures of the Cold War: it created a centralized and authoritarian state for the purpose of 'stable progress' – that is, of capital accumulation and the establishment of an industrial infrastructure with a minimum of social conflict.

There is no single answer to the question of how the party/state achieved forty years of relative stability, but a major feature of the successful formula was that it achieved the position of universal mediator of social conflicts and above all mediator of popular demands: a role which ranged from implementing to expressing to controlling them. One of the reasons why the PRI could always be the best mediator was that to become a member was to participate in a learning process, which produced good mediators, and good mediators achieved social success and power.[28] The tautology comes from the closed, self-reinforcing structure of the PRI and is part of the problem which has increasingly afflicted it in the past two decades. Mediation is also highly organized and classified according to family, alliance and profession and even includes a special group of hired mediators (coyotes). All of them 'fulfil old roles which come from the colonial period and which have been adapted to republican institutions'.[29] Thus on the one hand the led could become leaders, but on the other this took place within a particular closed structure. The problems generated by a party which monopolizes political life in this way include the weakening of any possible opposition parties, thus leaving a considerable part of the population, especially the marginalized and superexploited, without mediators.[30]

The universalism of the state includes, not surprisingly, the ideological sphere. Here 'the state presents itself as defender and intermediary of the ideals of the people': it interprets them and places them in the public arena, and this is done inside its wider role as 'depository of all national and human ideals'. 'The origin of this rhetoric', it has been suggested, 'is to be found perhaps in the long history of links between the middle classes and popular movements, and its origin can possibly be traced to life in the colonial period.'[31] The continuity with colonial structures relates also to the phenomenon of the colonial creole culture recorded by Lafaye (and discussed in Chapter 1), which constructed an intermediary synthesis between Spain and the Indian majority. And as for folk art, it could offer, as Salvador Novo declared in 1932, 'a heightened sense of racial identity and a national consciousness which we previously lacked'.[32]

It is widely agreed that the crisis of the PRI surfaced in 1968 with the massacre by government forces of students in Mexico City's Tlatelolco Square during the prelude to the Olympic Games: this marked the exit from consensus politics of important parts of the urban population. Since then, many popular struggles have become detached from PRI mediation, more pragmatic in their demands and directed towards solving the problems of everyday life. They have also become both de-ideologized and suspicious of pyramidal organization.[33] The phenomenon of *Superbarrio*, mentioned in Chapter 2, is an example. With the debt crisis and economic stagnation of the 1980s, the Mexican state has been deprived of one of its essential roles, that of redistribution, in that there is little to redistribute. This has dealt a body blow to the populist project and has been accompanied by growing separation between the economic sphere, increasingly dominated by neo-liberalism, and the political, where previously functional rhetoric cannot be replaced and becomes a dead mythology.

One of the keys to the PRI's hegemony was its use of education. To this day, primary schoolteachers who instil allegiance to the government and tell people who to vote for contribute to its success in the countryside. The possibilities of a new public education system were recognized in the 1920s, with the establishment of the Secretaría de Educación Pública. As Monsiváis puts it, with characteristic irony, the state in the 1920s recognizes that 'it is in its interest to encourage a *popular culture*, which will supply to those majorities of such undeniable physical presence (their brutal entry as armed men) elements of identity to confirm their belonging to the nation. The foundation of this popular culture designed by the state is elementary education.' Those who participate in the process learn that their own knowledge is 'insufficient, that theirs is not culture but popular culture'.[34]

The first stage of the new education programme began with José Vasconcelos, Secretary of Education from 1921 to 1924. The most innovative aspect of the new plan was the scheme for rural education, where ' "missionary" teachers ventured forth to study the needs and socioeconomic and cultural conditions of different areas'.[35] The scheme was paternalistic and based on the needs of the metropolis and of capitalist development. The assumption was made that peasants were isolated from the market economy, whereas their real situation was one of 'marginalized integration', as a source of cheap labour. This assumption, which probably derived from a nineteenth-century liberal view of the indigenous community as an obstacle to progress, reflects the Ministry of Education's goal of 'integration of the rural community as a productive unit within the nation'.[36]

The characteristics of the education programme were in line with Vasconcelos's own classicism and Europeanism. His teachers were to 'redeem' the masses through 'work, virtue and knowledge', values which were defined in terms of European civilization. He conceived artistic value in the same terms: in one of the cultural festivals he organized he had 'Mexican schoolgirls dressed in Greek togas dancing in the style of Isadora Duncan'.[37] His book *La raza cósmica* (*The Cosmic Race* 1925) claims the mixture of races in Latin America was producing a new and superior type of human being. As is usual in theories where race is substituted for culture, there is a hidden hierarchy, and the vision of integration depends on white creole strata for its accomplishment, while the touchstone of the civilized continues to be Europe.

However, despite the narrowness of these definitions of artistic value, Vasconcelos was responsible for giving state support to the Mexican muralist painters (Rivera, Siqueiros, Orozco), in whose work beauty is conceived not according to Vasconcelos's sublimatory and classical notions of beauty, but as a force to arouse mass social struggles. The fact that peasant and Indian figures were used by the muralists to represent the nation enraged the *gente decente*: middle-class students at first defaced the murals with graffiti. Over time, 'the functional role of mural painting has been to disseminate a common, national and secular culture'.[38] The creation of a stable repertory of national symbols was also an effect of the socialist education policies which were introduced under the presidency of Cárdenas in the 1930s. Here Vasconcelos's vision of Mexico achieving equality with European culture was replaced with an emphasis on anti-imperialism and social reform, and the conversion into national emblems of previously excluded referents such as indigenous culture and the heroism of Zapata.

Identity and National Identity

It is not possible to discuss the uses made of popular culture in the formation of the nation-state without examining the semantics of identity, a term whose meanings overlap with those of myth and are comparably diffuse. Intellectuals have been the foremost interpreters of national identity, an action which

populism has played a particular part in making possible. But first, the word
'identity', with its apparently transparent obviousness, should be located in a
critical and historical perspective. For this purpose, there are two more key
words to be placed alongside it: mirrors and masks. There is a short story
entitled '*O espelho*' ('The Mirror'), by the great nineteenth-century Brazilian
writer Machado de Assis, which explores the impact of transition from colony
to republic. A young man finds himself alone in a house in the country: the
slaves have escaped in the night and he loses any sense of having a self. Finally
he looks in a mirror and the figure he sees is vague, faded, diffuse: the outlines
decompose, the features are liquid and incomplete. He then starts to put on
his uniform – he is a lieutenant in the Republican National Guard – and the
image in the mirror restores his selfhood: 'it was me myself, the lieutenant'.[39]
His soul has returned to him: 'My soul which had gone away with the lady of
the house, and had fled and dispersed with the slaves; here it was reassembled
in the mirror.'[40] The moment of historical transition produces one of
ontological uncertainty, which is transcended when self is restored,
reterritorialized inside the republican uniform, the new repertoire of social
stereotypes. The story both opens up identity to analysis and places it
historically. The mirror becomes a projection of the social as a reflecting and
identifying surface. Historically, the act of self-recognition is placed at a time
when the fixed social positions of caste society are being replaced by the
fluidity and instability of a modern society – the story was written just before
the abolition of slavery and the declaration of the Republic. It is at this point,
the moment of individual identity, that a mirror becomes necessary.
However, the mirror can only offer images, not symbols. It is the uniform, an
icon of the state as order and of the nation as collectivity conferring identity,
that provides the stabilizing symbol, giving coherence and unity where there
was simply undefined individuality. Modern society both individualizes and
homogenizes.

The above interpretation is intended not as a model or formula but in order
to introduce some clarity into an issue that is often handled in an over-
simplified or over-complex way.[41] In particular, there is the problem of how
the 'I' becomes 'we' or 'us'. This is crucial not only to how dispersed or
divided populations can be made to experience themselves as members of a
collectivity known as the nation, but also to how intellectuals attain the
position of being able to articulate in the name of others this powerful,
identificatory 'we'. As Oscar Landi has stressed, all politics depends on
particular principles of individualization: rather than expressing pre-
constituted subjects, whether as individuals or classes, it actually plays a main

role in making human beings into subjects, into beings with an identity.

Let us examine, in this context, the language of Mexican intellectuals in relation to populism. A useful place to begin is the 1968 crisis, when the post-revolutionary consensus began openly to break up. As a result of the Tlatelolco massacre, Octavio Paz, the most important Mexican intellectual of the twentieth century, resigned his post as ambassador in India. However, despite this act of dissociation from the government, he continued, in the book which was a response to the events, to use the 'we' of national identity: 'What happened on the second of October 1968 was, simultaneously, the negation of what we have wanted to be since the Revolution and the affirmation of what we are from the Conquest and even before. . . . I scarcely need repeat that that other Mexico is not outside but inside us.' The Revolution can no longer be deployed as symbol of national unity. But national identity with its unifying effect (the 'we') is recuperated by Paz in terms of another layer, archaic and deeper: 'our subterranean and invisible history'.[42] The history of culture disappears into the perpetuation of a symbolic order which does not change and has no break in its continuity. Here a mythic discourse interprets the present as controlled by an unchanging past (expressed in the present tense): a different use of myth from the one Mariátegui had in mind. As a strategy for self-legitimation as representer of the nation, it is extremely common among twentieth-century intellectuals in Latin America. Populism makes this discourse possible insofar as the state which mediates the masses also supplies the intellectual's arena and status. In this connection, intellectuals in Mexico have prolonged the universally mediating role of the state: they can be seen as operating inside circuits of communication that prolong the political culture's production of specialized mediators.[43]

Paz's most influential book on Mexican identity, *El laberinto de la soledad* (*The Labyrinth of Solitude* 1950), assembles a definition of the Mexican character, supposedly valid for all Mexicans. In this assemblage two quite different types of language are woven together: on the one hand, there is a series of symbols going back to the Conquest and before which supply a language of origins; on the other, a modern rootlessness, expressed in the life of the *pachuco* (an earlier word for the *chicano*, the Mexican immigrant to the USA) who has at his disposal no essential identity but only a series of masks. The book thus offers both immobile archetypes and the unstable masks of a modern society, an opposition which reveals the dilemma of the intellectual as representer of national culture – given that change has to be stabilized into continuity, something that, since 1968, the PRI has been increasingly unable to do. As the Brazilian historian, Nicolau Sevcenko, has pointed out, intellectuals who exploit the populist position tend to use the past as a kind of bank which can always be drawn on, while at the same time offering themselves as prophets of the new. Their handling of the past in this way is helped by the fact that pre-capitalist rural culture tends to be relatively static over long periods of time, which facilitates making it look like an archetype.

For Roger Bartra, a member of a younger generation of Mexican intellectuals, metaphors of national character have become a prison that needs to be destroyed. In a recent book entitled *La jaula de la melancolía* (*The Cage of Melancholy* 1987), he criticizes the official national culture and its stabilizing mythology, stressing that popular culture plays no active part in the 'myth of national character'. Mexican character is in this sense 'a bundle of stereotypes codified by intellectuals but reproduced in the society and producing the mirage of a popular mass culture'.[44] These ideas have built up over time to become a self-perpetuating net in which both Mexicans and foreigners get tangled. Predominant among these ideas is the sentimentalism of the Mexican. What this image does, according to Bartra, is to cover over the cost of adjustment to modern urban life under capitalism, the destructiveness both of adaptation and of marginalization. Emotiveness and sentimentalism are supposed to protect the Mexican from 'the inhospitable world of modernity',[45] giving him a kind of permanent alibi. This is the wishful projection of intellectuals, not an accurate picture. Of course, such images include real aspects of actual behaviour, but give a distorting interpretation. The point can be illustrated by the imitation of popular speech used by the Mexican film comic Cantinflas, in his portrayal of the *pelado*, the stereotype of transition from rural to urban life. The effect of comically tangled speech Cantinflas produces takes away a key function of popular slang, which is to hold on to an awareness of the difference between the way things really are and the official version. Instead, he portrays the poorer strata of the cities as passive – and stupid – links in the machinery of political corruption, a machinery which can only function when oiled by bribery.[46]

Despite his critical attitude, Bartra offers very little actual investigation of popular culture. Like Paz, he makes connections between the Aztecs and the present, without considering the intervening history of how native cultures were affected by the dominant Spanish one. And he still resorts to the problematic inclusive 'us' which in populist discourse sustained fetishistically the programme of a single national culture.[47] Populism is still the main stance of intellectuals towards popular culture. In this context, Carlos Monsiváis may be taken as an example of someone who seeks to break with the language of populism. By refusing the unifying 'we' he refuses one of the central rules of the game. In its place, he puts the multiplicity of different meanings that lie within the terms popular culture and national culture, restoring the ethnic and class differences they have been used to obscure: '*popular culture* is, depending on who uses the term, the equivalent to the indigenous or the peasant, the synonym of forms of anti-capitalist resistance or the mechanical equivalent of the culture industry. The term ends up capriciously unifying ethnic, regional and class differences and inscribes itself in a political language'.[48] And instead of taking 'national culture' as an ideal unity, he exposes the actual uses of the term and shows that its contents are varied and often antagonistic, listing at least fourteen different possibilities.[49]

Monsiváis also subverts the immobile mythology of the PRI by drawing attention to the need to understand culture in Mexico as a historical process. Thus he introduces a crucial distinction when he points out that in the past two decades the state has abandoned 'national culture' and handed it over to the culture industry. At the same time, the popular urban masses have not passively taken on the national identity offered to them by the state or the culture industry: on the contrary, in the unstable world of urban survival, identity is something which is simultaneously affirmed, criticized and dissolved.[50] Finally, rather than interpret them, he documents the materials of popular urban culture as themselves valid interpretations of reality. In the same way, Elena Poniatowska's books are notable for their documentation of the lives of those who live at the margins and for respecting their own voices.[51]

There is a recurrent theme in Brazilian populism which links together its main points of tension. This is the idea that the evil is outside the nation, that if the influences of imperialism and the imitation of foreign ideas can be eradicated, then a genuine national culture could emerge. As the idea is very familiar in twentieth-century Latin America, it is important to look critically at how it functions and why it needs to be characterized as populist. In a theoretical sense, it is an example of the abstraction of one part of a more complex reality (the internationalization of political and economic relationships under imperialism) into a pseudo-autonomy (the nation as independent and original). However, this type of theoretical resolution is itself too abstract. In the first place, the idea of freeing the nation from external adulteration corresponds with a desire on the one hand and an ideology on the other. Second, this ideology has a particular internal and historical function within the society in question. As Roberto Schwarz has pointed out in his essay, 'Nacional por subtração' ('National by Subtraction'), there is a logic shared by both Right and Left, which consists in arriving at the genuinely national by 'the elimination of what is not native'; the residuum would then be the truly national, 'the authentic substance of the country', which amounts to a mythical purity and unity.[52] It is not that the emphasis on for example United States domination was not just, but that it was used for 'the mythification of the Brazilian community, as object of patriotic emotion and removed from the class analysis which would make it problematic'.[53] More specifically, populist nationalism, by emphasizing the imitation of the foreign as an evil whose remediation will produce an 'authentic' culture, obscures the inequalities within the internal social structure of the nation. Of historical relevance is the fact that the Brazilian bourgeoisie, who inherited the Enlightenment and liberalism, also inherited slavery, a social machinery of production which they had a vested interest in perpetuating, after its legal abolition, in whatever disguised forms were possible. Therefore to say that the problem is imitation is to obscure the 'organic' coexistence of liberal ideas with the prolongation of colonial society and culture. Schwarz's critical emphasis on the gaps and contradictions between populist nationalism as an ideology and actual cultural processes in a society which never came to terms with slavery, includes the crucial point that populists continue to inherit a social structure which they do not transform.

As a main component of state policies, populism in Brazil began with the setting up of the *'Estado Novo'* ('New State') under Getulio Vargas in the late 1930s and continued through a succession of regimes until the military coup of 1964. Vargas, known as 'the father of the poor', made the state the protagonist of trades union organization (the constitution of 1937 stipulated that only unions recognized by the Ministry of Labour were legal), so that rights were granted pre-emptively from above in order to prevent radicalization of the labour movement. Government sponsorship of unions was one of a set of policies designed to make the state, rather than any stratum of civil society, the site of hegemony. With this went a doctrine of social harmony, guaranteed by the state. And in this context, *o povo* (the people) became a central category in the language of Getulismo: on the one hand an alibi of identity between state and nation, on the other a way of referring to the condition of political availability of a large mass of urban population. As one critic has put it, it was not the people but 'the ghost of the people' which had entered Brazilian politics: simultaneously powerful and impotent, empty.[54] As Vargas said in a speech to workers during his presidential campaign: 'For the statesman, for the politician, your lesson of labourism – and I mean labourism in the best ideological sense – has the value of a social democracy, a harmonious reconciliation between individualism and socialism through the transcendence of both, in an original, fecund and typically Brazilian solution'.[55]

During the last ten years before the collapse of Brazilian populism in 1964, the debate about the nation and national identity was taken up systematically by the Instituto Superior de Estudos Brasileiros (Higher Institute of Brazilian Studies ISEB). For the ISEB, the central goal is defined as the achievement of nationhood, and underdevelopment is identified as a primary obstacle, since it involves being appropriated by the metropolitan countries, as opposed to a realization of the nation's own essence, defined as being-for-itself.[56] In this discourse, the nation transcends class differences, given that the conflict between periphery and metropolis is considered primordial. And 'the people' become all those groups, strata and classes engaged in the gigantic and progressive task of overcoming underdevelopment. The strategy here is to fuse an idea of personal identity with a notion of national identity as both already available (the true nation) and still to be achieved. The combining of two ideal coherences gives added traction to the language: on the one side, being-for-oneself, nation and true culture; on the other, being-for-others, anti-nation and reflex culture. By reflex culture was meant the 'transplanting' of European culture onto Brazilian 'soil', which of course calls for the foreign elements to be removed in order to return to purity, represented by 'the people'.

The term 'imitation', used as a criticism of the ruling elites' relationship with European culture is accurate on one level, but it has the disadvantage of carrying with it an ideological message: by explaining a divided society as the result of the imitation of the foreign it covers over the internal relations of power which perpetuate the division. The terms need to be reversed: instead of making the imitation of Europe the explanation of the lack of a common denominator between the ruling class and the popular masses, the 'copied' aspect of Brazilian culture must be accounted for as the result of 'brutal forms of inequality which exclude a minimal reciprocity . . . without which modern society was bound to appear artificial and "imported" '.[57] In other words, partial and distorted modernization, carried out for the benefit of a small ruling class, looks like a bad imitation of the 'advanced' countries. The lack of reciprocity, of a common denominator, indicates the bourgeoisie's failure to achieve hegemony, a gap which populism sought to fill with the rhetoric of an authentic national culture. At the same time the relationship between populist intellectuals and the true culture is made to seem organic, by contrast with the 'alienated' relationship between the ruling class and 'imported culture'. This has been the basic stance of populism throughout Latin America. Its beginnings can be traced to Haya de la Torre's complaint about 'imported ideologies' (for example Marxism), a stricture which carried considerable power until the 1980s when neo-liberalism, with its rejection of cultural nationalism, began to become the dominant political discourse.[58]

An extreme form of populist cultural politics can be seen in the Popular Cultural Centres (Centro Popular de Cultura – CPC) that operated in Brazil between 1962 and 1964. Instead of taking popular culture (for example, folklore) as something valuable to be preserved, they took it to be a force for political transformation, as the 'political action of the people'.[59] Here popular culture stops being the subaltern classes' conception of the world and becomes a political weapon to raise consciousness against the false culture of the dominant classes. For these purposes, it is intellectuals who bring culture to the masses, whose alienated culture is replaced by the authentic practice of the CPC.[60] A somewhat different conception was expressed in the Popular Culture Movements in the Northeast of Brazil (Movimento de Cultura Popular, Movimento Educação de Base), who argued against regarding the people as passive recipients of an already made truth. A decisive role was attributed to consciousness, subjectivity and experience in the process of overcoming underdevelopment; it entailed a form of *conscientização* (consciousness-raising), designed to develop the capacity to reclaim history as the active realization of 'man' as a 'creator of culture', and the privileged site for this was defined as popular culture. One of the ways in which such *conscientização* was to be achieved was through a nationwide adult literacy campaign using the revolutionary approach developed by the pedagogue Paulo Freire.[61] According to this method, learning to read and write also involves coming to a deeper structural understanding of social reality and the causes of oppression of which illiteracy is only one aspect. In conjunction with the inhabitants of a locality, a team of adult literacy teachers compile a list of words – generative words – connected with the essential social and economic dimensions of the learner's everyday life and expressing their 'existential situation'. Learning to read words such as *luta, sapato, pão, favela* (struggle, shoe, bread, shanty-town) is coupled with a discussion of the 'existential situation' embodied in the word and projected as an image together with the word on a screen; this is designed to lead learners to analyse their problems and come to see them as the product of a changeable social order.

The reasons why populism broke down in Brazil have to do with the increasing demands of workers and peasants and the strengthening of their organizations, together with the inability of the capitalists to make concessions. The state, for its part, was caught up in a conservative system of patronage, granting administrative favours in exchange for loyalty. In contrast, the regime brought in by military coup in 1964, and based on an alliance between the armed forces and national and transnational capital, immediately carried out a massive modernization programme. In the cultural sphere this took the form of the creation, under strict state control, of the vast culture industry to which we have referred in Chapter 2. The key concept for the authoritarian national security state was 'integration', a concept frequently used as a euphemism for violent incorporation.

'The Masses Do Not Think, They Feel'

The Left in Brazil, rather than creating an alternative to populism, had become involved in its methods and language. The aim was to gain the allegiance of the masses by alliance or infiltration into populist movements: 'in the majority of cases, however, they themselves became populists; they became entangled in the techniques, language and interpretations of populism'.[62] In Argentina, with Peronism, intellectuals at first kept a critical distance and it was not until the 1960s that Peronism appeared to be capable of transformation into a revolutionary alternative. Perón took power in the 1940s, the key date – in Peronism's version of its own history – being 17 October 1945. On that day there occurred a mass invasion of the Plaza de Mayo, symbolic centre of government and military power, demanding the liberty of Perón, at that time held prisoner by the armed forces. The invaders had come from the *cinturón industrial*, the workers' districts surrounding the genteel centre of town. In Peronist language they were the *descamisados* (literally, the ones without shirts), this renaming being a typical Peronist strategy of fabricating classless social identities. Peronist mythology re-elaborated the events of 1945, concealing the crucial fact that the invaders of the Plaza de Mayo were supported by the police and the army, and exaggerating the role of Perón's wife Eva in recuperating for the mass of workers their leader 'at the moment of definitive national liberation and of the triumph of all the aspirations for which they had fought for so many years'.[63] Two effects can be seen here: first, an attribution of autonomy to 'the people', concealing the role of army and police as actual supports of state power', and second, the use of Eva as mediatory figure between leader and masses. Both Perón and Eva become figures who were used to confer identity on the masses. The way this identity is constructed can be examined by considering the characteristics of Peronist language.

Two underlying discourses unite in the language of Peronism: a religious and a military. On the surface, however, an impression is given of a single vocabulary, uniting leader and led, unifying the nation. As Perón himself put it, 'the secret is to be penetrated and to penetrate, so that when one reaches the home of the people one is accompanied by, it is like being in one's own home. . . . Speaking the same language, we understand each other easily.'[64] It has been suggested that the leading edge of the Peronist cultural revolution was Perón's vocabulary, drawn from lower-middle and working-class speech but without any critical function.[65] Its actual function is laid bare in the many Peronist primary school texts, for instance the following: 'How easy it is to understand what general Perón says! Even children can understand when he speaks! . . . Because his words are for everybody: children, old people, poor and rich. They are words for the people!'[66] The most common icon of early Peronism was a shield (the *escudito*), which displays a pair of hands clasped diagonally, one above the other, recalling the vertical imagery used by Haya de la Torre: 'Why aren't the two hands at the same height?', a child asks a teenager in a schoolbook. 'Because one is trying to raise the other. It's as if you had fallen and I offered you my hand to help you get up.'[67] The phrases supplied for the first writing lessons are blatant: 'Perón loves us. He loves us all. That's why we all love him. Long live Perón!'[68] The Peronists' legitimation of popular culture was chauvinistic and included a 'rejection en bloc of anything foreign and an undifferentiated exaltation of the themes and language of the people, mixing both reactionary and progressive aspects'.[69] At the same time, the structure of Peronist language has to do with reconciling the vertical (hierarchy, social difference) with the notion of unity and mutuality. Its all-enveloping, all-penetrating aspect (for example, 'today is a Peronist day' or 'you can't be a good Argentinian without being a good Peronist') has a force which is both seductive and totalitarian. One of its key effects is the deployment of a full *nosotros* (we), the people, in opposition to an empty *ellos* (them) which refers to the anti-Peronists whom this discourse disqualifies and expels from the collective body of the nation.[70]

The political intentions that shape this language are exposed in statements addressed by Perón to party professionals. 'The people' is defined as 'an organized mass', the task being 'to convert an inorganic mass into an organic one'. The ability of leadership to control is at a premium: 'the mass goes where its leaders indicate and if not, it gets out of control, and God help me!' A notion of control at every point gets translated into Peronist sayings which have a proverbial, regulative function, such as 'From home to work and from work to home'. The relationship of leader to the masses is entirely hierarchical, like that of the brain to the muscles: 'the masses do not think, they feel'.[71] Saturated by these controls, the notion of a popular identity coheres in Perón himself. Perón is 'the first worker', or, in a poem published by the magazine *Mundo Peronista*, 'Perón is the Fatherland' for which the gaucho has given his life.[72] The masses are both subordinated and subsumed into the figure of the leader: domination and submission become popular.

It is not surprising to find Peronism reusing the mythology of the gaucho as the essence of the nation, including the land as expression of *argentinidad*. However, the telluric model of national identity did not prevent the Peronist government from urbanizing the pampas. As with other populist regimes, Peronism set out to stabilize forces unleashed by capitalist modernization. So although the cultural forms preferred by the subaltern classes, for example the tango, gained increased national presence, there was no attempt to effect the critical transformation of cultural habits. Sometimes weaknesses and defects caused by exploitation were consecrated, as in the slogan 'Shoes yes, books no'.

As indicated earlier, the other main principle of Peronist language was military. Perón was a serious student of military strategy and he brought this knowledge into his conception of politics. The leader pursued a single goal, victory – the key to which was the 'economy of forces'. The Peronist Party was organized in a hierarchy of commands, headed by the Single Command (*Comando Unico*). The 'organized forces of labour' constituted a 'pacific army' while the armed forces were 'part of the people, labouring for the people'.[73] The circular semantics confirm an interpenetration of state, politics and war which goes back in Europe to Machiavelli and has been taken up again in the twentieth century by Gramsci and Paul Virilio.[74]

The urgent question is what resources can be found within popular culture in Latin America for alternative modes of politics. Left Peronism in the 1960s and 1970s became part of an anti-imperialist, third-worldist discourse and offered to a new generation the vision of a nationalist revolution. The catastrophic outcome of Perón's return from exile (1973), followed by military government (1976–83) and the death of tens of thousands of young people, has stimulated a critique of the whole political culture of Peronism and especially of the Peronist Left. For Beatriz Sarlo, 'the foundation of a new democratic political culture on the left' is necessary,[75] which means overcoming the authoritarianism and militarism of the Left and their failure to acknowledge and foster cultural diversity. One of the most powerful critiques of Argentinian populism is offered in Josefina Ludmer's analysis of nineteenth- and early-twentieth-century gauchesque literature, which reveals the foundation of corporatist semantics in this earlier historical period, through the use of the body of the gaucho (of the subaltern classes) by the army as the basis for the use of the gaucho's voice as the voice of the fatherland.[76] The people become, tautologically, the voice of the nation/state (people = nation = people), effacing the differences between dominant and dominated.

Ernesto Laclau has argued that populism can be a feature of socialist as well as of non-socialist politics and that socialism is the highest form of populism. His argument is based on the notion that the popular is not specific to any type of politics and that ' "popular traditions" represent the ideological crystalliza-tion of resistance to oppression in general',[77] and can only be articulated politically in subordination to class ideologies. There are two main problems here. The popular is limited by Laclau to pre-capitalist cultures and can only become a political force in the national arena through being absorbed into strategies of class domination; this amounts to a pre-Gramscian position. At the same time, in Laclau's formulation, popular culture continues to be used for ideological purposes. What would be the alternative? The question is difficult to answer because of the scarcity of actually existing political experiences which break with the populist mould. It has been argued that one of the criteria must be that subaltern classes become 'subjects of historical action',[78] a process which includes breaking with the corporate identity (populist national identity, in the case of the present discussion) that has been placed upon them. That the popular classes should become subjects rather than objects of political action is one of the premises of national liberation movements, which we now turn to.

An Alternative Model of Development

It is not possible to understand the nature of the relationship between culture and politics in Central America and Cuba without considering the economic imperialism to which the region has been subject and which has been central in its historical formation. Of course, in many respects this condition has marked all the countries in the continent. In Central America and Cuba, however, special circumstances, in particular the overriding influence of the United States, have given this shared condition specific regional features.

Towards the end of the nineteenth century the economies of Nicaragua, Guatemala and El Salvador were restructured in order to satisfy the growing demand for coffee and bananas on the world market. Similarly in Cuba the export of a single crop, sugar – 'El Rey Azucar' – came to dominate the economy. This had various deleterious consequences for the autonomous development of the region. Reliance on a single crop was accompanied not only by a new dependency but also by a concentration of landownership and growing inequalities in wealth; this in turn led to social conflicts which would ultimately spark off the revolutions and civil wars that have characterized the region in the twentieth century. Indian and peasant lands were expropriated, releasing a mass of cheap labour to work on the vast coffee and sugar plantations, while the use of foreign capital to finance their expansion would transform the region into a virtual colony of the United States.

In Guatemala, the link between the United Fruit Company, owner of large tracts of banana lands, the Railways of Central America and the US-owned shipping companies which transported the produce, as well as other investments and loans, guaranteed United States control of its economy. By the mid nineteenth century, the United States had become the main consumer of Cuban sugar and US companies bought a sizeable proportion of the sugar plantations. In 1895, the struggle for independence from Spain, led by José Martí, revered in Cuba not only as one of its most original thinkers but also as the forerunner of Castro, led to even greater dependence on the United States. Anxious not to lose control of the Cuban economy, and on the pretext of defending its citizens after the explosion of a North American ship in Havana harbour, the United States declared war on Spain and militarily occupied Cuba. A few years later, Cuba was granted its independence, but with the proviso that it would comply with the Platt Amendment whereby the USA had 'the right to intervene for the preservation of Cuban independence, the protection of life, property and individual liberty'.[79]

In Nicaragua, the US government intervened on various occasions in the early part of this century. It supported a conservative revolt against the liberal President Zelaya, who sought to reduce North American control of the economy by granting concessions to national capital. When subsequently the liberals revolted against the conservative government, US Marines occupied Nicaragua and the conservatives granted the United States the right to construct a canal from the Atlantic to the Pacific Ocean.

Like José Martí, who fought to achieve Cuba's economic and political independence a few decades earlier, Augusto Cesar Sandino, a liberal officer in Nicaragua, organized a guerrilla force of miners, peasants, workers and Indians in order to expel US troops and, in his words, 'take the reins of political power to proceed with the organization of large cooperatives of Nicaraguan workers and peasants who will exploit our own natural resources for the benefit of the Nicaraguan family in general'.[80]

Sandino's thinking is an extraordinary eclectic synthesis of various influences. It is based partly on a form of anarchist communism acquired during his stay in post-revolutionary Mexico and partly on a theosophy of liberation grounded in freemasonry, the spiritualism of Alain Kardec and Zoroastrianism.[81] Characteristic of Sandino's thinking and subsequently of the FSLN, with significant repercussions for its concept of culture, was a belief not only in a fraternal society based on an economy managed by workers and peasants but in the revolution as a form of spiritual redemption or awakening to the 'Spirit of Light and Truth'.[82]

In contrast to the scientistic materialism of the Communist International, Sandino stressed that communism was a way of life and not merely a transformation of the mode of production, that it was necessary to forge links with the workers and peasantry by addressing their needs and hopes in their own language and religious symbolism. Sandino's patriotism – expressed in the FSLN motto 'Patria Libre o Morir' ('Free Country or Death') – included not only uncompromising defence of national honour as a 'sacred duty' and inviolable right, but also an awareness of the religious and cultural heterogeneity of the Nicaraguan people. Moreover, since defence of national sovereignty was an expression of the 'sacred right' of the weak to human dignity and justice, patriotism also comprised the struggle against poverty, exploitation and underdevelopment as well as the realization of Simón Bolívar's dream of unification of the Indo-Hispanic peoples.[83] Sandinista nationalism thus also contained a Pan-American and internationalist dimension, grounded in a particular conception of the marriage between the national and the popular. Finally, and crucial for an understanding of the role of culture under Sandinismo, is the emphasis Sandino – subsequently reinforced by Guevara and the Cuban Revolution – placed on the need to create a 'New Man' as the subject who would actualize the universal brotherhood of humanity.

In 1961, when the FSLN was created, Sandino's legacy was recovered and amalgamated with the New Marxism of the Cuban Revolution to form the basis of its revolutionary vision. José Martí, who Fidel claimed was the true intellectual author of his attack on the Moncada Barracks, prefigured and reinforced Sandino's anti-imperialist nationalism, and this in turn became the basis of the FSLN's argument that only a form of Marxism rooted in the experience and language of the people could have an authentically liberating function and become a hegemonic force in society. In line with Mariátegui's emphasis on the importance of popular myths in creating a revolutionary morality – in sustaining, to use Gramsci's formulation a 'concrete phantasy' of an alternative social order – the FSLN gave its support to the progressive Christianity of the Theology of Liberation. This in turn was part of a broader project of social transformation, to be achieved not only through changes in the economy, but through a cultural revolution which would lead to the formation of a new humanity. Such a transformation was only possible if the institutions of civil society – the school, the Church, the family, the media and political organizations – questioned the values of the pre-revolutionary dominant culture while simultaneously becoming vehicles for the recovery of the past as the patrimony of the popular classes. It is against this background that the Sandinistas' often repeated phrase that 'the revolution was the most important cultural event' makes sense.

While there was a marked populist element in Sandinismo, in that it was based on a broad alliance of classes and social groups, defined as 'the people' and brought together under the banner of Sandino's mythologized presence, it needs to be distinguished from Peronism and Getulism. The principal difference lies in the fact that, while in Argentina and Brazil the purpose of the process of popular mobilization was to obtain support for a capitalist path of development, in Nicaragua it institutionalized forms of political participation designed to ensure that development benefited primarily the popular classes. It is as an allusion to this difference that the statement by Tomás Borge – a member of the government directorate during the Sandinista Revolution – needs to be understood: 'Nicaragua has a mixed economy at the service of the workers . . . in other countries it is a mixed economy at the service of the bourgeoisie.'[84]

One of the hallmarks of this model of development lies in the fact that democratic participation is not restricted to guaranteeing civil and political rights but also involves the creation of egalitarian social and economic structures and the political education of 'the people'. Sergio Ramírez, writer and member of the Sandinista directorate, defined 'popular democracy' in the Nicaraguan context as a 'permanent dynamic' in which 'the people' participate in a variety of political and social tasks:

> the people who give their opinions and are listened to; the people who suggest, construct and direct, organize themselves, who attend to community, neighbourhood and national problems; a people who are active in the sovereignty and the defence of that sovereignty and also teach and give vaccinations; a daily democracy and not one that takes place every four years . . . for us democracy is not merely a formal model, but a continual process capable of giving the people that elect and participate in it the real possibility of transforming their living conditions, a democracy which establishes justice and ends exploitation.[85]

Popular democracy was manifested in a variety of ways. It entailed for example nationwide discussion of the constitution in town halls and the opportunity to directly question party members and government officials on official policy. It entailed the creation of a multiplicity of mass organizations: the Committees of Sandinista Defence (CDS), neighbourhood organizations responsible for distributing basic foods and representing citizens' needs to the state; the National Union of Farmers and Cattle Raisers and the Rural Workers' Association representing the peasantry and agricultural workers; the Luisa Amanda Espinosa Association of Nicaraguan Women representing the interests of both rural and urban women; and in the sphere of culture the Association of Cultural Workers.

Obviously it is necessary to distinguish between the aims of Sandinismo and their realization. It would be unrealistic to expect a political culture forged against the background of dictatorship, United States intervention, male supremacy and semi-feudal labour relations to evaporate in the new social and political context. The Sandinistas have, particularly since their defeat in the elections of 1990, been criticized for the vertical structure of the FSLN and for using the state for clientelistic purposes. However, despite these and other possible shortcomings, it should be stressed that the FSLN introduced a new and emancipatory model of democratic politics in Latin America which recognized the important role of culture in the formation of a new polity. It is against this that not only the FSLN but also future governments and parties will be judged.

In Sandinista thinking the Somoza decades were an era in which the collaboration of a sector of the local dominant classes with US imperialism not only governed the country through terror, but in doing so failed to generate an autonomous Nicaraguan identity and culture. In a more grotesque and openly brutal manner, the ruling Somoza elite shared with other fractions of the dominant classes in Latin America a contempt for 'the people' and the indigenous element of their *mestizo* culture.[86] Thus it could be argued that the Somoza regimes had maintained what the Brazilian pedagogue Paulo Freire termed 'the culture of silence', a condition of oppression wherein people are deprived of the ability to know, to express and to transform their lives. In this sense, the Sandinista project can be seen as an attempt to enable the people to have a 'voice', encompassing not only the expansion of education, a nationwide literacy campaign which includes political education, but a wide-ranging series of cultural activities and policies designed to promote the growth of a national-popular culture. Sergio Ramírez explains the cultural significance of the national liberation struggle: 'Once we lifted the Yankee stone which weighed Nicaragua down everything that was fundamental and authentic had to surface again, dances, songs, popular art and the country's true history. And we discover a history that is based on a continuous struggle against foreign intervention . . . our people are beginning to perceive their history, their traditions with a popular meaning . . . and we teach people to defend that history.'[87]

This process of liberation and the creation of a national-popular culture was to be achieved by a series of interconnected policies:

1. To give the people access to the products and means of cultural creation, enabling them not only to receive educational benefits but first and foremost to actualize themselves as subjects of cultural creation. In a speech to the Association of Nicaraguan Artisans, Daniel Ortega stated: 'If there is one piece of advice we would like to give artisans it is that they develop their imagination, their creativity, as best they see fit. It is a question of releasing everything which was oppressed and dammed up, assimilating what comes from outside the country, which allows us to grow and advance without any restrictions . . . for we will be on good terms with the Revolution to the extent that we are capable of being increasingly creative, of generating new forms and ideas, of making our imagination work continuously, of breaking with any and every dependent mentality.'[88]

2. Artists and intellectuals must not produce art for art's sake. At the first Assembly of Cultural Workers artists were exhorted to accomplish the difficult task of creating works which, without sacrificing aesthetic quality and experimentation, could be understood by the people and 'help them transform themselves'.[89] Indeed, for the poet and Minister of Culture Ernesto Cardenal, there was no contradiction between aesthetic value and political content; in his view 'every great artist is also revolutionary'.[90] The term revolutionary here seems to imply that both the content of artistic works and the institutional framework which make them possible, must be grounded in a revolutionary concept of culture as creative transformation of the self and the objective world.

3. A culture which is firmly grounded in the history and traditions of Nicaragua 'which reflects reality and is nourished by life' was not xenophobic but open to 'universal' art.[91] In this sense, the Nicaraguan Revolution hoped to accomplish one of the fundamental aims espoused by preceding modernist movements in Latin America, namely to contribute to international culture by the discovery and affirmation of local traditions, identities and symbolic forms previously silenced and marginalized by official culture.

The Sandinista concept of the role of culture in creating a historical force of transformation was reflected in the plethora of cultural institutions and projects that emerged, particularly during the years following the insurrection of 1979, before the country's energies had to be channelled into the war effort against the US-sponsored Contras.

Under the direction of Minister of Culture Cardenal, regional Centres of Popular Culture were erected as places in which the people were able to consult libraries and participate in poetry workshops and community theatre. A new Research Institute of Sandinista Studies was created to carry out research into Nicaraguan festivals and the role of folklore in the revolutionary process, and to keep a record of all individuals who had perished in the war. A mobile cinema, part of the Nicaraguan Institute of Cinema, brought films and documentaries to rural areas while the state-funded Association of Artisans was created in order to fuse aesthetic sensibility and utility and to encourage the development of an intermediate technology capable of substituting imported products.

One of the most important expressions of popular democracy and of the Sandinista cultural politics of creating a 'New Man' (and woman) was the 1980 adult literacy crusade carried out by the Ministry of Education headed by the Jesuit priest Fernando Cardenal. The literacy crusade could perhaps be seen as one of the most highly developed examples of the pedagogical character of the Sandinista Revolution. First, it involved the organization and training of a large mass of voluntary literacy teachers (180,000) recruited among professional teachers, factory workers, public employees and above all among students and women.[92] Second, it was complemented by the use of traditional Nicaraguan ballads containing revolutionary texts, designed to raise the people's awareness of their role as protagonists of a new society. During the revolutionary struggle the record 'Guitarra armada' by the brothers Mejia Godoy, taught revolutionaries how to fabricate explosives, while after the revolutionary triumph, their 'Convirtiendo la oscurana en claridad' urged teachers and learners alike to transform the darkness of oppression into the light of social justice through learning/teaching to read.[93]

The literacy crusade encompassed both urban and rural areas, including among its learners the army, the police and political prisoners, many of them former members of the National Guard. In the rural areas, in order not to inhibit food production and thus jeopardize economic recovery and development, the *brigadistas* worked on the land during the day alongside the peasantry. The literacy crusade thus took place not only outside the conventional institutional framework of the school – thus transcending the separation between the sphere of culture and society, between school and production, between learning and doing – but also involved society as a whole in an educational process of emancipation [Plate 11].[94] Moreover, becoming a literacy teacher also entailed becoming a learner: the teachers also had the task of recording the myths, legends, music, culinary traditions and oral history of their assigned region as well as compiling an archive of regional medicinal herbs and samples of its flora and fauna.[95] The unity between learning and doing was additionally emphasized by the use of Paulo Freire's literacy method discussed earlier. In Nicaragua, however, the literacy crusade set itself the difficult task of trying to combine the learners' open and critical discussion of their 'existential situation' with the use of a ready-made *cartilla* – an educational booklet with the history, development and consolidation of the Revolution in twenty-three lessons – on the assumption that the process of the learner's *concientización* would coincide with the Sandinista interpretation of the people's experience and history. While in Freire's original method the 'generative' words which constitute the themes of discussion and which the learners subsequently learn to read arise out of a given particular situation, in Nicaragua the generative word was taken from an already existing sentence. While this conflation between the people's experience and consciousness and Sandinista ideology appears impositional, it is necessary to take into consideration the fact that Sandino symbolized in the Nicaraguan context the attainment of the dignity of a free nation.

The overarching project of fomenting popular culture as a process of self-discovery, transformation and liberation through critical insight into past relationships of domination is clearly manifested in the cultural programme of the rural Enrique Peñã School. Members of a peasant community were invited by 'cultural promoters' of the 'Popular Investigation Workshops' to paint a large chart of their region including images of the flora and fauna, of themselves and their tools, as well as data on the past land-tenure system. This was accompanied by the written recording of the community's history from 1910 to the present, as recounted by various members, and was followed by a dramatic re-enactment of their daily suffering as landless peasants subjected to the foreman's demands (a role which the actors seemed thoroughly to enjoy). Through this form of re-enactment in which a collective history is externalized, the peasants gained distance from their historical experience; as a result it ceases to appear 'natural', creating in them an awareness that the social world is open to transformation through knowledge and action.

A further example of the emphasis on creativity in the Sandinista experiment were the *talleres de poesía* (poetry workshops) organized by the Ministry of Culture throughout the country and also amongst the army, the police force, the air force, the state secret police and Somocista prisoners. Originally the idea of creating poetry workshops, in which the people would learn and then practise capturing the poetry of everyday life in free modernist verse, emerged before the Revolution in the Catholic peasant commune called

Nuestra Señora de Solentiname where Fernando Cardenal acted as priest and where not only poetry but also 'primitive painting' workshops flourished.[96] It was inspired in a form of thinking that would subsequently become important in the Revolution and which fused the New Marxism of Cuba, with the tenet put forward by the Theology of Liberation that Christ's message of love could only be actualized in a society without exploitation. Advocating a 'simple' poetry defined as *exteriorismo*, which concentrates on verbal economy and observed reality, Cardenal's 'rules for writing poetry' used in the *talleres*, were a significant departure from the conception of poetry held by pre-revolutionary official culture with its preference for rhyme and ornate language. In a broader sense, the *talleres* could be seen not only as an attempt to widen access to poetic creation, but also to create new audiences and develop forms capable of expressing Nicaraguan experience, two pre-conditions for the growth of an autonomous national artistic tradition. The following poem, 'Eufemia mi novia guerrillera', illustrates clearly the way in which a poetics of everyday life is interlaced with the broader theme of the revolution:

> Standing beside the stove I kissed you
> on the days I could see you.
> Then I was told
> that you had left for the mountains to fight
> and I saw you no more
> until that afternoon
> when you came from Leon wearing olive green trousers
> and a red shirt.
> You were lovely
> as we walked down the road to Pueblo Nuevo.
> Standing beside the stove you kissed me
> and you told me you wanted to be a guerrilla of the FSLN.
> Again I saw you no more
> I don't know where you are Eufemia.[97]

Although the Sandinista tradition was, as we saw, inspired by and shares many features of the Cuban example, its cultural policies are distinctive for their accommodation of religious and ethnic diversity.

At the beginning of the Cuban Revolution, the sense of liberation from oppression and the belief in the realization of a socialist utopia on American soil gave rise to a great surge of cultural creativity. Hitherto marginalized popular traditions were made central to national culture; the educational system was expanded and a literacy campaign reduced illiteracy to 2 per cent of the population; mass organizations and trade unions were involved in cultural activities including participation in community theatre organized by a New Theatre Movement in local Centres of Popular Culture. Inspired by the work of the Brazilian Augusto Boal, groups belonging to the New Theatre Movement performed plays aimed at both political and aesthetic education through the use of themes pertinent to the audience/community's concerns and of music, masks, costumes, dances and poetic forms reflecting local cultural traditions.[98] Journals such as *Revolution*, *Lunes* and *Cuba Socialista* flourished, publishing both avant-garde, Cuban black literature and critical discussion on the nature of socialism.[99] Cuban film, both documentary and fictional, concentrated not only on Cuban history and identity; it also attempted to develop critical audiences by producing films which exposed the devices used to create cinematic illusion. As the director of the Cuban Institute of Cinematographic Art and Industry, García Espinosa, explains, the deconstruction of form is as vital as content in this endeavour: 'It is impossible to question a given reality without questioning the particular genre that you select or inherit to depict that reality . . . to make a new cinema is, in fact, to reveal the process of destruction of the one that came before. . . . We have to make a spectacle out of the destruction of the spectacle. This process cannot be individual. . . . What is needed is to perform this process jointly with the viewer.'[100] However, following the Bay of Pigs invasion by the USA in 1961, Castro proclaimed the well-known dictum which was to become the general principle governing Cuban cultural policy: 'Dentro de la Revolución Todo. Fuera de la Revolución Nada' (Within the Revolution Everything, Outside the Revolution Nothing), which was subsequently clarified as meaning those cultural forms and activities compatible with the 'scientific conception of the world established and developed by Marxism–Leninism'.[101]

Marx viewed religion as a compensatory construct for the deprivation and self-alienation hitherto endured by humankind, which with the advent of communism would disappear. In accordance with this view, religion in Cuba was not seen as being 'within the Revolution', in contrast to Nicaragua where it formed part of revolutionary ideology. The Sandinistas took into consideration Mariátegui's warning that Christianity was an essential component of the people's consciousness and that to ignore it would allow reactionary forces to use it for their own purposes. The Christian conviction that the poor are God's chosen people was interpreted as the collective longing for a just society, expressed idealistically. This stance was concisely articulated in the Sandinista slogan that 'between the Revolution and religion there is no contradiction'. In Cardenal's thinking Christianity and Christ's

Second Coming were given a non-individualist interpretation: 'The Son of Man will not come as an individual, as he did the first time; he will be a collective Christ, he will come as a society, or rather a new species, The New Person. . . .'[102] Thus while in Cuba All Saints Day, Easter and Christmas have been abolished, in Nicaragua posters displayed during Christmas in 1980 in Managua portrayed Christ and the Virgin in the stable protected by armed Sandinistas.[103] Moreover, in Cuba African religious cults continue to exist in semi-clandestine form, but its religious rites are seen as a form of superstition, or as 'folklore' to be performed by the National Folklore Group. In this sense Cuban socialism follows in the tradition of the Enlightenment view inherited by the Left, that 'the people' need to be educated to transcend their irrational passions and superstitious beliefs so they may constitute a rational and enlightened society. The additional fact that sexual 'deviants' such as homosexuals are persecuted could be taken as further indication that Cuban official cultural policy finds it difficult to tolerate plurality and ambiguity.

In Nicaragua, however, it would appear that within the predominant aim of creating a nation-state in order to promote the development of the forces of production, there has, despite initial difficulties and mistakes, particularly in relation to the Miskito groups, been an attempt not to override the distinct Amerindian and creole English-speaking cultures on the Pacific coast. The fact that festivities celebrating the patron saint, characteristic of popular Catholicism, have been regarded by the Ministry of Culture as expressions of a 'concrete utopia', of life lived in a genuine human community in which 'the needs of the community and the individuals of which it is made up are satisfied',[104] also indicates that the model of development and modernity of the Sandinista state was not predicated on the extirpation of popular religion and mythology.

In the aftermath of the February 1990 elections, the disastrous economic consequences of the United States embargo and prolonged war were put forward as explanations of the unexpected defeat of the Sandinistas; but also the very ambiguities and to some extent the successes of the Sandinista revolutionary process were seen as important causal factors.

Perhaps the main ambiguity which faced the Sandinistas arose out of their commitment to a mixed economy. Although its bias was ostensibly in favour of meeting the needs of the popular classes, as the economic crisis worsened, policies which favoured private farmers and entrepreneurs were implemented in order to sustain production and political unity in face of US and Contra hostility.[105] These concessions to the private and wealthier sector were made at the cost of deteriorating services, a lowering in the standard of living of workers, peasants and public employees and an erosion of the achievements in health and education in the early stages of the Revolution.

One of the political consequences of these policies, which imposed sacrifices on the less advantaged in the name of the Revolution while in comparative terms exonerating the privileged, was to reduce the level of participation in the mass organizations, which came increasingly to be seen as executive branches of the Sandinista state. The overall effect was to reinforce those authoritarian elements of the political culture inherited from the Somoza era that the cultural politics of Sandinismo had been designed to transform. At the same time it seems that, despite these shifts in the economic and political sphere, the very success of Sandinismo at the ideological level in mobilizing national-popular symbols to forge a new independent Nicaragua, led the FSLN to mistake mobilization for political support. It has been suggested that its success in establishing the right to self-determination backfired in the sense that 'now many people could feel proud of being Nicaraguan and still vote against Sandinismo'.[106] Perhaps the most serious consequence of this effectiveness at the ideological level was the fact that 'Observers and analysts projected the rationality of the Sandinista line onto the electorate, assuming voters would choose on the basis of general ideological reasoning rather than on the concrete and specific issues of living conditions.'[107] In 1984 66 per cent of the electorate voted for the FSLN despite the war with the Contras, the threat of invasion and growing economic difficulties. In 1990, however, in an incomparably more serious situation, the material reality of unremitting war, food shortages and the deterioration of health and education was no longer compatible with Sandinista ideology, which had already been undermined in reality and thus in effect no longer offered a *concrete* utopia.

Nevertheless, it could be argued that the Sandinista Revolution was founded on an alternative model of development, on a civilizing rationality that attempted to combine rational strategies for development with popular participation and a positive recognition of the importance of popular culture for the creation of a specifically Nicaraguan and Latin American modernity. Another model of development, to which we turn now, has emerged from Indian Politics groups, who speak of 'ethnodevelopment'.

Indian Politics

Over approximately the past fifteen years Indian Politics movements have begun to appear throughout the subcontinent, even in countries like

Colombia and Venezuela whose native populations had until recently received little political attention. They claim that the overall Indian population is between 55 and 80 million; other estimates would place it at possibly 26 million, distributed among some 400 ethnic groups.[108] These movements base themselves on the principle of ethnic autonomy and therefore contest the notion of the single nation, which is the goal of liberal, left and new right politicians. Historically, 'Indianism' (*indianismo*) needs to be distinguished from 'Indigenism' (*indigenismo*). The latter may be defined as a recognition of the native population as a fundamental part of the nation, and therefore of the need to put an end to its isolation. Its beginnings can be traced to the late nineteenth century in Peru, when the shock of defeat by Chile in the War of the Pacific in which the Indians did more to defend the territory than the bourgeoisie, led the writer Manuel González Prada, himself a member of the bourgeoisie, to declare, 'the true Peru is not made up of the groups of creoles and foreigners who inhabit the strip of land situated between the Pacific and the Andes; the nation is formed by the masses of Indians scattered to the east of the mountains'.[109] *Indigenismo* first gained a continental presence through the First Interamerican Indigenist Congress held in Pátzcuaro, Mexico, in 1940. President Cárdenas gave the inaugural speech, in which he declared that the Indian population was a 'factor for progress' and should therefore be incorporated into the nation: the objective was not to 'indigenize' Mexico, but to 'Mexicanize' the Indian.[110] Mexican and Peruvian Indigenism differed considerably, especially in the sense that Mariátegui in Peru had developed it into a key feature of a programme for revolution. Nevertheless, by the 1960s, Peruvian Indigenism had lost its radicalism and become absorbed into populist politics.[111]

The Indian movements substitute for the notion of a single nation the idea of territories made up of a plurality of nations and cultures. As a result even the concept of hegemony becomes untenable. And in place of modernization modelled on the advanced capitalist world, there is the idea of ethnodevelopment. For Barre, Indianism is 'an ideological response to the universalist ideology of the West'.[112] In some cases, the extreme is reached of denying that Indians have anything to learn from the West. For Díaz-Polanco, what he calls 'ethno-populist' separatism is particularly dangerous in Central America because it diverts Indians from joining with other social forces in self-defence against imperialist-backed oppression. In this context, he draws attention to the Indian Law Resource Centre (ILRC), a right-wing foundation based in Washington, which declared at the United Nations Conference on Indigenous Populations, held in Geneva in 1985, 'When the Indian peoples and nations see their rights threatened they have the right to self-defence and can request the intervention of a third country.'[113] It is difficult to imagine who could fulfil the role of third country except the USA. The ILRC, which was engaged in using Nicaraguan Indian groups against the Sandinistas, was not supported by the Latin American delegates. In 1982, it had attempted to win over the Guatemalan peasant leader Rigoberta Menchù by offering her one million dollars.

What seems to be missing from Indianist politics is any clear notion of what might replace the nation-state as a viable principle of social cohesion. Some of the Peruvian movements insist on the viability of Inca forms of organization, without taking into account that an Indian form of modernity, though imaginable, has yet to be constructed. This tradition has recently been taken up by the Peruvian anthropologist Rodrigo Montoya, in the notion of 'magical socialism', wherein the mythical dimension of Andean culture is deployed not as populist identity but as a critique of rationalism as the supposed basis of Western political practice. The implication is that there is a need for a new form of political culture. The contribution of the indigenous peoples would be their tradition of reciprocity, solidarity and non-Cartesian thinking. On the other hand, the idea of ethnic autonomy would not be sufficient to resolve the political problems of Peru. The key Western achievements of freedom and modernity must be included, though this modernity must include a criticism of capitalism.[114] The task, needless to say, remains to be performed. 'Unfortunately, human beings, brothers, there is a lot to be done', as César Vallejo, the Peruvian poet, wrote.[115]

Patchwork, Machismo and New Social Movements

The Indian Politics movement bears similarity to various important new social movements that have emerged in Latin America during the last twenty years, due among other things to the repressive measures of the military regimes, the new constituencies created by rural–urban migration and the failure of the Left to break with the hierarchical structure and clientelistic practices of political parties. In contrast to Europe and the USA, where the new social movements have tended to focus on the consequences of advanced industrialization, in Latin America they are primarily concerned with the satisfaction of basic needs. In Brazil, the neighbourhood associations involved in the struggle for provision of services, housing and land, brought the concerns of everyday life and the sphere of consumption into the public sphere of politics. The feminist movement and incipient black movement have drawn attention away from the arena of class conflict, creating in the process new forms of collective identity and political organization. In Chile, where neighbourhood associations became one of the main sites of resistance to the military, the call for a return to democracy was coupled with a new emphasis on the democratization of civil society and social customs. Moreover, the comparatively non-hierarchical structure of these movements has been associated with the large numbers of women who participate in them both in the ranks and as leaders: indeed Rosa María Alfaro has used the term 'maternidad social' to describe neighbourhood associations led by women. Thus in contrast to European feminist assumptions about the role of the family, in this context 'the historical role of the people becomes meaningful to the extent that the family is part of the social movement in terms of its organizational structure and as the basis of motivational hope in the future.[116]

Perhaps one of the most significant contributions of the new social movements has been the creation of a new political culture manifested in a broader concept of democracy and new methods of political resistance, entailing novel forms of organization and of cultural action.[117] A particularly striking example of popular culture as resistance, expressed not only in the language of opposition but in an attempt to transform personal experiences of loss, separation and destitution into testimonies of political events, are the arpilleras or patchwork pictures produced by groups of working-class women in Chile during the military dictatorship of Pinochet. Using scraps of cotton and wool to create images of everyday life, the delicate and child-like form of the arpilleras stands in shocking contrast to their content. They depict relatives waiting outside the gates of mass detention centres; dead civilians deposited in an army truck on the day of the military coup; scenes of soup kitchens in the shanty towns; imaginary scenes of reunion with missing relatives; and of a life of plenty without hunger or sorrow.

The arpilleras emerged as a result of the formation of a committee set up by the Catholic Church, with the purpose of denouncing human rights abuses and supporting the families of the thousands who have 'disappeared' under recent military dictatorships in Latin America. The Church sponsored the workshops, buying the arpilleras and sending them abroad for sale to provide an income and a means of financial independence for the arpilleristas. The committee also set up communal kitchens in suburban areas suffering hardship due to the monetarist economic measures of the Chilean government junta; and in 1974 it created the Association of Families of the Detained/ Disappeared. This Association consisted mainly of women, who organized forms of protest remarkable for their symbolic content and power. With photographs of their disappeared relatives, women of the Association chained themselves to the fence around the National Congress Building [Plate 9]. In 1978 the Association formed a human chain connecting the capital, Santiago, with a mine in which a mass grave containing the partially burned bodies of 'disappeared' farmers was found. Another protest action involved enveloping the walls of a renowned torture centre in Santiago with a white cloth, spraying it with red paint to represent the blood of the disappeared and writing on it the names of persons tortured to death at the centre.[118] What these forms of collective action and the *arpilleras* have in common is their use of personal metaphors to counter the aggression of the state: photographs of the disappeared which highlight the fact of absence or death; human chains to denote the power and importance of interconnection; fragments of coloured cloth sewn together by the delicate movement of the hand.

In societies characterized by a sexual division of labour wherein the female element is subordinate, masculine supremacy is maintained in culture through the devaluation of femininity and the spheres of life – the body, the personal, the domestic – with which it is connected. In such male-dominated or phallocentric societies, emotions in general – and in particular feelings of weakness, dependence and vulnerability – have been relegated to a position of marginal importance within a dominant male culture which above all prizes mastery and control. In the case of the *arpilleristas*, it is in their role as women – identified in Latin America first and foremost as mothers and thus as marginal to the central and masculine institutions of the state and public discourse – that they have been successful in articulating the hidden truth of the regime. And it is through the use of the marginalized language of the personal, of grief, emotional attachment and hope, that this suppressed truth has been recovered. While all forms of public dissent were censored, the seemingly innocuous and 'feminine' embroideries of the *arpilleristas* bore witness to daily events, chronicling and commenting like the storytellers of oral poetry not only on acts of persecution and hardship experienced by the people, but also expressing their faith that other forms of human existence are possible. In the words of one *arpillerista:* 'I put an enormous sun in all my *arpilleras*, because even though I might not have a cup of tea to my name I never lose my faith.'[119]

Guy Brett in his work on the way in which people's experience of modern history is given visual form indicates how the *arpilleras* communicate this faith and transform it into resistance: the depiction in loving detail of the familiar objects of everyday life – trees, vases, kitchen utensils, the interiors of houses, food – constitute a 'resistance against dehumanization' while the image of the

Andes 'towering over Santiago and running the whole two thousand mile length of Chile, are both the most obvious feature of the landscape and also the symbol of grandeur and promise against which to measure the cramped, grinding existence imposed by the present day social system'.[120] In the process of producing the *arpilleras* a new aesthetic emerged. The use of wool and cloth to weave tapestries or make patchwork quilts and jackets is a widespread practice in Latin America.[121] In Chile the embroideries of the women of Isla Negra, a coastal fishing village, have gained public recognition through the writings of the poet Pablo Neruda and the work of the Chilean singer Violeta Parra, who developed this technique of embroidery in her own tapestries. However, the employment of these techniques outside their traditional context transforms them into powerful symbols. Due to the alienating effect produced by the disjuncture between form and content, the viewer is shocked into a realization of what the *arpilleras* depict. Moreover, the fact that they are frequently made with materials used in the *arpilleristas'* daily life – cloth from a skirt, a lock of hair – reinforces their connection with the personal and the body, linking art and life in a very direct manner.

By including the marginalized 'metaphors of the personal' in the struggle against the military dictatorship, the *arpilleristas* contributed, in conjunction with a multiplicity of women's organizations that emerged during this period, to the development of a new concept of democracy and politics. Women's participation as mothers, wives or sisters in the strategies for survival and movements of resistance under the dictatorship placed them in a contradictory position: as women moved primarily by their family attachments they entered the public sphere of politics only to come into conflict with the system which relegates them to silence within the domestic sphere. Out of this contradiction arose the demand to participate on an equal footing with men in the opposition to the military; hence the growth of feminist politics, which in focusing on the democratization of daily life and gender relations, revealed the links between military rule, the reproduction of authoritarian culture in the family and women's subordination.[122] Under Allende's Popular Unity Government women had been active in working-class organizations without questioning their own subordinate role in society. Indeed, Allende's government was significantly weakened by the failure of the Left to include the liberation of women as part of its socialist project; this failure accounts in part for the support given by women to the Right and its strategies to undermine the government. Paradoxically, then, the politicization of daily life in resistance to military rule led to a realization of the need for a broader concept of democracy, encompassing both gender and cultural politics.

Notes

1. Populism has been the subject of considerable debate. See Ernesto Laclau, 'Towards a theory of populism', in *Politics and Ideology in Marxist Theory*, London 1977.

2. The point is made by José Martí in his seminal essay 'Nuestra América', in *Obras completas*, La Habana 1963–65.

3. See Antonio Gramsci, *Selections from Prison Notebooks*, London 1971.

4. León Enrique Bieber, *En torno al origen histórico e ideológico del ideario nacionalista populista latinoamericano*, Berlin 1982, p. 27.

5. Ibid., p. 5.

6. Víctor Raúl Haya de la Torre, *La Defensa Continental*, Lima 1967, p. vii.

7. Bieber, p. 45.

8. The image is reproduced in Steve Stein, *Populism in Peru*, Wisconsin 1980, p. 177.

9. Stein, p. 164.

10. Ibid., pp. 207, 212.

11. As Alberto Flores Galindo points out in *La agonía de Mariátegui*, Mariátegui was a pioneer of Marxist theory in this context; Marx's writings on the Asiatic mode of production were not known until later.

12. Alberto Flores Galindo, *La agonía de Mariátegui*, Lima 1982, p. 31.

13. Ibid., p. 50.

14. Gramsci, pp. 130–31.

15. Ibid., pp. 19–20.

16. José Carlos Mariátegui, 'El hombre y el mito', in *El alma matinal*, Lima 1959, p. 18.

17. Ibid. pp. 19, 22.

18. *¿He vivido en vano? Mesa redonda sobre Todas las sangres*, Lima 1985.

19. Gramsci, p. 126.

20. Ibid., p. 129.

21. Mariátegui, p. 21.

22. Ibid., p. 56.

23. Bieber, p. 45.

24. Jean Meyer, *La révolution mexicaine*, Paris 1973, p. 282.

25. Jean Meyer, *The Cristero Rebellion: the Mexican People Between Church and State, 1926–1929*, Cambridge 1976, p. 181.

26. José Revueltas, *El luto humano, Obra Literaria*, Mexico 1967, Vol. 1, p. 274.

27. See John Womack, *Zapata and the Mexican Revolution*, London 1969.

28. González Casanova, *El estado y los partidos políticos en México*, Mexico 1981, p. 121.

29. Ibid., pp. 122–3.

30. This point is made in ibid., p. 128.

31. Ibid., p. 134.

32. Néstor García Canclini, 'Las políticas culturales en América Latina', Part 2, *Unomásuno*, No. 303, 10 sept. 1983, p. 6.

33. Sergio Zermeño, 'El fin del populismo mexicano', *Nexos*, No. 113, may 1987, p. 35.

34. Carlos Monsiváis, 'Notas sobre el Estado, la cultura nacional y las culturas populares en México', *Cuadernos Políticos*, No. 30, oct.–dic. 1981, p. 35.

35. M.K. Vaughan, *The State, Education and Social Class in Mexico, 1880–1928*, Dekalb 1982, p. 138.

36. Ibid., pp. 144–5.

37. Ibid., pp. 140–41, 252.

38. Alistair Hennessy, 'Artists, Intellectuals and Revolution: Recent Books on Mexico', *Journal of Latin American Studies*, Vol. 3, No. 1, p. 76.

39. *Obra Completa*, Rio 1962, p. 357. English translation, *The Psychiatrist and Other Stories*, Berkeley 1963.

40. Ibid., p. 352.

41. The work of Freud and Lacan, which is crucial here, tends to dehistoricize the process of identity. See J. Laplanche and J-B. Pontalis, *The Language of Psychoanalysis*, London 1980, pp. 205-8.

42. Octavio Paz, *Posdata*, Mexico 1970, p. 107; see also p. 40.

43. See Gramsci, pp. 6-10, on how intellectuals are specialist in those techniques of organizing and controlling which are distributed through the whole society. See also Roderic Camp, *Intellectuals and the State in Twentieth Century Mexico*, Austin 1985.

44. Roger Bartra, *La jaula de la melancolía*, Mexico 1987, p. 17.

45. Ibid., p. 150.

46. For a more positive view of Cantinflas's early films, see 'Instituciones: Cantinflas. Ahí estuvo el detalle', in Carlos Monsiváis, *Escenas de pudor y liviandad*, Mexico 1988, pp. 77-96.

47. See p. 26 for example.

48. Monsiváis, 'Notas sobre el Estado', p. 33.

49. Ibid., p. 34.

50. Ibid., p. 40.

51. Her *Hasta no verte, Jesús mío* is discussed in Chapter 4.

52. Roberto Schwarz, *Que horas são*, São Paulo 1987, p. 33.

53. Ibid., p. 32.

54. F. Weffort, *O populismo na politica brasileira*, Rio de Janeiro 1978, p. 71.

55. Getulio Vargas, 'A campanha presidencial', quoted in Octavio Ianni, *O colapso do populismo no Brasil*, Rio de Janeiro 1971, p. 161.

56. See Vivian Schelling, *Culture and Underdevelopment in Brazil (1920-1968): Mário de Andrade and Paulo Freire*, PhD Thesis, University of Sussex 1984, p. 214 for discussion of intellectual sources.

57. Schwarz, p. 46.

58. See Mário Vargas Llosa, 'El elefante y la cultura', in *Contra viento y marea*, Barcelona 1986, Vol. 2, pp. 313-22.

59. Renato Ortiz, *Cultura brasileira e identidade nacional*, São Paulo 1985, p. 71.

60. The critique is Ortiz's. See pp. 72-4.

61. Paulo Freire, *Culture: Action for Freedom*, 1970.

62. Ianni, p. 208.

63. Alberto Ciria, *Política y cultura popular: la Argentina peronista 1946-1955*, Buenos Aires 1983, p. 275.

64. Ibid., p. 72.

65. See ibid., p. 310.

66. Ibid., pp. 223-4.

67. Ibid., p. 285.

68. Ibid., p. 219.

69. Néstor García Canclini, 'Las políticas culturales en América Latina', Part 2, *Unomásuno*, No. 303, 10 sep. 1983, p. 6.

70. Silvia Sigal and Eliseo Verón, 'Perón: discurso político e ideología', in Alain Rouquié, ed., *Argentina, hoy*, Mexico 1982, pp. 190-91.

71. Ciria, pp. 76-7.

72. Ibid., pp. 279, 291.

73. Ibid., p. 282.

74. Paul Virilio, *Speed and Politics*, New York 1986.

75. Beatriz Sarlo, 'Argentina 1984: la cultura en el proceso democrático', *Nueva Sociedad*,

No. 73, 1984, p. 80.

76. Josefina Ludmer, *El género gauchesco: un tratado sobre la patria*, Buenos Aires 1988, pp. 31–41.

77. Ernesto Laclau, 'Towards a Theory of Populism', in *Politics and Ideology in Marxist Theory*, London 1977, p. 167.

78. Juan Carlos Portantiero and Emilio de Ipola, 'Lo nacional popular y los populismos realmente existentes', *Nueva Sociedad*, No. 54, 1981, p. 7.

79. Quoted in Peter Marshall, *Cuba Libre: Breaking the Chains?* London 1987 p. 32.

80. Keen and Wasserman, *A Short History of Latin America*, Boston 1984, p. 46.

81. See David Hodges, *The Intellectual Foundations of the Nicaraguan Revolution*, Austin 1986.

82. See Sandino's 'Manifesto of Light and Truth' in *El pensamiento vivo de Sandino*, ed. Sergio Ramirez Mercado, 5th edition, San José 1980.

83. D. Hodges, pp. 75–9.

84. Quoted in James Dunkerley, *Power in the Isthmus*, London 1988, p. 294.

85. Ibid., p. 281.

86. In this context it is worth remembering that training for the National Guard was accompanied by call-response drills in the following vein: 'Who is the enemy of the Guard?' 'The People.' 'Who is the father of the Guard?' 'Somoza.' 'Up with the Guard.' 'Down with the People.' Quoted in George Black, *The Triumph of the People*, London 1981, p. 55.

87. Sergio Ramírez speaking in a television documentary for Channel 4, *The Making of a Nation*, by Marc Carlin.

88. Daniel Ortega, 'La Revolución es creatividad y imaginación, in *Hacia una política cultural de la revolución Sandinista*, Managua 1982,p. 87.

89. See Comandante Bayardo Arce in 'El dificil terreno de la lucha: lo ideologico' in *Hacia una política cultural*.

90. Ernesto Cardenal, 'La Cultura: los primeros seis meses' in *Hacia una política cultural*.

91. Sergio Ramírez, 'Los intelectuales y el futuro revolucionário, in *Hacia una política cultural*, p. 127.

92. George Black & John Bevan, *The Loss of Fear*, Nicaragua Solidarity Campaign pamphlet, London 1980.

93. See R. Pring Mill, 'Convirtiendo la oscurana en claridad', unpublished handout; also 'The Role of Revolutionary Song – a Nicaraguan assessment' in *Popular Music 6/2*, 1987.

94. See Carlos M. Vilas, *The Sandinista Revolution*, New York 1986.

95. See G. Black, *The Triumph of the People*; Ernesto Cardenal, 'La democratización de la cultura', in *Hacia una política cultural*.

96. See Robert Pring Mill, 'The Workshop Poetry of Sandinista Nicaragua', in *Antilia*, Vol. 1., 1984, No. 2.

97.   Junto al fogón te besé
los días que llegué a verte.
Después me dijeron
que te habías ido a la montaña a combatir
y no te volví a ver
hasta aquella tarde
que venías de León con el pantalón verdeolivo
y la camisa roja.
Te vi hermosa
mientras caminábamos por la carretera que va de Pueblo Nuevo.
Junto al fogón me besaste
y me dijiste que querías ser guerrillera del FSLN

De nuevo no te he vuelto a ver..

No sé dónde estás Eufemia.

José Antonio Rodríguez from the Esteli Workshop, in *Poesía Libre*, No. 7, Managua n.d.

98. See J.A. Weiss, 'The emergence of popular culture' in S. Halebsky and J.M. Kirk, *Cuba Twenty Five Years of Revolution 1959–1984*, New York 1985.

99. See Marshall, *Cuba Libre*.

100. Quoted in Julianne Burton, 'Film and Revolution in Cuba' in S. Halebsky and H.M. Kirk, *Cuba: Twenty Five Years of Revolution*, p. 151.

101. See Marshall, *Cuba Libre*.

102. Quoted in D. Hodges, *The Intellectual Foundations of the Nicaraguan Revolution*, p. 281.

103. Ibid., p. 260.

104. Ernesto Cardenal, 'La democratización de la cultura', p. 255.

105. See Carlos M. Vilas, 'What Went Wrong' in *NACLA, Report on the Americas*, June 1990.

106. James Dunkerley, 'Reflections on the Nicaraguan Election', *New Left Review* 182, July/August 1990.

107. C. Vilas, 'What Went Wrong', p. 15.

108. Marie-Chantal Barre, *Ideologías indigenistas y movimientos indios*, Mexico 1983, p. 8.

109. 'Discurso en el politeama', in *Sus mejores páginas*, Lima n.d., p. 26. See Efrain Kristal, *The Andes Viewed from the City: Literary and Political Discourse on the Indian in Peru 1848–1930*, New York 1987.

110. Barre, pp. 34, 61.

111. See Sebastián Salazar Bondy, 'La evolución del llamado indigenismo', *Sur*, mar.–abr. 1965, pp. 44–50.

112. Barre, p. 297.

113. Héctor Díaz-Polanco, '*Neoindigenismo* and the Ethnic Question in Central America', *Latin American Perspectives*, Vol. 14, No. 1, Winter 1987, pp. 90–91, 96.

114. The above points were made by Rodrigo Montoya in a seminar on 'Culture, Identity and Politics', given at the Institute of Latin American Studies. London on 16 May 1990.

115. In 'Los nueve monstruos', *Poemas Humanos*. English translation: Clayton Eshleman, *César Vallejo: the Complete Posthumous Poetry*, Berkeley 1978.

116. Quoted in Jesús Martín-Barbero, *De los medios a las mediaciones*, p. 216.

117. See Ilse Scherer-Warren and Paulo J. Krischke, eds, *Uma revolução no cotidiano?, Os novos movimentos sociais na America do Sul*, São Paulo 1987.

118. M. Agosin, *Scraps of Life*, London 1987.

119. Quoted in ibid., p. 83.

120. G. Brett, *Through our own Eyes*, London 1986, p. 47.

121. M. Agosin, *Scraps of Life*.

122. See Patricia M. Churchryk, 'Feminist Anti-Authoritarian Politics: The Role of Women's Organizations in the Chilean Transition to Democracy', in *The Women's Movement in Latin America*, ed. Jean Jacquette, Unwin Hyman, Boston 1989.

FOUR

Popular Culture and

High Culture

One of the problems with using an opposition like 'popular' versus 'high' is that it tends to bring in its wake others like vulgar versus polite; impure versus pure, and so on. As a result, the whole cultural field becomes polarized by these apparently symmetrical oppositions. However, the symmetry is merely apparent: it is produced by making an opposition such as high versus low into an imposed either/or by placing everything inside one or other category. At the same time, the tendency is to line up these binaries with each other until they make a complete intellectual grid, with high and low, human and animal, domestic and savage, and so on, corresponding to each other. To think in this way is to rigidify the cultural field, eliminating whatever is transitional, hybrid, multiple, or ambiguous. It is to ignore the fact that these polar opposites are no more than 'terminal points of the process of becoming'.[1]

A vocabulary which places the high against the low, and so on, is obviously hierarchical, and in a historical sense has reinforced the hegemonic controls exercised by bourgeois ruling classes. The most seductive way out of the problem is to reverse the terms, and play off the low, the vulgar, the plebeian, the uneducated, against the pretensions and rigidity of 'classical' or 'high' culture.[2] This type of attitude, in its familiar forms of social messianism – the notion of the world upside down, and the cult of Carnival as subversion – has become extremely common in cultural studies. Such reversals of categories end up as utopian gestures (or alibis, in fact) on the part of the intellectual, who is obviously on the side of the angels – or rather, in this case, the devil, the low, the marginalized. The hierarchical language remains. Although it matches the symbols actually used by social groups, it will not do as a method for cultural analysis. By approaching the issue of power on a merely symbolic level, it does not confront the social articulation of power. To identify with the marginalized does not increase understanding of social power. At the same time, in a practical historical sense, distinctions between high and low culture no longer serve as markers of social stratification. With the increasing spread of the electronic media, shifts in consumption have occurred. The tendency in recent decades has been towards a single cultural repertory across the social classes with the result that popular culture tends to become less available as a store of symbolically resistant attitudes.

Stallybrass and White, in their useful book *The Politics and Poetics of Transgression*,[3] attempt a critique of idealizations of Carnival, fairs, and other forms of low culture, with particular reference to the work of Bakhtin. The context of their discussion is British and European culture over the past four centuries, and there are important differences when studying Latin American culture, a point we will come to shortly. Their book only goes part of the way in criticizing this intellectual fashion, and illustrates the danger of remaining within the control of the terms while seeking to analyse their operation. Thus they criticize the idealization of the low, without criticizing the use of hierarchical classificatory symbols. Indeed, they assume that any critique has to stay inside this 'framework of discourse'. It has to be so, given their assumption that this particular discourse is a type of basic cultural grammar, by which all meaning is controlled. 'The high/low opposition in each of our four symbolic domains – psychic forms, the human body, geographical space and the social order – is a fundamental basis to mechanisms of ordering and sense-making in European cultures. . . . Cultures "think themselves" in the most immediate and affective ways through the combined symbolisms of these four hierarchies.'[4] To rigidify and universalize the terms in this way gives them a semantic solidity that conceals their role as conceptual controls, controls which reduce and stabilize the multiplicities of any culture. The work of cultural history, in our view, should be to restore the multiplicities, while at the same time exposing how they have been reduced. One of the most effective allies in this task are works of art and we make extensive use of them below.

The lining up of binaries, especially if one includes that of gender, is a commonplace of current literary and cultural criticism. One set of classifications, particularly that of gender, tends to be used as a totalizing explanatory device for a text or texts, on the tacit assumption that other binaries will fall in behind it. One thing Stallybrass and White's work shows is the fact that the lining up of central binaries, whereby one set will mesh with another, is a historical achievement of the European bourgeoisie in their 'production of status and identity through a repudiation of the low'.[5] 'The division of the social into high and low, the polite and the vulgar, simultaneously maps out divisions between the civilized and the grotesque body, between author and hack, between social purity and social hybridization.'[6] The historical action of the bourgeoisie is there in the 'simultaneously', which is taken too much for granted, and which depends upon a long complex process of cultural and linguistic homogenization.[7]

In Latin America attempts to enforce dichotomic thinking in terms of high/low, inside/outside and so on have been a characteristic of repressive regimes, most recently the Chilean dictatorship, as Nelly Richard has pointed out.[8] The homogeneous symbolic space, which has been an instrument of bourgeois hegemony in Europe, pertains much less in Latin American societies. The main reasons for the difference can be set out as follows. There are still great differences of cultural system and code between native, *mestizo* and Westernized social groups. As a consequence, even within a single national territory people do not speak the same languages, or share the same iconographical traditions, or think of themselves as having the same identity. In addition, there are combinations of very different economic formations, pre-capitalist and capitalist. As one of the results of all this, the formation of nation-states has been incomplete.

Let us consider, for a moment, the case of Peru, where the Andean population continues to maintain traditional forms of sociality which do not fit with attempts by successive ruling groups to establish a nation-state. A major problem has been the chronic racism of the state's authorities and representatives. During the past decade, in the civil war between the army and the Maoist Sendero Luminoso, the unresolved historical agenda, which goes back to the sixteenth century, has once again been exposed, above all in the shape of massive state violence against the highland population. The following song offers a response and a diagnosis:

> When the eyes of children
> fill with hate
> can my song continue to be song
> can my tears continue to be tears? . . .
>
> They cut off my cow's head
> they take away my radio
> they say 'Your mother's a *cholo*'

and still they say 'Long live the fatherland'
and still they say 'Long live the fatherland'.[9]

The composer is Carlos Falconí, from the city of Huamanga, Ayacucho, and the text is in Quechua; it articulates the separateness of the world of the native peasantry. The Spanish words 'viva la patria' fail to bring about social unity. On the contrary, the shattering of any shared sense of society exposes the meaninglessness of that language, introduced from the French Enlightenment at the time of emancipation from Spain, which enshrines the idea of a national society. Moreover, the exposure of the language of patriotism as a farce is carried out from a more profound sense of rupture. The basic coherence between things and meanings, the coherence of culture, is ruptured. The very possibility of a mutuality of human feelings, which might make sociality possible, is being destroyed. What price the nation? No response by any political group, no statement by any intellectual has come anywhere near the capacity of this and other current Andean songs to confront and understand the process of social violence in Peru.[10]

Patriotic symbols, like flags and national anthems, derived from the iconography and language of the European Enlightenment, have had varied success in penetrating Latin American populations, depending on their different histories. However, the major move towards homogenization – that is, the disappearance of cultural divisions – has occurred not, as in Europe, through literacy, schooling and the press, but through the culture industry and the electronic media, and predominantly during the past three decades. There has been no classical age of the bourgeoisie – which does not mean there have not been attempts to imitate it, as in the case of Vasconcelos in Mexico. As well as deterritorializing symbols and memory – that is, detaching them from a particular location in space and time – the mass media have brought about a process of hybridization whereby cultural signs flow across social, ethnic and nation-state boundaries, and the notion of high culture as a separate sphere becomes impossible. The term 'postmodern' used by some to describe this situation, has been the subject of considerable debate in Latin America.[11] A degree of consensus has arisen around the proposition that the distinctiveness of Latin American modernism is that it occurred without modernity, and that given that a partial and distorted modernization has generally occurred only in recent decades, it is inappropriate to speak of a postmodern condition in Latin America. It is from key differences like these that the contribution of Latin America to cultural studies needs to be made.

One of the necessities of a Latin American approach is a redefinition of art, and for the rest of this chapter we will be using artistic creation as an investigation of cultural divisions. High culture in Latin America needs placing as *cultura ilustrada, erudita, letrada* (enlightened, erudite, literate), terms with implied though less easily defined opposites whose common denominator is non-literacy. High culture has used art as a key distinguishing mark, with the judgement that the aesthetic productions of the popular sectors do not qualify as art. Indeed the term 'aesthetic' has been denied to works of popular art, given their embeddedness in ritual and other uses. Clearly, therefore, the opposition high culture/popular culture is not symmetrical, and simply reversing it does not help in getting rid of the distortions it generates.

One solution, favoured by Mirko Lauer, is to avoid using the word art altogether when referring to native productions.[12] The danger here is that they remain in a sense disqualified, when what is needed is to challenge the dominant terms of definition. In particular, there is the difficulty of vindicating the aesthetic power of such objects if they are not to be called art. The Paraguayan critic Ticio Escobar opts for a different strategy, insisting on the need to use the terms native art and popular art, precisely because they refuse the currently hegemonic uses of the word art. Conceptual oppositions which have become dominant in Europe fragment what is unitary in native and popular art: 'certain pairs of oppositions deployed by the theory of art (such as useful–beautiful, art–society, form–content, the aesthetic–the artistic, etc.) cannot simply be applied to a reality which does not yield separate elements which would support such oppositions'.[13] The imposition of inappropriate oppositions includes the hierarchical dualism of art versus *artesanía*, arising from assumptions to do with the autonomy of form as defining genuine artistic experience. 'It is assumed that the word *art* applies to a series of cultural phenomena in which form predominates over function and constitutes a separate domain, to be considered for itself, in opposition to *artesanías* or *minor arts* in which use prevails over formal aspects.'[14] The idea of the gratuity of the work of art goes back to the Enlightenment programme of achieving the autonomy of different cultural activities, together with the autonomy of the individual person, notions which receive a classic formulation in the philosophy of Kant. The world of art, as Bourdieu puts it, was made into 'a sacred island systematically and ostentatiously opposed to the profane, everyday world of production . . . like theology in a past epoch'.[15]

Once again one is dealing with assumptions that involve social conditions which do not pertain in Latin America. If the aesthetic function is assumed to be the distinguishing factor in art, popular art is excluded, given its close welding together of 'ritual, aesthetic, religious, political and even ludic functions'.[16] The non-aesthetic functions make *artesanía* into the poor relative of 'genuine' art. And yet, examined carefully, they express particular types of sociality and cultural synthesis rather than inferior qualities of the artistic object. The extreme instance is the native ritual celebration, which 'as maximum intensification of communitary experience, is the culmination and corollary of indigenous art; in ritual there converge, intensified, the different aesthetic manifestations (visual elements, dances, music and representation). It is total art in the current meaning of the term.'[17]

Ticio Escobar's concern is popular rural cultures. If one turns to urban mass culture, the notion of the autonomy of art as opposed to lesser, utilitarian practices is yet again inappropriate in Latin America. With literature, among the conditions in nineteenth-century Europe which made that autonomy, or at least its ideological appearance, possible are a massive increase in literacy and an expansion of the market for the printed word. This enabled literary writing to become a self-supporting activity, occupying a restricted ambit within generalized literacy, and the writer to inhabit a 'higher' sphere, separated from the vulgarity of mass culture. However, in nineteenth-century Brazil – and the example holds for the rest of Latin America – such a polarity failed to arise. Due to the fragility of capitalism, and the limitation of literacy, the cultural market remained restricted. The frontier between mass and erudite culture (for example in terms of journalism and literary writing) was not as clearly marked as in Europe. At the same time, different types of intellectual work were not clearly separated, so that politics and the study of society were included in literature. The lack of autonomy of literature vis à vis other discourses ceased around the 1940s, precisely when the social division of labour and the autonomy of the professions, along with the capitalist infrastructure as a whole, became consolidated.[18]

The differences referred to have also become an issue for literary history and literary criticism. The dominant tendency has been to locate modern Latin American literature inside a process of 'catching-up' with the European paradigm of autonomy and professionalization. In this view, the so-called 'boom' of the Latin American novel in the 1960s and '70s was taken as the final achievement of 'maturity'. Still predominant among European academics and critics, this attitude was also until recently common even among Latin American critics. To assume that Latin American literature exists to compete with European literature is a teleological approach: it cannot explain the actual production and reception of literature in the region. The strong development of Latin American literary criticism over the past two decades is reversing the tendency to impose Eurocentric paradigms and thereby obscure differences. A pioneer of Latin American criticism, Angel Rama, gave a new, counter-hegemonic sense to the critical term 'intertextuality'. Normally designating the references and echoes connecting one text to others, the term has been used to dehistoricize Latin American works of literature by locating them in a field of European and North American literary references. Rama gave the term a strategic reversal, by speaking of intertextuality with European literature or intertextuality with Latin American culture, as alternatives that need to be faced by critics.[19]

Literature and the Nation

The tendency to mix what in Europe were separate intellectual discourses is exemplified in Sarmiento's *Facundo* (1845), one of the great founding texts of Latin American literature. Concerned with the formation of Argentina as a modern nation, it was written in favour of the unity of the nation, with Buenos Aires as the central civilizing force, and against federalism, the ghost which had haunted liberals through the nineteenth century in their fear of fragmentation and chaos. It continued one of the first debates in the political history of Latin America after Independence, that of centralism versus federalism, with which Bolívar had been intensely concerned. But it adds a new dimension. Placing Argentina inside a colonial discourse which made it the destiny of capitalism to dominate 'savagery' in Africa, Asia and the Middle East, *Facundo* seeks to make civilization and barbarism the foundation of a set of hierarchical binaries. In this reinforcement of cultural frontiers, the cities are 'a continuation of Europe', while the interior rural areas threaten to dissolve the most basic principles of social cohesion.[20] The type of hierarchical oppositions that fortify the cultural frontier can be gathered from the questionnaires Sarmiento sent to various rural areas which were designed to measure how widely 'enlightenment' ('las luces') had been disseminated. The interlocutor in the following is 'una persona respetable' ('a respectable person'):

Q. How many notable citizens reside in [the city of La Rioja]?
A. In the city there would be six or eight.
Q. How many lawyers practise there?
A. None.
Q. How many doctors attend the sick?
A. None.

Q. How many men wear morning dress [*frac*]?
A. None.[21]

Clearly there is no capitalist or professional class, and a considerable degree of poverty. Sarmiento compares this with the destruction caused by the Turkish invasion of Greece, while *frac* becomes the fetishistic indicator of the presence of civilization.

However, despite the attempt to impose a European, high cultural paradigm upon Argentina, Sarmiento's text is marked in a number of crucial ways by the Latin American context within which it was produced. In the first place, it combines politics and sociology with imaginative literature. But the imaginative, poetic dimension – which Sarmiento calls 'the lies of the imagination' – cannot find its material in the life of cities and civilization.[22] Expansive individualism and the need for release from the confining doctrine of progress by education, hard work and social gentility, can only be satisfied by the pre-capitalist rural culture of the gaucho, to which Sarmiento's attitude is profoundly ambiguous. Although it means a dissolution of sociality, it is also attractive: 'the gaucho does not work; food and clothing he finds ready for him at home; both are supplied by his herds, if he is a proprietor, or by the house of a landowner or relative if he possesses nothing. The attention required by the herd is limited to pleasurable excursions.'[23] The vast, desolate landscape of the pampas, setting of gaucho life, supplies an inspiration whereby the imagination can break the moulds of outdated neo-classical aesthetics. This 'solemn, grandiose, immeasurable, silent nature' resists mapping according to the grids of European civilization.[24] The land cannot be read by an outsider. For this the traditional skills of a *baqueano* (guide) are necessary. By observing, smelling or touching the minimal changes of land surface and the sparse vegetation, he is able to produce a precise location. Sarmiento recognizes the *baqueano*'s skills as a legitimate form of knowledge: 'he is the most complete topographer; he is the only map the general takes with him to direct the movements of his campaign'.[25] Here quite clearly Sarmiento's admiration for European capitalist society loses its centrality, and popular forms of knowledge are recognized. The *baqueano* is one of four gaucho types which Sarmiento displays as essential to the foundation of a genuine 'national literature'. The others are the *rastreador* (pathfinder), the singer (composer of oral poetry) and the 'bad gaucho'. The latter classification attempts to put social violence inside a Christian symbolic order and thus control it: a step which became crucial in later uses of the gaucho, as mentioned in Chapter 1. What begins to emerge in Sarmiento is that the civilizing project of the Argentinian liberal bourgeoisie failed to supply the affective connections necessary for the construction of a national identity. For this, it was necessary to make use of popular culture.

The problem posed itself much more sharply for the ruling elite of Paraguay during the War of the Triple Alliance, fought by Paraguay against Brazil, Uruguay and Argentina from 1865 to 1870. The patriotic newspaper they published at the time of the war reveals their difficulties. Its title, *Cabichuí*, is in Guaraní, the national lingua franca. But given that the use of Guaraní is restricted to oral communication, the contents of the paper had to be written in Spanish, in the hope that the minority of literate members of the troops would transmit its message to the illiterate majority. For the illiterate, a visual mode of communication was offered: on every page there were a number of wood-block drawings, which used the style of popular art forms and would not only be recognizable to the majority but could also mediate their experience of the war. As a means of social communication, *Cabichuí* showed an extraordinary heterogeneity: on the one hand, a patriotic discourse drawing on the vocabulary of European Enlightenment, Latin tags and references to classical mythology, and on the other the grotesque popular visual style of the woodcuts.

Let us take one further example of the heterogeneity of literary production in Latin America. In a number of Latin American countries in the nineteenth century there was wide circulation of what are known as *pliegos sueltos*, large folded sheets, similar to the twentieth-century *cordel* literature in Brazil mentioned earlier. Sold on street corners, they offered in traditional ballad form accounts of political events and stories of crime and love. In Chile, they began to appear from the 1860s.[26] Their format, inspired by the multitude of printed sheets and small newspapers which appeared in the early Republican period, reflects the fact that many artists and intellectuals passed through journalism. The main audience of the *pliegos sueltos* were workers who used to meet after work and listen to one of them read aloud: in this sense they constituted a transition between orality and literacy. For their readers they represent 'the conquest of the space of writing', from which previously they had been excluded.[27] What they reveal in terms of boundaries between 'high' and 'low' cultural strata is that such divisions were relatively fluid: the readers were obviously capable of combining different strata.

In the twentieth century, there is a broad shift from transitional art forms to hybrid ones. The hybrid can be defined as a break with the notion of tradition as accumulation over time and an emergence of new simultaneities whereby elements from previously separated territories and histories can be combined.[28] It is a phenomenon greatly accelerated by the spread of the mass media. An initial phase can be traced in the early twentieth-century avant garde movements, such as Brazilian Modernism. The Brazilian Modernists proposed a dissolution of cultural boundaries which would entirely refashion the national. But their vision of a new national identity arising out of modernization was a 'fantasy' (Renato Ortiz's word), unaccompanied by actual economic development.[29] The fact that the project of modernity arose before the real social changes which would constitute it, helps to explain the Brazilian tendency to an acritical attitude towards the modern, whereby the external forms of modernity, such as architecture, are treated as if in themselves they represented social and economic modernization.

A key emphasis in the Brazilian Modernist manifestoes was on the need to bring together the primitive and the modern. These were taken to be the crucial dimensions through which the objective could be achieved of a national-popular culture which would also be 'universal'. 'We have a double and present basis – the forest and the school': 'barbarians, credulous, picturesque and gentle' and at the same time 'newspaper readers'.[30] 'A language without erudition' was necessary, 'natural and neological'. The programme involved a re-evaluation of the primitive, against the deadweight of the *doutores*, the academics: 'the counterweight of native originality in order to make academicism useless'. On the agenda was a 'plunge' into what the official culture considered barbaric, especially the black and Indian cultures.[31] The 'Cannibalist Manifesto' ('Manifesto Antropófago') went further, proposing cannibalism as metaphor and method for a primitive assimilation of the civilized Other, through the idea of assimilation and digestion of the useful powers of the colonial master and his epigones – the opposite of colonial domination by white *doutores* and the calamity that had brought. This schematic did not have a lot to do with actual tribal culture, the anthropological study of which occurred later in the century. Nevertheless, it proposed a radically new vision of Brazilian culture. As Antonio Candido has commented, the Modernists' 'attitude, analysed in depth, represents an effort to destroy the class character of literature, and to transform it into a common good'.[32] The Cannibalist Manifesto stood against 'all forms of catechism' and for the liberation of the primitive, pagan, African and Indian elements which were not burdened by the plagues of 'Western culture': 'We were never catechized. We created carnival.' 'What obstructed the truth were the clothes, water-proof sheet between the inner and outer world. . . . We never permitted the emergence of logic amongst us. . . . We never had grammars. . . .'[33]

For Mário de Andrade, a major poet and theoretician of the movement, Modernism meant adopting the position of a 'primitive intellectual'. This included liberation of the unconscious in a context of hallucinated fascination with the modern urban landscape of São Paulo: 'When I feel a lyrical impulse, I write without thought everything which my unconscious screams to me.'[34] At the same time, he was concerned with the need to bridge the inherited opposition between the European idea of art as disinterested and the social embeddedness of primitive art: 'It is self-deception to imagine that the Brazilian primitivism of today is aesthetic. It is social. . . . Because all socially primitive art, including ours, is social, tribal, religious, commemorative art. It is circumstantial art. It is interested art. All exclusively artistic and disinterested art has no place in a primitive phase, a phase of construction.'[35] The new stance includes commitment to explore and validate those elements condemned by official high culture as barbaric and not worthy of consideration in order to transform them aesthetically and thus create the preconditions for the development of an autonomous national culture.[36]

Macunaíma, the eponymous hero of his novel, is pursued and finally destroyed by the simultaneous pressure of two worlds, the tribal and the modern.[37] During his infancy Macunaíma lives in harmony with nature in the tropical world of the Amazon. He spends his adulthood in São Paulo, searching for the lost talisman given him by the Empress of the Amazon but now in the possession of a São Paulo industrialist/cannibalistic giant. Vei, the Sun Goddess, offers him help, but he betrays her by making love to a Portuguese woman. As a result of her punishment, which is to seduce him to his destruction with the image of a ravishing European woman reflected by her rays on a lake, he loses a leg, his genitals and the talisman. Presented with grotesque realism, his irreverence, his many deaths and resurrections, his exuberant sexuality, his *palavrões* (vulgar language) and laughter, and the absence of repressive integration denoted by his lack of character, can be taken as metaphors for the unfinished, developing 'body' of Brazil, its people and culture. *Macunaíma* offers a multiple mirror to Brazil's heterogeneity, returning a parodic image of colonial views of the tropics. It also successfully synthesizes modernist aesthetic devices and popular cultural forms. While the formal narrative structure is based on the compositional principles of a rhapsody – the 'popular romance' sung by the travelling singers of the Northeast – in its open non-realist structure and its deployment of aesthetic devices such as simultaneity and the fusion of fantasy and reality, it is also a typically modernist work, in the sense of the international late-nineteenth- and early-twentieth-century cultural revolution described by Marshall

Berman, among others.[38] Mário de Andrade's use of the primitive (that is, tribal material) thus occurs in a context of fluidity and migration of aesthetic forms and in this sense is not a continuation of folklore by other means. Rather, it belongs to the interest in tribal art characteristic of early-twentieth-century avant gardes.[39]

Macunaíma, although concerned with the formation of a national identity, is not a classical bourgeois novel either in content or form. It parodies the *Bildungsroman* idea of a protagonist who learns through an accumulation of experiences, and it subverts narrative conventions with grotesque humour. Benedict Anderson's thesis that the novel was the main vehicle for forging the 'imagined community' of the nation corresponds more to the desires of the bourgeoisie than to the works that were actually produced. Andrés Bello, in an essay entitled 'Autonomía cultural de América' ('America's Cultural Autonomy' 1848), argued that the development of the narrative mode was essential for achieving a proper sense of Latin American history. The Argentinian statesman Bartolomé Mitre, in a prologue written in 1847, gives to novels a nation-building function, in the same sense as law.[40] However, despite the attempts of the literate elite to make use of narrative in this way, what the major works of literature display are the fundamental divisions of culture, language and territory that made the formation of modern nation-states difficult. One such example is the Colombian novel *María* (1867), called familiarly *La María* by Colombians and compulsory reading for every Colombian adolescent from the middle or upper class.[41] This family romance allegorizes the formation of the nation as erotic drama. The heroine is of Jewish extraction, and the hero does not belong to the ruling families of Bogotá. However, their moral qualities make them a model for the nation-as-family, capable of generously incorporating and converting outsiders. Nevertheless, despite the many marriages celebrated in the novel, there is one which does not take place. María becomes ill and dies before Efraín, who has been away studying in England, is able to reach her. The obstacle is the jungle terrain he has to cross to reach the Cauca valley and which becomes the major presence in the final chapters. The landscape which intervenes so powerfully is a cultural landscape, in Karl Sauer's sense of the term.[42] Rather than the physical features that are its perceived force, the decisive factors are the modes of transport, the forms of production and the social structures of those who inhabit the land. *La vorágine* (*The Vortex* 1924),[43] a novel of the early twentieth-century rubber boom, similarly places the lack of consciousness of national territory on the part of rubber tappers in the jungle – they are unable to differentiate between Colombia and Peru – as a barrier to an effective sense of the nation-state as a territorial entity.

Cultural Boundaries

A great part of artistic creation in Latin America is critical of cultural boundaries, revealing their relationship to social forces and to historical change. The texts chosen for consideration here are ones that articulate popular culture as an active principle and not just an exotic referent. In them popular cultures intervene structurally, altering inherited high cultural forms, such as the novel, through the use of popular aesthetic forms. Our examples are literary, though the same processes could have been illustrated in music or the visual arts. There are a number of reasons why the literary field is particularly appropriate to this discussion. In the first place, the written word has tended to play an oppressive role in Latin American history. This goes back to the legal instrument called the *requerimiento* (requirement), a written document explaining the history of the world from Adam, justifying the authority of the Pope and the Catholic monarchs, and requiring the Indian populations to submit and be converted. The *requerimiento* was designed to be read out by the Conquistadors before making just war on the Indians, who were unlikely, of course, to have understood a single word of it. Colonial and republican uses of the written word to keep a ruling elite in power make it a place of particularly acute contradictions. The novel offers an especially good probe into these given that it has been both a main site for the accumulation of middle-class cultural capital and at the same time a strategic place for transculturative actions, where subordinate cultures have had a transforming effect upon dominant ones.[44] Our aim is to suggest a reverse view from the one that legitimates Latin American literature by reference to the European canon of 'great literature'. The order in which authors and works have been placed is thematic rather than chronological and begins with rural and ethnic cultures before moving to urban culture and the experience of women.

Let us return to the family as founding principle of national coherence. This is a key theme in perhaps the most famous of all Latin American novels, García Márquez's *Cien años de soledad* (*One Hundred Years of Solitude* 1967). Here, in contrast to *María*, the problem is the excessive cohesiveness of the family. Its members are sucked into the solitude of Oedipal desire, incapable of sufficient solidarity for the construction of a society. The historical issue is the chronic weakness of the state in Colombia. Riven by factional disputes between feudal-type political parties and their personnel, its failure to provide a framework of coherence led to the frequent degeneration of politics into violence. The most recent prolonged period of generalized social violence (1946–66), known simply as *La Violencia*, was the result of a partial collapse of the state in the face of the new forces unleashed by capitalist development.[45]

Two different ideas of Colombian history can be traced in García Márquez's fictional work. On the one hand there is the view of the provincial aristocracy (for example, the Buendías in *One Hundred Years of Solitude*), who experience the penetration of capitalism (the arrival of the Banana Company) as a disaster. They have no sense of history as a process; it is timeless, static, repetitive. But there is also a popular memory, concerned not with the perpetuation of a way of life, but with preserving a counter-version of events to that put about by the dominant groups. In *La mala hora* (*In Evil Hour* 1962), a novel set in the period of *La Violencia*, there is a sharp contrast between the notables of the town, preoccupied with scandals which undermine their pretension to gentility, and the poor, who refuse to give any recognition to the authorities 'until you bring our dead back to life'.[46] Popular counter-memory provides the main thrust of the narrating voice in García Márquez's dictatorship novel, *El otoño del patriarca* (*The Autumn of the Patriarch* 1975). The life and death of the 150-year-old dictator, a fictional amalgam of a number of actual historical figures, are told by a multiple and multitudinous voice which gathers into itself popular experiences of abusive power stretching from the arrival of Columbus to the twentieth century. This voice simultaneously fashions the myth of the dictator's power and presence and destroys it through parody and laughter so that finally there is nothing actually there in the palace, the seat of power, except the continuity of popular memory and desire.

The title story of *La increíble y triste historia de la cándida Eréndira y de su abuela desalmada* (*Innocent Eréndira* 1972) narrates the enforced prostitution of a fourteen-year-old girl by her grandmother. She has accidentally burnt down the grandmother's house; to repay the debt she must sleep with a vast number of men, over a period of many years. In order to place the business on an entrepreneurial footing, the grandmother organizes a travelling tent, with a throne-like bed in the middle for Eréndira. But every single item of the infrastructure (transport, bed, tent, and so on) must be paid for by Eréndira's body. Although the economy of this arrangement has capitalist characteristics (for example, accumulation, the body as commodity), it takes place alongside popular, pre-capitalist forms of exchange. The following conversation takes place between the grandmother and a postman who passes by on a mule:

'Do you like her?' asked the grandmother. . . .
'Not bad for a hungry man,' he smiled.
'A hundred pesos', the grandmother said.

'It would have to be made of gold!' he said. 'That's what it costs me to eat for a month.'

'Don't be tight-arsed', the grandmother said. 'The air mail postman earns more than a priest.'

'I'm the national mail', the man said. 'The air mail is the one who goes in a van.'

'Anyway love is as important as food', the grandmother said.

'But it doesn't nourish you.'

The grandmother understood that a man who lived on other people's hopes had too much time on his hands for bargaining.

'How much have you got?' she asked. . . .

'I'll give you a reduction', she said, 'but on one condition: you spread the news everywhere.'[47]

The key features of a meeting of traditional and modern economies are given here: time measured as time to bargain, as opposed to time equals money; demand relative to need, as opposed to the creation of demand from supply ('the algebra of need', in William Burroughs's phrase); localized and specific exchange, as opposed to universalized exchange. The grandmother, in a daring and imaginative act of exchange between one system and another, uses the distributive network of the traditional economy (itself a mixture of a localized form of transport and a national, homogenizing service – the post – which distributes the written word) in order to universalize her commodity.

Neither the modern nor the traditional occurs in a pure state; rather, elements of each combine in different ways. Once the news has been spread by the postman, the tent becomes surrounded by food and lottery stalls and a photographer arrives – a fair establishes itself. At first the grandmother will only accept cash, but over the months she learns 'the lessons of reality' and accepts 'medals of saints, family relics, wedding rings';[48] after a period of time, there is enough to buy a donkey and move to new locations: the old gold pays for new mobility. Nor is each form of economy, traditional and modern, precisely equivalent to traditional and modern cultural strata. Although the grandmother conducts her business like a capitalist, her treasured objects are feudal and colonial, the most important being a viceregal throne: capital accumulation is used only to perpetuate feudal privilege, a satire perhaps on the distortions of modernization in Colombia. Popular culture, however, preserves a difference on both cultural and economic levels. The grand-mother's sacred symbols, her dreams of the perpetuation of colonial privilege, are the object of burlesque laughter. The story's viewpoint, the economy of its meanings, arises from a continuity of popular experience. A group of ordinary prostitutes, angry at Eréndira's privileges, which rest ultimately on political favour, capture her and parade her round town on her bed like a saint, in a parody of Catholic processions. The endless accumulation of wealth, at the expense of Eréndira's body and of the reduction of love to money, is also a burlesque of capital accumulation. The economic activity which receives most frequent mention is smuggling. It takes place at the margins of the nation-state: the smugglers (*contrabandistas*) are better armed than the police, and their activities depend on a constant evasion of national frontiers. Eréndira is finally liberated by a smuggler called Ulysses.

While García Márquez uses popular voices and iconography to satirize feudal privilege, Juan Rulfo's story 'Luvina' carries out a humorous demolition of populism. It takes the form of a one-sided conversation, the speaker being a rural schoolmaster who has been sent, in the tradition of Vasconcelos's missionary teachers, to enlighten the inhabitants of an isolated village somewhere in Jalisco.[49] There is, apparently, an interlocutor, the teacher's successor, who is about to depart for Luvina. But he is totally silent. What is it that destroys the possibility of dialogue?[50] It is true that the speaker gets increasingly drunk, until he falls asleep at the end. Getting drunk seems to be a response to frustration and depression at what happened to him in Luvina, but it does not explain the silence which surrounds his speech and also penetrates and erodes it. This has to be thought socially. It is not that the schoolmaster is unable to express, to find words for what happened to him. The act of communication is broken at some other level. When he first arrived in Luvina, the teacher was 'full of ideas'. He tried to persuade the inhabitants to leave their arid land and, with government support, settle elsewhere. 'But if we go away, who will take our dead?' they reply. 'They live here and we can't leave them on their own.'[51] The dead represent memory, a collective memory threatened by extinction through the dislocations of modernization in post-revolutionary Mexico. The peasants of Luvina also have something to say about the government:

> Do you say that the government will help us, sir? Don't you know the government?
> I told them I did.
> We also know it. It so happens we do. What we know nothing about is the government's mother.
> I said it was the Fatherland. They shook their heads, saying no. And they laughed. It was the only time I have seen the people of Luvina laugh. They bared their molar teeth and told me no, the government had no mother.[52]

There is no place inside educated discourse from which this can be said or answered. Not only are the meanings of the great symbols like the Fatherland

and the rhetoric of government = nation = great family made inoperative, so also are the assumptions which guide everyday life and its meanings. For instance, there is no sense of a forward-moving progression of time in Luvina: 'there time is very long. No one keeps an account of the hours and no one is worried about how the years mount up. The days begin and end. Then night comes. Just day and night until the day of death, which for them is a hope.'[53] The staticity of time in Luvina has penetrated the teacher's thinking: he is capable only of repeating himself, without progress or development. The speech which flows through him stumbles, falls silent, and receives no answer. The populist notion, that the nation can come together in a single voice, crumbles. There are not even the conditions for dialogue.

In what way does the popular manifest itself in Rulfo's writing? Certainly not as a voice expressed (the voice of the peasants, the people, and so on). It is more a question of a voice, or more precisely speech, which penetrates, interrupts, laughs, causes to stumble. The world of his characters cannot manifest itself directly as writing (it is an oral not a written world), but it can and does interfere with the codes of the written world. Rather than the illusory pretension of a direct transcription of orality, Rulfo opts for tracing the contours of an oral world through its clashes with the written. Another story, 'They Have Given Us the Land' ('Nos han dado la tierra'), shows how the dominant historical process moves in the opposite direction: the silencing of oral culture through the power of the written word. Some peasants have been allocated land under the Revolutionary Government's Agrarian Reform programme. When they complain that the land is so arid as to be useless, the bureaucrat in charge answers, 'Put it in writing. And now go away. It's the big estates [latifundios] you should be attacking, not the Government, which gives you land', and refuses to listen any more. What this means for the peasants is 'they did not let us say our things'.[54] Speech here has to be understood as action, and power. One is a long way from the creolist and indigenist literature of the earlier part of the century, in which normal Spanish is used for the narrative (the world of the author and reader), and the different language used for the peasants' speech illustrates from outside their mentality, rather than being an action in a field of power relations. In other words, in creolism and indigenism, the cultural universe within which novels are written and read is cut off from that of their referent (the peasantry, the rural hinterlands);[55] Rulfo, however, exposes and criticizes the division from the side of the dominated.

Augusto Roa Bastos's work achieves a similar effect. The story 'Borrador de un informe' ('Draft Report') places two cultural universes beside each other.[56] On one side is that of an army officer, sent to preserve public order during a popular Feast of the Virgin, and charged with writing a report on the events. On the other is that of the popular festival, which combines popular Catholic religiosity with the activities of a traditional fair. The result is a collision, both of two landscapes and of two symbolic orders. The officer arrives in a convoy of military vehicles, along a newly tarred road paid for by United States development money. But his way is blocked by a woman dragging a huge cross which makes a curving groove in tar softened by the hot sun. The woman does not listen to demands to clear the way and the officer's jeep has to leave the flat-surfaced road. As the vehicle moves onto the broken terrain, it is not clear whether the 'obscene shaking of her breasts' is the viewer's perception from the lurching jeep or caused by the uneven movements of the woman herself.[57] That the woman is a prostitute, seen in representation of Jesus himself, shocks the officer. In his cultural world, the sacred and the body, the virgin and the whore, are hierarchically separate. The symbolic order, which polarizes good and evil, must be kept intact. However, he is obsessively attracted to the woman whose presence, nevertheless, causes attacks of an illness which makes him vomit. These are some of the multiple ambiguities that occur as the two cultures interact. A dense irony, characteristic of all of Roa Bastos's writing, is produced as words, gestures and images mean different things according to which culture they are interpreted from.

However in the story there is no habitable middle space between the two cultures, no *mestizo* culture of the type promoted by Mexican intellectuals. The lack of a stable mixture is expressed in the fact that there is no solution to how two enigmatic murders took place during the festival; the hinterland between cultures produces disparate modes of explanation, which do not cohere. The lack is also expressed in the officer's body, torn by illness, a kind of semiotic illness arising from the unspeakability of his desire for the peasant woman. And finally, it is displayed by his discourse (his draft report with its bracketed sections not meant for publication), torn by different versions. The officer's written draft, self-contradictory, repeatedly doubling back on itself, is all that the reader is given. There is no additional layer of explanation capable of resolving the divisions.

Where the sense of history, of a meaningful sequence of events in time affecting a whole social group, depends upon spoken memory rather than written reports, then it requires living human beings to pass it on from one generation to another. The actual process and mode of non-written transmission is a key preoccupation of Roa Bastos's novel *Hijo de hombre* (*Son of Man* 1960). The continuity of popular memory, preserved by word of mouth, is also given material permanence by the inscribing or gouging of marks on the land, tracks made by human beings or vehicles moved by human beings, which outlast their death and can be read by future generations. History becomes not just words but seeing, touching, smelling. But Roa Bastos's novel is of course a written text; it can only subvert inherited forms of written transmission from within. This it dramatizes through the figure of the main character, Miguel Vera, whose name, meaning truth, alludes to a mode of verification parallel and antagonistic to the popular one. Vera is a military officer, trained in logistics, whose Euclidean ideas of space and individualistic ideas of history are broken down by the different world of popular rural culture.

Son of Man uses the written word, but in order to create new possibilities of meaning in writing through the force of popular culture. It includes two utopias: that of the oral universe as a historical continuity, 'written' on the land, and that of writing, whose meaning can break free from a particular place and time, creating its own space rather than needing the land to be inscribed on, and with a new mobility which can be placed at the disposal of popular experience. These are explorations which continue in Roa Bastos's massive novel, *Yo el Supremo* (*I the Supreme* 1974), which also gives to Guaraní, the ordinary spoken language of everyday life in Paraguay, a central role. The interferences of Guaraní in the Spanish text occur on three main levels: linguistically, it introduces wordplay, breaking up Spanish words into unaccustomed units; logically, it reformulates Western philosophy; and discursively, it projects speech as action rather than expression, and reality as essentially verbal.[58] One of the concerns of this novel is to invent that middle ground lacking in the earlier story 'Draft Report': to invent it, not as a populist programme of making the differences disappear, but as a viable multiplicity, demonstrating alternative possibilities for a future society.

Popular culture in the work of García Márquez, Rulfo and Roa Bastos is rural and traditional, rather than modern and urban. Nevertheless, their writing, in its use of modernist techniques, implies the experience of modern urban culture and requires a reader with that experience. In this sense, their fiction reflects particular biographical circumstances without which it would have been impossible: the experience of life in the regions where the social and cultural weight of the capital city is at its least, and contact with the international ambiance of big cities. None of them is actually a member of the popular classes and therefore they cannot express directly the experience of the latter. On the other hand, they reject the option of paternalistic substitution where the writer adopts 'the voice of the people'. Instead, their method has been to bring the cultural practices of subaltern social groups into the centre of narrative art, a tendency manifested in a number of other key Latin American writers of the past forty years. The outstanding writers in this very large field include the Guatemalan Miguel Angel Asturias and the Brazilian João Guimerães Rosa.

These cultural practices include oral narratives, visual art, music and dance. Probably the most extensive and inventive use of these forms by a major writer is José María Arguedas's *El zorro de arriba y el zorro de abajo* (*The Fox From Above and the Fox From Below* 1971). Born in Andean Peru of parents who belonged to the caste of 'whites', Arguedas spent a crucial part of his childhood in the care of an Indian community. In this novel, set in a large modern fishing town, Arguedas explores the invasion of the other, Westernized Peru by the 'avalanche' of Andean immigrants in the 1960s. A crucial aspect of Arguedas's strategy for bringing together native art with twentieth-century poetics has to do with the language of mythology. In the language of native myth, objects become signs without losing their place in the world as objects, as explained by Lévi-Strauss in the idea of 'the science of the concrete':[59] the world is perceived, in Baudelaire's phrase, as a forest of symbols. Arguedas places the sign-objects of myth in a field of twentieth-century poetic techniques, in an act of translation which can be compared with Jerome Rothenberg's translations of tribal poetries in *Shaking the Pumpkin*.[60] Arguedas's act of translation is also a vindication of an autonomous Andean knowledge: 'I have learned less from books than from the differences which exist, which I have felt and seen, between a cricket and a Quechua mayor, between a sea fisherman and a fisherman from lake Titicaca, between an oboe, the plume of a reed, the bite of a white louse and the plume of a sugar cane. . . . And this knowledge has, of course, as also does erudite knowledge, its circles and depths.'[61]

Let us consider his use of a particular Indian art form, the scissor-dance. Like other instances of native art, this is embedded in ritual occasion. In Arguedas's narrative it has been detached from its original occasion and resignified, although without losing all of its ritual connotations. The scissor-dance, traditional to the Lucanas and Huancavelica regions of Peru, involves competition between two kinship groups (*ayllus*) each with their own dancer, accompanied by harp and violin. The winner of the competition is the dancer who is able to carry out the most difficult feats. These require extraordinary agility and resistance to physical pain. The dance has infernal and diabolical associations for the Christian symbolic code, whereas in the Indian context it involves the traditional Andean notion of complementarity, whereby instead of excluding each other as polarities (like God and the Devil), social oppositions are conceived as complementary to each other. This makes the scissor-dance an essentially dialogical form.[62]

In *The Fox*, the scissor-dance becomes the controlling aesthetic form, as dialogue, dance and theatre, in a long episode which takes place inside a fishmeal factory. Diego, an anthropomorphic figure who is fox, mythic hero and a character in the novel, enters into a dialogue with the factory manager and the machinery. More accurately, he dances the machinery: 'He breathed not with his chest but with that of the eight machines.' As he dances, the workers watching him 'felt that the force of the world, so centred in the dance and in those eight machines, reached them, made them transparent'.[63] The dance transforms and refunctionalizes industrial technology through an Andean cosmology where the social is based in complementarity. And this occurs in a context of rapid modernization, bringing hybridization of cultural forms. Andean culture becomes fragmented and dispersed. But the loss of traditional coherence for modern hybridization gives Andean culture a new capacity to penetrate into the social fabric. The pink smoke at the factory, which rises 'without borders', like Diego's dance, becomes a *huaca*, a sacred object. To give a sense of the new cultural and social mobilities, the novel adopts a modernist montage technique, deploying an extraordinary multiplicity of voices through which different cultural worlds converge: a convergence of differences without uniformity.

This bears no similarity to Vargas Llosa's novel *El hablador* (*The Storyteller* 1987),[64] where the desire for a single national language is legitimated through a satire on the attempt of an anthropology student to make himself into a native shaman/storyteller. Not unexpectedly, *El hablador* is presented as written in Florence, symbolic of European high art and of a supposedly homogeneous culture. Arguedas's novel does not in fact pretend to 'give' a voice to subordinated groups. It shows a range of possibilities for the invention of new social and aesthetic forms, which require a new way of reading and a new reader – a reader of the future, with a knowledge both of literary reading and of Quechua culture, a type of reader who has recently begun to exist in Peru, where Quechua-speaking migrants to the cities are laying claim to the space of writing.[65] The conditions which make this type of book possible – the existence of a bicultural reading public – having ceased in Peru by the early seventeenth century, are now reappearing. At the same time, Arguedas's text implies a project of modernity, but an unprecedented, Peruvian modernity, based in the multiplicity and inventiveness of popular cultures. It bears no resemblance to the usual populist paradigms of inter-cultural processes with their culinary and metallurgic metaphors drawing on the crude mechanics of soup and melting pots.

A brief note on magical-realism seems appropriate here, given that it has been removed by critics from its sources in popular culture and as a result dehistoricized. If we take it, broadly, as the suspension of Enlightenment rationalism with its demotion of superstition, a rethinking of magical-realism from popular culture might start with how the imposition of the label 'idolatry' upon native cultures both foregrounded magic and denied it any cognitive dimension.[66] Thus the magic that continued to be practised by the lower orders of society became an alternative knowledge, from below. This is the 'colonial magic' referred to in Chapter 1. It was a syncretism of native Indian, African and popular European belief, shared by different social classes, located in the interstices rather than the official structures of society, and was primarily the province of women. This is the case in the work of García Márquez, whose insistence that what seems fantastic in his fiction is perfectly real needs to be understood in the context of readers whose everyday life is shaped by this historical inheritance. In a second sense, insofar as the term has been used say of Arguedas's work, it involves native ritual practices which include not only the idea of magic as action produced by 'irrational' agencies but also a network of shared meanings which the practitioner engages with and reproduces.[67] In neither of these first two meanings is it connected with fantasy, with which it has tended to be elided. This is because it is not a projection of individual desire, as in European Romanticism, where magic becomes merely aesthetic, separate from social uses, the final stage of which being the degeneration of magic into a 'drug', as William Empson puts it, referring to Walter de la Mare.[68] The difference is clear, if one thinks of Diego's dancing the machinery, in Arguedas's *The Fox*. In a third and connected sense, magical belief is not always treated as positive. For example, in Rulfo's *Pedro Páramo* the characters, who are literally dead, live in the hell created by Catholic ideology.[69] Finally, to legitimate magic can be a vindication of pre-capitalist culture, against the logic of capitalist accumulation and positivist social engineering. When García Márquez presents a world governed by magic he is breaking with those rationalist philosophies of nationhood which exclude popular culture as superstitious and valueless. Different from magical-realism in European art, in Latin America magical-realism arises in an encounter between modernism and popular culture.[70] In Arguedas, exceptionally, Andean magic not only confronts modernization and its technology as themselves magical, in the sense that they are not as rationally controlled as they pretend to be, but also proposes an alternative way of controlling them socially.

Mass Culture and the Novel

The process of modernization took a very particular form in Argentina, as was shown in Chapter 1. In the aftermath of massive immigration from Europe in the late nineteenth and early twentieth centuries, a large part of the population found itself without inherited models for social improvement. These they found in films and radio programmes. The elaboration of unifying social models passed through radio and cinema. The first novel by the Argentinian novelist Manuel Puig is entitled *La traición de Rita Hayworth* (*Betrayed by Rita Hayworth* 1969). Its characters live in a small town in the province of La Pampa. The most powerful cultural influence in their lives is cinema, and cinema means Hollywood films of the 1940s, providing images of female beauty and desirable lifestyles. These are films whose codes of evasive (in fact repressive) sublimation are more easily negotiable by US audiences, for whom Hollywood film and everyday life can be more easily compared. For Puig's characters, a social referent for film images is lacking, enlarging the gulf between their circumstances and what they see on the screen and making the difficulty in negotiating it that much greater. What makes the negotiation possible is the existence of a common process in life and films: the conversion of lifestyle (food, clothes, speech, and so on) into cultural commodity. In this sense Puig is tracing a key moment of the history of how the capitalist market for cultural goods became consolidated in Argentina.

In Puig's second novel, *Boquitas pintadas* (*Heartbreak Tango* 1969), popular forms supply the narrative procedures. He attempted to publish it first as a serial (*folletín*): the plot is divided, for this purpose, into episodes. Not only the materials but the type of reading invited draw on the *folletín* tradition. 'I enjoy very much certain manifestations of what they call bad taste and I find, in its habitual rejection, a form of repression', Puig stated in an interview. 'When a book gives a very immediate pleasure I believe it makes people suspicious, I think that at the bottom of this there's a factor of puritanism, which the lower classes don't have.'[71] This break with high-cultural prejudice has been followed subsequently by many other novelists, among them Mario Vargas Llosa in *La tía Julia y el escribidor* (*Aunt Julia and the Scriptwriter* 1977). *Heartbreak Tango* includes tangos, boleros (by the late 1930s rivalling tangos in popularity), newspaper articles, radio serials and films, the latter two serving as the principal models of narrative method. But this approach does not result in a single, unifying language; on the contrary, the characters are places of intersection of different languages: written, spoken, middle-class, working-class, police reports, boleros, and so on. In this crucial sense, it does not follow the usual roles of soap opera, which seduces with its pretence that despite their differences all social groups in the end speak the same language. The British serial *EastEnders* can be taken as an example of this phenomenon, in that despite its accuracy to different sociolects, it promises a single, shared meaning behind them. Puig's world, in contrast, is irremediably divided – at least, on the level of verbal language. Because at the level of image there is unity across the social divisions, suggesting that film in Argentina from the 1930s has generated a unified imaginary, shared across social groups, against the dividing effects of verbal language.

Another sense in which *Heartbreak Tango* is not simply a *folletín* or soap opera, but produces a distance from its models, has to do with the relationship between the characters and the social stereotypes in play. As the Cuban novelist Severo Sarduy puts it, 'in a serial, literally, there are no characters; between the clichés and the actors who inhabit them . . . there are no gaps, no interstices, both correspond to the other in an ideal way'.[72] In other words, identity is treated not as a process but as a myth. The difference in Puig's novels is that the process is displayed. 'The urgent need for models, for mythical directives, is so compelling, and the absence of them is lived so much like a *lack* – the lack or need which drug addicts speak of: these characteristics are *drugged with clichés* – that all communication has to be preceded by their consumption.'[73] The dependency shown to the reader highlights the gap between characters and stereotypes. Person and media stereotype cannot perfectly coincide – there is always a residue.

Let us consider Puig's approach to the popular media from a different angle, that of Armand Mattelart's critique of the effect of mass communications in an underdeveloped society. Taking Marx's analysis of the fetishism of commodities, whereby commodities seem to be endowed by a power and life of their own whereas in fact they are social products, as a model for explaining the functioning of the mass media, Mattelart argues that their meanings are not inherent to them but derive from the social and economic system, a fact which they seek to hide by appearing to be free and natural. In an underdeveloped society, films and television offer a way of life the vast majority will never enjoy: they passively consume objects and lifestyles without having the conditions for their production, which means that they consume their own underdevelopment.[74] For the reader of Puig's work, however, there are two possible effects: either 'seduction' or 'catharsis'. These are Puig's words; others might be either identification or critical distance: a reflective distance not just from verbal languages but from the cinematic image itself.[75]

The following is from the social page of a provincial newspaper, reporting a dance and naming two of the novel's characters:

> SPLENDID CELEBRATION OF THE FIRST DAY OF SPRING
> In observance of a practice which custom requires, the Social and Sports Club inaugurated the arrival of the vernal season with a splendid dance, held on Saturday 22nd September to the pleasant sound of the band The Harmonics, from this locality. At midnight, during an interval, the enchanting Nélida Fernández, whose slender silhouette adorns these pages, was elected Queen of Spring 1936.[76]

The key quality of this language is the role played by the adjectives, which serve as intensifiers of glamour. They add no specific qualities to the people or events, only a gloss which makes social desirability appear to be inherent. It is here, in the fetishism displayed, belonging to an older medium (the newspaper), that cinema and later television move in. What is important is that it is displayed, critically, as an area of mystification and potential demystification within which Puig's characters actively negotiate. They calculate their chances, and measure distances between the idealized and the real world, while pretending to themselves and others that they are not doing that – the imaginary allowing a certain freedom to shape and negotiate which ideology does not. The critique of sublimation, as non-distance between person and filmic image, and of filmic imagination Hollywood-style is taken further in *The Buenos Aires Affair* (1973). *El beso de la Mujer Araña (The Kiss of the Spider Woman* 1976) explores a possible different use of popular media, as a counter-manipulation to dominant machista values. These are the terms of discussion Puig's work suggests, a good deal more useful than the notion of audience passivity or than what the autobiographical protagonist of Puig's first novel was able to learn: that treachery is a characteristic of female attraction and, by implication of films.

Any idea of popular culture in Latin America as either nostalgic and out of date or as a political fiction is banished by Luis Rafael Sánchez's recent novel, *La importancia de llamarse Daniel Santos (The Importance of Being Daniel Santos* 1989). Here it is music which cuts across social divisions and national frontiers, feeding 'the machine of the emotions', one of the many ironical phrases whereby Sánchez breaks down the supposed incompatibility between the culture industry and authentic feeling. Daniel Santos's boleros (Santos was a famous Puerto Rican singer) penetrate through the whole of Spanish America, fulfilling that vision of unity dreamed by Bolívar and by the great Nicaraguan poet Rubén Darío, among others. The issue of a Spanish-American cultural identity is of course particularly acute for those like Sánchez whose native country is Puerto Rico. Popular culture, 'the great museum of collective memory', is for Sánchez both object and method of research and belongs to the vast majority, who are poor.[77] One of the sections of his book is headed: *'Dictated in the bar. The Birth of Paricutín amongst mariachis, tequilas, juke box and other research resources'*, pointing to the multiplicity of its sources and the variety of its locations. Interviews and sociological observation are carried out in bars, record shops and streets throughout the subcontinent. The end of the presentation, which is entitled 'The method of discourse', announces: 'The importance of being Daniel Santos is a hybrid frontier narrative, exempt from the rules of genre.'[78] It laughs at high-cultural seriousness by quoting and misquoting Descartes, Plato, Shakespeare, Quevedo, and so on but nevertheless uses these materials seriously in order to invent a theory and practice of popular discourse.[79] It invades other discourses and intellectual provinces with disrespectful respect, combining novel, essay, sociology, philosophy, linguistic treatise (on the history and geography of popular language), and what Sánchez calls 'fabulation'. Through all of this, the bolero supplies both content and form, discourse and emotion.

Daniel Santos is shown to be entirely modern, in three key senses: first, because he has outlasted many fashions, such as Presley, the Beatles, Raphael and Willie Colón; second, because in an epochal sense, he marks the mass experience of the modern; and third 'because he risks everything, he radicalizes the senses', applying the lessons of Rimbaud, Darío and the twentieth-century avant garde.[80] But it is a different modernity, not that of the American dream, from which the poor are excluded, and not that of the Latin American elites with their skyscrapers and other fetishes of the modern: 'Because of its ardent attunement with the huge population of the poor, of those who scratch a living together, of the nobodies, the modernity of Inquieto Anacobero Daniel Santos grows and perpetuates itself. Tuned to the marginalizations of feeling.'[81] Tuning is a metaphor from radio, as medium for the massification of emotion. 'Marginalization of feeling' is a repeated phrase used by Sánchez with considerable ambiguity as to whether the emotional dimension precedes or follows its medium (primarily bolero and melodrama) and how far it is a product of or a response to social conditions. It does not apply exclusively to any social sector: Sánchez refuses to totalize his discourse, to make any part signify the whole, differing here from much sociology and from those like Octavio Paz who seek through dialectics to make the marginalized, the periphery into a new centre.[82] There is no centre to Sánchez's discourse, only moving fragments. Nevertheless, the *barriada* (shanty town) is the key site of the modern and its new movements. Poverty, in the sense of social marginality, does not prevent cultural innovation; on the contrary. 'Reader, do you now understand why I travel in the *guagua* [bus] which goes where modernity swarms and continues, straight ahead, to the other stops which fragment totality? . . . To the powers of music. . . . To the juke box as adviser to the unwary. To Our Night Which Is Here On Earth.'[83] The *barriada* and its mode of transport offer, against Catholicism, a parodic counter-transcendence. The only transcendence possible in this world is love.

Sánchez offers an archive of the popular musical culture of twentieth-century Latin America. His text, which constantly invites the reader into dialogue, is a patchwork, a parodic dialogue of song texts, through which the emotions of the public pass: 'the public . . . rummages through the words of the boleros and *guarachas* which it sings, convinced that they are the hidden corners of its own existence transformed into song'.[84] America, 'the bitter America, the shoeless America, America in Spanish' is 'orphic to the point of rashness';[85] music is *the* major mediation, in love, in revolution, in death. It is also a key resource of the poor, as is laughter too, and 'healthily neurotic melodrama', that 'curtain-raiser for carnal love'.[86] The book is also an archive of a particular emotional style, irreverent and transgressive, and of 'the tics of machismo', one of whose sacred places is the billiard hall, 'the Vatican of virility', 'the mosque to which the wild herd of machos turns its eyes, five times daily'.[87] But what it celebrates, with pleasure, exuberance and irreverence, is the distinctive modernity of Spanish America, for Sánchez a fundamentally popular one.

Double Marginalization

The world of Jesusa Palancares, the speaker of the oral autobiography transcribed by Elena Poniatowska as *Till We Meet Again (Hasta no verte Jesús mío* 1969) begins in rural Oaxaca before the Mexican Revolution, in an ambience of traditional Zapotec and *mestizo* culture, and ends, via a series of migrations, in Mexico City in the 1960s. If her cultural world is pre-modern, it is nevertheless heard (or strictly speaking read) within modernity. The genre whereby a member of the dominant culture interviews a member or members of the subaltern goes back to the sixteenth century in Latin America, when priests of the Spanish religious orders took down native accounts of religious practices and historical memory. The Franciscan friar Sahagún, for example, is responsible for crucial information about the native experience of Conquest in Mexico.[88] The practice of ethnography is also pertinent, whether in the form of native materials transcribed and assembled by an anthropologist, or where anthropological skills are used by members of a native community, with the help, direct or not, of a professional anthropologist. And in a more general sense, we should mention the considerable impact of anthropology upon Latin American writing, for instance in the work of Asturias, Arguedas, Guimarães Rosa and Darci Ribeiro. For a voice from one culture to be 'heard' in another, two main methods are possible. Either an imaginary ethnic author is required, from 'inside' the ethnic culture, as is the case with what has been called ethnofiction; or alterations are needed in the communicative models of the receiving culture. A number of the latter occur in Poniatowska's book. There are references to the moment of speaking and being listened to, source of the written text, and acknowledgements of the time-lapse between the moment of Jesusa's spoken account and the actual events, particularly when these have a special intensity, such as her meeting with Emiliano Zapata during the Revolution. There are also occasional references to the presence of the interviewer herself. These details, which are departures from the codes of written autobiography, are often eliminated by ethnographers when present-ing oral materials in written form, thus obscuring the process of their textual production.[89]

However, in Till We Meet Again it is in certain qualities of the language that the effects of orality are most perceivable. Apart from the lexical and morphological inventiveness of popular speech, there is an exceptional use of the sensuousness of sound, as in the following description of how her father would bring oysters fresh from the sea: 'Then with his machete pácatelas! my father pulled off the big oyster shells, opened them and we ate the oysters in their shell because they're alive and fresh' ('Entonces con su machete ¡pácatelas! mi papá arrancaba las grandes ostras, las abría y en la misma concha comíamos los ostriones porque están vivitos, fresquecitos').[90] Apart from specific onomatopoeic sounds, the language often verges on onomatopoeic effects. Both can be heard in this account of bathing in the sea: 'It looks so beautiful when the wave comes up and zas! it covers us and then goes away, and to wait for the next one which is just coming flicking its tail as if all the water had gathered there in a single cloudburst' ('Se ve tan bonito cuando se

220

acerca la ola y ¡zás! nos tapa y luego se va, y esperar la otra que allí viene dando coletazos como si toda el agua se hubiera juntado allí en un solo chubasco').[91] Here there are also traces of Indian beliefs, the water moving like snakes' tails.

It is difficult, however, in this text to perceive the effects of the editing which has been carried out between Jesusa's speech in its raw state and its written version. Take the issue of repetition, a prime characteristic of oral utterance. It is present at the level of the phrase, as in Jesusa's description of the prison where she worked as a girl: 'It was an old-style prison, with a very big dome, long long and in the middle a grille and then more bars and bars....'[92] However, at the level of the sentence, repetition is less frequent and at the larger narrative level it is virtually absent, which is highly uncharacteristic of oral utterance. Thus there would seem to have been a selective elimination of oral features. The actual process of editing is not shown to the reader. Where this applies most importantly perhaps is to the features of continuity and progression in time in the written narrative which are clearly the result of the refashioning of materials supplied by an oral memory whose workings become to some extent obscured. The result of this attenuation of oral form is that the book is probably more easily readable for those who have grown up in a world of print culture. What it manifests, in a historical sense, is the replacement of a world of oral memory with one of written memory.

As a survivor from a pre-capitalist culture, Jesusa has effected the same transitions made, wholly or partly, by millions of Mexicans – and other Latin Americans – in the twentieth century. Her cultural archive includes elements of Zapotec Indian as well as Hispanic *mestizo* culture with the additional experiences of massive population displacement during and after the Revolution, including her own move to Mexico City. There, as in many Latin American cities, spiritism serves as a continuation of popular rural religion. Radio, film and television, however, appear to have impinged very little on her consciousness. The book offers an alternative history of twentieth-century Mexico, seen from the point of view of women's experience. The account of women's role and of everyday life among the forces engaged in the Mexican Revolution is particularly valuable as a corrective to the dominant versions. Jesusa's intelligence is manifested in the fineness of her perceptions, her sensibility for language, her linguistic ability (in Zapotec, English, Catalan and Japanese, as well as Spanish). There is also her capacity for survival and her uncompromising independence. These are not 'psychological' qualities of a single individual but aspects of a whole social layer, which Jesusa calls 'this old race'. In this sense her speaking includes the voices of many. There was an extraordinary amount of violence in her life, from the death of her mother when she was eight years old to other deaths, journeys and discontinuities. 'Of all my relatives . . . I was the only wanderer, the walker, the one who has been everywhere. Because my father never saw what I saw.'[93] In death too, which she faces with stoical humour, she desires the journeys to continue: 'I want very much to go and die there where I went wandering. May God remember me because I would like to end up under a tree far away! Then the vultures would surround me and that's it; they'd come and ask for me and I would be so happy there flying in the vultures' guts.'[94]

Jesusa's story is one of marginalization due to both gender and poverty. She is in conflict with the dominant order because although a woman and poor she is also independent. Her interpretation of her life does not confirm a fixed set of symbolic hierarchies. She accepts the mobility of her life and her identity, in its transitions to the modern world. Although her autobiography marks the end of a particular experience, of older, pre-modern cultures, nevertheless the fragmentation and dispersal is accepted, without the professional nostalgia and romanticism of so many intellectuals. The old culture, fragmented, becomes reformulated, through a written narrative, itself disengaged from the pressure of dominant values. In this sense, the book *Till We Meet Again* is exemplary of and contributes to a Latin American experience of popular modernity.

Notes

1. Bakhtin, quoted in Peter Stallybrass and Allon White, *The Politics and Poetics of Transgression,* London 1986, p. 17.

2. Historically, in Europe, the word 'culture' became separated from popular and mass culture in an attempt to resist the conversion of culture into a commodity. See Raymond Williams, *Marxism and Literature,* Oxford 1977, pp. 153–4.

3. London 1986.

4. Stallybrass and White, p. 3.

5. Ibid., p. ix.

6. Ibid., p. 191.

7. For examples of how historically specific distinctions of hierarchy are made into a general classification, see ibid., pp. 3, 23, 194.

8. Nelly Richard, 'Estéticas de la oblicuidad', *Revista de Crítica Cultural,* Vol. 1, No. 1, p. 6.

9. Rodrigo, Edwin and Luis Montoya, *La sangre de los cerros,* Lima 1987, pp. 648–9. *Cholo* is a derogatory racial term for people showing characteristics of Andean culture.

10. The point was made by Rodrigo Montoya, in a talk given at the Institute of Latin American Studies, London, 16 May 1990.

11. See, for example, Fernando Calderón, ed., *Imágenes desconocidas: la modernidad en la encrucijada postmoderna,* Buenos Aires 1988.

12. Mirko Lauer, 'La estructura del objeto plástico', in *Critica de la artesanía*, Lima 1982, pp. 145–63.

13. Ticio Escobar, *El mito del arte y el mito del pueblo*, Asunción 1986, p. 14; see also p. 16.

14. Ibid., p. 18.

15. Pierre Bourdieu, *Outline of a Theory of Practice*, Cambridge 1977, p. 197; see also p. 178.

16. Escobar, p. 24.

17. Ibid., p. 37.

18. See Renato Ortiz, *A moderna tradicão brasileira*, São Paulo 1988, pp. 25–9.

19. Angel Rama, 'Literatura y cultura', in *Transculturación narrativa en América Latina*, Mexico 1982, pp. 11–56. See Patricia D'Allemand, *Hacia una crítica literaria latinoamericana: nacionalismo y cultura en el discurso de Beatriz Sarlo*, London 1990.

20. Domingo F. Sarmiento, *Facundo*, Buenos Aires 1963, pp. 38, 58, 65.

21. Ibid., pp. 67–8.

22. Ibid., p. 41.

23. Ibid., p. 38.

24. Ibid., p. 40.

25. Ibid., p. 47.

26. Gina Cánepa, paper given at AELSAL meeting, 3 June 1990. See also, 'Folletines históricos del Chile Independiente y su articulación con la novela naturalista', *Revista de Crítica Literaria Latinoamericana*, Vol. XV, No. 30, 1989, pp. 249–58.

27. Jesús Martín-Barbero, *Procesos de comunicación y matrices de cultura*, Mexico, n.d., p. 133.

28. See Néstor García Canclini, 'Escenas sin territorio: estética de las migraciones e identidades en transición', *Revista de Crítica Cultural*, Vol. 1, No. 1, p. 9, and 'Culturas híbridas: el espacio comunicacional como problema interdisciplinario', unpublished paper.

29. Ortiz, p. 35.

30. Oswald de Andrade, 'Manifesto Pau-Brasil' (1924), in G.M. Telles, *Vanguarda Europeia e Modernismo Brasileiro*, pp. 266–72.

31. See Vivian Schelling, 'Mário de Andrade: A Primitive Intellectual' in *Bulletin of Hispanic Studies*, Vol. LXV, 1988, pp. 74–5.

32. Antonio Candido, *Literatura e sociedade*, São Paulo 1976, p. 164.

33. Oswald de Andrade, 'Manifesto Antropofago', in Telles, pp. 293–300.

34. *Pauliceia Desvairada (Hallucinated City)*, Poesías completas, São Paulo 1966, p. 13.

35. Schelling, p. 80.

36. Ibid., p. 76.

37. *Macunaíma* [translation], London 1984. See Vivian Schelling, 'Brazilian Journeys', *Third World Quarterly*, January 1988, pp. 312–17.

38. The narrative structure of *Macunaíma* may also be compared with *Bumba-meu-Boi:* discussed earlier, in which the central theme, the death and resurrection of the ox or in this case, of Macunaíma, is complemented by various digressions and side-plots.

39. James Clifford, 'Ethnographic Surrealism', *Comparative Studies in Society and History*, Vol. 23, No. 4, 1981.

40. Prologue to *Soledad (Solitude* 1847).

41. English translation by R. Ogden, New York 1890.

42. Karl Sauer, 'The Morphology of Landscape', in *Land and Life*, Berkeley 1963, p. 333.

43. Translation: New York 1935.

44. For a discussion of the term transculturation, see Angel Rama, *La transculturación narrativa en América Latina*, pp. 32–4.

45. See P. Oquist, *Violence, Conflict and Politics in Colombia*, New York 1980, pp. 4–17, 194–5.

46. *La mala hora*, Buenos Aires 1969, p. 77.

47. *La increíble y triste historia de la cándida Eréndira y de su abuela desalmada*, Barcelona 1972, pp. 109–10.

48. Ibid., p. 111.

49. See pp. 160–61.

50. See Roberto Schwarz, 'Grande Sertão: a fala', in *A sereia e o desconfiado*, Rio 1965, p. 38; Angel Rama, *La transculturación narrativa en América Latina*, Mexico 1982, p. 46; Carlos Pacheco, *The Oral Hinterland: Cultural Orality in Contemporary Latin American Fiction*, PhD Thesis, University of London King's College 1989, Chapter 4; and William Rowe, *Rulfo: El llano en llamas*, London 1987, pp. 61–67.

51. Juan Rulfo, *El llano en llamas*, Madrid 1985, pp. 127–8.

52. Ibid., p. 127.

53. Ibid., p. 126.

54. Ibid., pp. 41–2.

55. See Antonio Cornejo Polar, 'El indigenismo y las literaturas heterogéneas: su doble estatuto socio-cultural', *Revista de Crítica Literaria Latinoamericana*, Nos. 7–8, 1978, p. 12 and *Literatura y sociedad en el Perú: la novela indigenista*, Lima n.d., pp. 16–23.

56. In Augusto Roa Bastos, *El baldío*, Buenos Aires 1966, pp. 61–77.

57. Ibid., p. 66.

58. See Rubén Barreiro Saguier, 'Estratos de la lengua guaraní en la escritura de Augusto Roa Bastos', in J.M. López de Abiada, ed., *Perspectivas de comprensión y de explicación de la narrativa latinoamericana*, Bellinona 1982, pp. 181–97.

59. Claude Lévi-Strauss, *The Savage Mind*, London 1966, Chapter 1 and p. 268.

60. New York 1986.

61. José María Arguedas, *El zorro de arriba y el zorro de abajo*, Buenos Aires 1971, p. 204.

62. This crucial point was first made by Martin Lienhard in *Cultura popular andina y forma novelesca*, Lima 1981, pp. 130–9.

63. Arguedas, p. 145.

64. *The Storyteller*, London 1990.

65. Martin Lienhard in Cornejo Polar et al., *Vigencia y universalidad de José María Arguedas*, Lima 1984, p. 19.

66. See Carmen Bernand and Serge Gruzinski, *De l'idolâtrie: Une archéologie des sciences religieuses*, Paris 1988.

67. See Lévi-Strauss, pp. 220–21, and William Rowe, *Mito e ideología en la obra de José María Arguedas*, Lima 1979, pp. 88–93.

68. William Empson, *Arguifying*, London 1988, p. 94.

69. See Julio Ortega, *The Poetics of Change*, Austin 1984, p. 4.

70. See Wieland Schmied, *Neue Sachlichkeit und Magischer Realismus in Deutschland 1918–1933*, 1969.

71. Ana María de Rodríguez, 'Manuel Puig ¿De lo cursi al arte?', *Eco*, No. 206,. dic. 1987, pp. 212–213.

72. Severo Sarduy, 'Notas a las notas a las notas', *Revista Iberoamericana*, Nos. 76–7, 1971, p. 562.

73. Ibid., p. 565.

74. Armand Mattelart, 'The Nature of Communications Practice in a Dependent Society', *Latin American Perspectives*, Vol. V, No. 1, pp. 23, 26.

75. 'The Puig affaire, o de la literatura como espectáculo', *Postdata*, Vol. 1, No. 2, 1974, pp. 31, 32. Cf. Lois Zamora, 'Clichés and Defamiliarization in the Fiction of Manuel Puig and Luís Rafael Sánchez', *Journal of Aesthetics and Art Criticism*, IV, 41, pp. 421–36.

76. Manuel Puig, *Boquitas pintadas*, Buenos Aires 1969, p. 20.

77. Luis Rafael Sánchez, *La importancia de llamarse Daniel Santos*, Mexico 1989, p. 132.

78. Ibid., p. 16.

79. See Julio Ortega, *Teoría y práctica del discurso popular*, London 1989.

80. Sánchez, p. 82.

81. Ibid., p. 92.

82. Octavio Paz, *El laberinto de la soledad*, Mexico 1959, Chapter 1.

83. Sánchez, p. 87.

84. Ibid., p. 88.

85. Ibid., p. 103.

86. Ibid., pp. 110, 115–6.

87. Ibid., p. 122.

88. For a collection of native responses to the Conquest, including those transcribed by Sahagún, see Miguel León Portilla, *La visión de los vencidos*, Madrid 1985.

89. The extremely valuable autobiography of Gregorio Condori Mamani, recorded and transcribed by Ricardo Valderrama and Carmen Escalante, is a good test case. See Gregorio Condori Mamani, *Autobiografía*, Cusco 1982. Cf. Martin Lienhard, 'La etnoficción o la mala conciencia del intelectual colonizado', *Tilalc*, vol. 3, no. 4.

90. Elena Poniatowska, *Hasta no verte Jesús mío*, Mexico 1969, p. 24. Note the temporal shift to the present tense, dramatizing the past in the present, a device typical of oral narrative.

91. Ibid., p. 25.

92. Ibid., p. 34.

93. Ibid., p. 315.

94. Ibid., p. 316.

CONCLUSION

Memory, Destruction, Transformation

This book began with the destruction of cultures and the precariousness of memory. There have been in the twentieth century many examples of cultures which have disappeared in Latin America as a result of the struggle for the domination of territories, resources and populations. One such is a group of Guaraní forest dwellers in Paraguay, called the Axé, now reduced to becoming servants in white households. They expressed their response to being eradicated as an identifiable human group in a number of songs, which have been recorded and transcribed. One of these is the 'Song of Kanexirigi', which celebrates the founding symbols of a culture at the moment of its death:

> We, who were Axé
> do not ever go out any more
> among the columns of the forest.
> Our great father
> with his chief's cap
> even though he has ceased to live
> we will never abandon him any more.

This type of document makes the fashion for claiming primitive origins as part of one's identity, to say the least of it, look disrespectful. The response which is needed is to historicize memory and continuity: whose memory, preserved in what way, and under what circumstances?

Our song
is those who will never again be men
is the old men
they grow with the rain
they whom we have left far away
their head folded on crossed arms.[1]

The circumstances of this poem and the hazards of its preservation make imaginary continuities of identity like the collective unconscious or even the 'melting-pot of cultures' idea seem fairly irrelevant.

Unless the violence, the discontinuity, is remembered by some means or another – in the case of the Axé song, by the intervention of ethnography – a proper historical understanding becomes impossible, and cultural history runs the risk of becoming a comfortable ideological exercise. Part of the violence produced by global homogenization is the illusion that there is only one history, an illusion which suppresses the differences between the different histories lived by different groups of human beings. There is a further point: historical memory is a vital cultural action in the making and preservation of those differences, and the destruction of memory a prime means of domination. Social memory is not just continuity and unchanging identity, it is also memory of destruction and discontinuity. Nor is it appropriate to speak of a single popular memory: there are a variety of differentiated memories.

The military dictatorships in the southern cone countries (Chile, Argentina and Uruguay) during the past two decades have given new urgency to these questions of social memory and historical record. The study which we discussed in Chapter 3 shows that the Argentinian dictatorship produced an effect of public amnesia, which depended on the eradication of the normal spaces in which memory is exercised and sedimented. Nevertheless, means were found to defend and preserve a memory of the 'disappeared', the victims of extra-legal execution and imprisonment carried out by military and paramilitary forces. The most important of these has been the action of the 'Madres de la Plaza de Mayo' (Mothers of the Plaza de Mayo), whose weekly occupation of the main public space of Buenos Aires acquired the force of a ritual of counter-memory. Even after the 'Ley de obediencia debida' (law of due obedience), passed during the democratic regime which followed in order to grant middle- and lower-ranking officers immunity from prosecution for atrocities against civilians, the Madres de la Plaza de Mayo continue their action.[2] These and other refusals to accept the 'official version' (title of an important film by Luis Puenzo), exemplify one way in which popular memory can be made. In Guatemala, El Salvador, Colombia, Peru and Brazil, the operations of state-protected death squads continue. There has been minimal democratization in Guatemala, one of the worst areas of unacknowledged violence. Thirty years of civil war, still continuing, has included repeated genocidal attacks on Indian groups. Information is scarce, and dangerous to obtain.[3] How far will it be possible to reconstruct a history of this period?

After the defeat of the Great Rebellion of Tupac Amaru II in 1780 against Spanish colonial rule in Peru, everything was done by the authorities to erase the memory of its leader. But in the myths of Andean peasants he is still alive, and his body, drawn and quartered by the Spanish, has joined that of sixteenth-century Inca rulers in a corpus of utopian mythology which re-members the severed limbs and head, and imagines their return as future social justice and a new social body.

Popular practices of memory in the Andes are distinguished by the notion that the dead continue to exist alongside the living, either in a contiguous space or on a not too distant mountain. In a piece of contemporary Andean theatre, the dead are simultaneously on the stage with the living, and among them is the young man to whose disappearance by the military the play is a response. The dead, who are memory, preserve the past alongside the living, in a version of historical time very different from the prevailing Western one, with its necessity for constant and minimal change.

Overall, there is a need to distinguish the processes of popular memory from official, state and ruling-class forms of memory. In this connection, the body of Tupac Amaru represents that of his followers and their descendants, a distinct and oppressed social group. By contrast, official historiography creates heroes who represent the nation, and this began with the heroes of Independence: 'In a conscientious attempt to expand the levels of popular identification with the public action of the privileged, historians presented heroes of Independence as stripped of class representation, regional affinities, or religious zeal.'[4] And, as a Chilean historian has remarked, 'if history does not offer us model men, it is the duty of the historian to make them'.[5] These heroes are to be found throughout Latin America, in every public square of any importance, seeking to take possession of that space with the symbolism of the liberal nation-state.

Popular versions of these selfsame heroes are often very different, as happens with the figure of Simón Bolívar, conserved in the oral traditions of the rural black population of Venezuela. This Bolívar had a black mother, and is protected by magical powers. The differences here have to do both with the mode of storage of memory (oral narratives) and with the popular imaginary as matrix of beliefs and images, characterized in particular by confidence in magic. We cannot here give an account of the differences from the politically dominant liberal historiography, and its construction of an official memory. But one might begin with the ideas of Sarmiento, representative figure of authoritarian liberalism in nineteenth-century Argentina, whose educational programme aimed to undo emotional ties and reattach them to the nation, and included the idea of girls' schools where pupils were forbidden to touch each other. Another starting place might be the custom of awarding carbines as school prizes, which typifies the militarization of the social imagination.[6] But those human beings who were eliminated in order to ensure the continuity of the militarized imagination as national consciousness, the Indian populations to the south of the Río Negro, were forgotten, an amnesia which needs interpreting in the light of later amnesias of the last two decades.

The carbine, which in the twentieth century becomes the rifle, is a symbol reappropriated in the Nicaraguan peasant mass, celebrated by Ernesto Cardenal and other Sandinista priests, where the guerrillas hold their rifle in one hand and receive the host in the other. Similarly, a distinction needs to be made between sacrificial triumphalism, with its conversion of the dead into heroes – which is not actually to remember them, since their real particularity, including their membership of a distinct social group, is forgotten – and that localized and connective memory displayed in the Nicaraguan Gioconda Belli's poem, 'Free Country; 19th July 1979':

> How many deaths stick in my throat,
> loved dead with whom we once dreamed this dream
> and I remember their faces, their eyes,
> the assurance with which they knew this victory,
> the generosity they built it with
> sure that this moment was waiting in the future
> and it was worth dying for.[7]

One of the basic tenets of the Nicaraguan poetry workshops was the weaving of memory and everyday life, so that the war against Somoza would be recalled not in an idealized official version but as moments of personal affectivity, as faces, names, gestures.

(The poetry workshops, which fostered the first acts of writing of people who had just come into literacy, were concerned with individual memory and creativity, in an attempt to reverse the oppressive role of the written word in Latin America, particularly insofar as it is the medium of official history.) But many more people watched *telenovelas* than attended the poetry workshops.

The mass media, with their vast expansion in the past three decades, raise the question of how far they destroy the bases of popular memory and how far they stultify creativity. There are no simple answers. It is certain, however, that setting up an opposition between the culture industry and an idealized pre-industrial culture produces little insight into the actual processes. In the first place, these are not 'stages' in some inevitable cultural evolution, whether positive or negative. Too often cultural patterns are abstracted from a particular version of European history and essentialized. In this sense, the particular content of both pre-capitalist and capitalist cultural forms is different in Latin America, because their history is different.

When considering the culture industry, two types of transformation are especially relevant: hybridization and deterritorialization. By hybridization we mean the ways in which forms become separated from existing practices and recombine with new forms in new practices. An example would be how rural ceramic forms 'travel' to the city and a new consuming public and in the process are changed. The ceramic from Michoacán, Mexico, mentioned in Chapter 2, represents a bus taking people from rural areas to the industrial cities; the passengers inside the bus are devils, the devil figure being a traditional rural motif, used in a new way in order to negotiate a major transition. With the transition, symbols become detached from their previous contexts: the devils acquire new significance outside traditional rural religion, as do handicraft objects which become ornaments in cities instead of being used for eating, cooking and so on. Similarly, musical motifs and styles travel from fixed ritual occasions to new combinations and recombinations with music from elsewhere: Peruvian *chicha* combines Caribbean rhythms with Andean melody. Without radio broadcasts and the mobility of cassette recordings, these migrations would not have been possible. The term deterritorialization we use to refer to the release of cultural signs from fixed locations in space and time.[8]

An account of the ways in which the practices of popular memory can continue, transformed, through the mass media might begin with the use made of radio by the Brazilian *cantadores*, oral poets whose traditional role was to process and disseminate information in a rural locality. Over the past ten years the *cantadores* and their audience have through radio produced a means of reformulating their role and at the same time created a national network which reaches beyond the context of migrants. A vital part of the circuit of communication is the letters received from listeners, providing *motes*, two-verse themes, which the *cantadores* have to improvise upon. Another significant use of radio is the experience recounted by Rosa María Alfaro, whereby women stallholders in a Lima market placed their stories of migration to the city within the format of a radio serial. These two examples may seem peripheral to the main thrust of the culture industry – especially the second one, which is an example of alternative use of media – but they both show potentialities for the popular use of media: a yardstick in the argument as to whether mass media are inimical to popular memory.

The *telenovela*, the particular Latin American style of television serial, is the leading edge of the culture industry's penetration into everyday life. The number of people watching one episode of a *telenovela* is greater than the total copies of all García Márquez's work sold in Spanish – one of the reasons he gave, in a recent interview, for turning to writing a *telenovela*.[9] The first popular mass form with a similar influence was cinema. In many regions of the subcontinent, the predominant, and often virtually exclusive type of cinema was what Hollywood exported. Mexico was exceptional in creating a strong national film industry in the 1930s. And it was through film images, as Carlos Monsiváis has pointed out, that the popular masses in Mexico saw themselves, their own faces and gestures, represented in the new public space of the nation, their previous sense of identity being confined to regional or local communality. The images may have been in many ways vulgar and debased – for instance exalting machismo – but the masses celebrated in and through them their new social presence. The national culture industry could not exist without the masses, nor could the modern nation-state which was constructed after the Mexican Revolution. The two processes in fact relied upon each other: the formation of the modern nation and the construction of a national culture industry.

Film, surprisingly, has not had a major influence in the making of the *telenovela* as a genre. What, then, is the generative history of the *telenovela*? It can be traced through a series of popular forms, beginning with the *folletín*, or newspaper serial, itself transitional in that it was a first step whereby traditional oral themes and styles entered the medium of print at the same time as their audience negotiated literacy. Intermediate between the *folletín* and the *telenovela* is the *radioteatro* (radio serial), with its family romance plots. Running through all of these is melodrama, as plot, time structure, emotional ambience and moral emphasis. On each of these levels, the *telenovela* is capable of transmitting popular memories. By making everything pass through the family, it also includes, as Martín-Barbero suggests, a principle of opposition to the reduction of the whole of life to a marketable commodity: 'melodramatizing everything, through family relationships, the popular classes take revenge, in their own way, upon the abstractness imposed by the commodification of life and dreams',[10] a commodification represented by the very advertisements which sponsor the programme.

Another vehicle of popular memory and identity is the music which spread through the subcontinent via the radio and the record industry. One example is the bolero, whose smoochy sounds and brash/tender words entered millions of households in the 1930s. Through the century and into the 1990s, sounds of the bolero – or tango, cumbia, salsa, *chicha*, samba, lambada – have become the soundtrack of everyday life, shaping memory and desire. In *The Importance of Being Daniel Santos*, Luis Rafael Sánchez reveals in the voice of one of the great bolero singers a display of irreverence, transgression and retaliatory laughter, qualities which are resources of the poor who are the majority. Sánchez's book reconverts literature, traditionally the province of high culture, into a hybrid medium capable of translating the bolero, a mass-cultural form of music which formulates the emotions of millions.

When Sánchez writes 'the great theatre of obsessions' and 'the great museum of collective memory',[11] referring to the bolero as cultural model, the irony is serious because the vocabulary of heightened representation and of legitimate continuity is being reclaimed from high culture.

Over time, popular forms of life have been both suppressed and transformed. To think of a single, continuous popular memory is to indulge in mythology. And without forgetting, or the alteration of the structures of memory, there can be no invention or creativity. Gratuitous, wasteful destruction should be distinguished from the other destruction which permits transformation: as in Hegel's famous metaphor, the eggs have to be broken before the omelette can be made. What is difficult but vital is to hold the two processes together in the mind, without reconciliation.

Notes

1. Augusto Roa Bastos, ed., *Las culturas condenadas*, Mexico 1978, pp. 269, 272.

2. See John Kraniauskas, 'Hebe Bonafini, Madres de la Plaza de Mayo', *Index on Censorship*, Vol. 19, No. 9, p. 42.

3. See James Painter, *Guatemala: False Hope, False Freedom*, London 1987.

4. Mark D. Szuchman, *The Middle Period in Latin America: Values and Attitudes in the 17th–19th Centuries*, Boulder 1989, p. 5.

5. Diego Barros Arana, quoted in Szuchman, *The Middle Period*, p. 6.

6. See Szuchman, 'Childhood Education and Politics in Nineteenth Century Argentina: the Case of Buenos Aires', *Hispanic American Historical Review*, Vol. 70, No. 1, pp. 109–38.

7. Gioconda Belli, *Amor insurrecto*, Barcelona 1986, pp. 116–17.

8. The term is used extensively by Néstor García Canclini. For a thorough exposition of its possible uses, v. Gilles Deleuze and Felix Guattari, *A Thousand Plateaus*, London 1988.

9. See Holly Aylett, 'Of Love and Levitation', *Times Literary Supplement* 20–26 October 1989, p. 1152.

10. Jesús Martín-Barbero, *Procesos de comunicación y matrices de cultura*, Barcelona n.d., p. 117.

11. Luis Rafael Sánchez, *La importancia de llamarse Daniel Santos*, Mexico 1989, p. 132.

Index

LATIN AMERICA BUREAU

The Latin America Bureau is an independent, non-profit making research organisation established in 1977. *LAB* carries out research, publishes books and maintains support links with Latin American groups.

New *LAB* books include:

Faces of Latin America
DUNCAN GREEN

A wide-ranging portrayal of Latin America's peoples in their fight for a brighter future, five hundred years after Christopher Columbus' arrival in the Americas.

200 pages, ISBN 0 906156 59 9 Pbk, 0 906156 61 0 Hbk

Brazil: The War on Children
GILBERTO DIMENSTEIN

Reportage and interviews on life for Brazil's ten million street children.

100 pages, ISBN 0 906156 62 9 Pbk, 0 906156 63 7 Hbk

Columbus: His Enterprise
HANS KONING

Reveals the personality and motivation of a man who changed the course of history.

144 pages, ISBN 0 906156 60 2 Pbk
Published in the USA by Monthly Review Press

Panama: Made in the USA
JOHN WEEKS and PHIL GUNSON

Explores the unanswered questions behind the invasion of December 1989 and the challenges facing the US-installed Endarra government.

132 pages, ISBN 0 906156 55 6 Pbk, 0 906156 56 4 Hbk

For a complete list of *LAB* books, write to Latin America Bureau, 1 Amwell Street, London EC1R 1UL. *LAB* books are distributed in North America by Monthly Review Press, 122 West 27 Street, New York, NY10001.

LAB is a UK subscription agent for NACLA *Report on the Americas*, the largest English language magazine on Latin America and the Caribbean. Write for details.